W9-CZF-607

Creative HANDS

AN INTRODUCTION TO CRAFT TECHNIQUES

DORIS COX AND BARBARA WARREN WEISMANN

New York • JOHN WILEY AND SONS, INC.
London • CHAPMAN AND HALL, LIMITED

Copyright, 1945
by
Doris Cox Thomas and Barbara Warren Weismann

All Rights Reserved

This book or any part thereof must not be reproduced in any form without the written permission of the publisher.

FOURTH PRINTING, NOVEMBER, 1946

PRINTED IN THE UNITED STATES OF AMERICA

to

HARRIET and VETTA GOLDSTEIN———

in acknowledgment of an inspirational association

Preface

FREQUENTLY IN CONNECTION WITH OUR TEACHING WHILE MEMBERS of the faculty of the University of Minnesota, we were asked to recommend books or other material dealing with the problems that made up the practical activities experienced by our students in the craft work. Since the class projects were keyed to the abilities of individuals who had little or no pre-training in either the fine arts or the craft techniques, the good books available were beyond the range of the ability of everyday folk. This book is our answer to that need as voiced by so many people. This group can be divided into the following classifications:

1. The person who lacks training.

   The individual who has developed a keen interest but because of circumstances has never received formal art training.

   The person who does not know whether he possesses ability because he has never attempted creative work in this field.

2. The person lacking self-assurance.

   The individual who has no confidence in his originality.

   The individual who has had a taste of art training but who, because of his limited background, feels insecure in going ahead in this field.

The individual who thinks he "cannot even draw a straight line."

3. The person who is budget-conscious.

   The individual whose eyes are bigger than his purse.

   The individual who appreciates and yearns for beautiful surroundings but who has felt he cannot afford them.

4. The person who lives in cramped quarters.

   The individual who is making an effort to create an attractive home in a single room.

5. The person who desires a creative hobby.

6. The person who needs therapeutic handicraft.

7. The person engaged in teaching, or in camp, social center, or club work; such as, 4-H or county extension groups.

   The individual who needs a manual of craft technique based upon sound design principles and purposes (life situations) for use in educational pursuits.

   The person who has minimum equipment for craft work.

In this compilation of numerous craft techniques we have attempted to explain the principles and techniques simply and directly in order not to overwhelm the beginner. Most books limit themselves to the development of one craft; this book offers condensed methods of procedure in a wide variety of crafts in order that one may experience many, select the few best adapted to his interests, then specialize with the aid of books dealing with more advanced technique.

Making an article without any thought of relating it to the individual who is to use it, or to the room in which it is to be used, is a frequent practice. We do not hold with the theory, "Art for Art's sake." Any well designed, beautifully made object merits a suitable setting, which ordinarily is most surely achieved if considered when the craft project is begun.

For the crafts discussed in this book, the average home would provide all the needed equipment; if not, less than a dollar would suffice to cover the cost of needed tools for one or more of the problems. The cost of the actual materials used would be governed by the choice of the individual.

We hope that this book will be a solution to the needs outlined above, and that it will open the door to many diverting and profitable hours of creative work.

We wish to acknowledge with all sincerity the encouragement given us by members of the faculty of the University of Minnesota; the assistance with photography given us by Miss Helen Ludwig, Mr. Lloyd Matterson, and Mr. George H. Thomas; the generosity of students and friends who permitted us to photograph their handiwork; the coöperation of the Milwaukee and Minneapolis WPA Handicraft Projects; and the patience and kindness of our friends, families, and not in the least, our husbands, G. H. T. and D. L. W., while this book was in preparation.

DORIS COX (MRS. GEORGE H. THOMAS)
BARBARA WARREN WEISMANN

January 1, 1945

Contents

Chapter I

A Word to the Wise

IT IS DIFFICULT TO DEFINE THE INTANGIBLE QUALITIES OF SO elusive a heritage as taste in anything incorporating artistic principles. Taste is influenced by our cultural heritage and is based upon certain principles. The application of those principles tends to fluctuate slightly with fashion changes in any generation. It has always been the tendency of the current generation to judge most harshly those who lived just prior to themselves because it sees an unselected array of material evidences by which these people expressed themselves. This lack of selection embraces both the temporary aspects of fashion and the more sound phases of good taste. Such a situation arises because there has not been a sufficient lapse of time between the two generations for the development of an unbiased appraisal of their creative works.

With a well developed understanding of the principles of design one is better able to eliminate the superficial fashion traits from the more meritorious works of the generation before his, as well as from contemporary creative expression.

With the rapid development of industrial production methods and widespread advertising techniques one is faced with the necessity of selecting from a seemingly unlimited array of merchandise those comparatively few articles with which he associates. Since one judges his fathers by the things with which they associated, must one not realize that in like manner his neighbors evaluate his character? The things with which one surrounds himself are usually of his own selection and therefore indicate the stage to which one's taste has been developed as well as being reflections of one's personality.

Cost is no indication of the artistic worth of the object under consideration, and a realization or knowledge of the principles of design will destroy the smugness which is often an outgrowth of price consciousness. This knowledge will help one, therefore, to become an intelligent consumer of all objects whether their appearance or function is the prime consideration. A low cost article which meets all of the principles of design has just as high an artistic value as a higher priced article that fulfills the same principles. A realization of this will aid in the development of a more intelligent consumption of present day industrial products. It likewise will aid in forming a keener appreciation for well designed and executed craft products. It will lead to the realization of the futility of spending large amounts of time in producing by hand poorly designed articles.

Since there are no absolute or exact measurements by which a design may be catalogued as good or poor, it will be necessary to develop one's taste or appreciation to the point where the recognition of the beautiful in design becomes second nature. This is a long, slow process which may be hastened by constant and close association with objects of recognized aesthetic quality. Unless one has had adequate training by competent instructors in the appreciation of the beautiful, one should not depend solely upon one's own likes and dislikes, since these are often based upon childhood associations and may have been colored by false standards and sentimentality.

Chapter II

Design

DESIGN IS ANY CONTRIVANCE OR PLAN INTENDED FOR ANY DEFINITE purpose. This may be an actual object such as a chair, a flatiron, a transport plane, a beautiful textile, or a plan on a piece of paper.

Design is anything to which man has put his mind and his talents to the alteration or the reorganization of natural materials or forms. For example, one might cite a wood carving or the turning of a crude piece of wood into an object of art. The plan in the mind of the artist-craftsman will determine whether it shall become the leg of a chair, a salad fork, or a piece of sculpture. Any of these things has its uses and may be equally important to both the physical and aesthetic requirements of man. Whether the final result is good or poor is dependent upon the intrinsic worth of the plan as it was originally conceived and upon the quality of craftsmanship employed in the construction of the object.

Tools of the Trade

Structural Design

Structural design is that phase of design represented by the object without benefit of embellishment. In other words, it is the contour by which that object is distinguished from others. The

THOMAS

SCULPTURED HEAD
by Barbara Weismann

The plan in the mind of the artist-craftsman will determine whether a piece of wood shall become the leg of a chair, a salad fork, or a piece of sculpture.

structural design is one of the most important means of identification. It is the fundamental character of the article under consideration. This basic quality determines whether the article may be considered good or poor in design. Structural design also encompasses the texture and color of the foundation material.

The first consideration in the construction of any article is function. The use to which any object is to be put should be the determining factor in the selection: first, of the materials from which it is to be made; second, the shape and proportions it will assume; and third, the color it will be given. Every material has inherent characteristics which make it suitable to certain uses and definitely unsuitable to others. The importance of the native personalities belonging to construction materials has been recognized by the directing staff of the Bauhaus, formerly located at Dessau, Germany, and now in Chicago, Illinois. There an introductory course is devoted to the analysis of materials, their reaction to manipulation, and their relationships to each other.

EMBROIDERED MITTENS

THOMAS

To make the consideration of function more concrete, reference will be made to the mittens shown in the accompanying photograph. Since the purpose of the mittens is to protect the hands, the material from which they are to be made must have certain qualities: namely, warmth, flexibility, durability, surface quality pleasing to the touch, a fabric which lends itself to the process of construction, and one which is harmonious to the garments with which the mittens are to be worn. A good quality of wool fleece coating was found to be satisfactory on all of these points.

In order that the mittens be truly functional, it is necessary that they be made to conform to the contour of the hands which they are to cover permitting, at the same time, freedom of movement. Other factors contribute to the final shape of this hand-covering which was primarily designed for warmth. The body of the mitten encases the four fingers together, which increases its heat retaining qualities. The thumb is enclosed within a separate unit in order that the hand can perform more easily.

Normally, such detailed analysis of the steps involved in any one part of construction would be telescoped because of familiarity gained through previous experiences. The foregoing reasoning is illustrative of the *way of thinking* in the evolution of any idea from the abstract to the concrete.

The structure of an object is limited by its function; however, it is composed of proportionate relationships which one should endeavor to keep as pleasing as possible. Beauty in space relationships should never be achieved at the expense of proper function, but it is an important contributing factor to the ultimate appearance.

Referring once more to the mittens, it is necessary to consider the occasions upon which they would be worn, since these occasions will in turn determine the types of garments with which they are to be combined. Naturally this demands that color receive due attention. Color should be thought of in its relation to the texture of the fabric, the particular occasion for which the mitten is to be worn, and to the other colors of the ensemble.

The foregoing discussion has been devoted exclusively to those things which comprise the structural design of an object. If the principles as outlined have been successfully realized, the object will already have a beauty and character of its own. Sometimes this object may be further enhanced by the addition of a decorative design which is also governed by the principles stated for structural design. It should be borne in mind that this enrichment should not only be in harmony with, but should also complement, the structural design.

Decorative Design

Decorative design is the surface treatment which is intended to enhance the underlying structure.

Any attempt to create a beautiful object, regardless of its magnitude, involves a thoughtful consideration of the structural and decorative designs and their relation to the purpose for which the object is intended.

Decorative design stimulates a person's interest in an object. If it is good it causes one to look again. A delectable looking frosting on a cake whets one's appetite, increasing one's desire to taste the cake beneath. Likewise a suitable decorative design will increase appreciation for the article at hand. It must be remembered, however, that the structure beneath must bear up under close inspection. No amount of decorative design, no matter how good it may be, will be able to camouflage weak structural design. Likewise, many a fine example of structural design is weakened by the application of poor decorative design. Excessive decoration has the same tendency. Robert Henri is credited with the well known statement, "Simplicity is the soul of art," a statement which may well be used in judging a decorative design.

Intelligent Integration

One might reasonably say that there exists only one standard for the evaluation of design. For the purposes of simplification it is possible to consider all the usual principles of design—harmony, unity, proportion, emphasis, rhythm, balance—as being merely ramifications of this one major maxim, *ORDER*. This is a term which implies absolute accord not in its narrow sense, but with a broad consideration for all of its related aspects.

To make the discussion of the aspects as concrete as possible let us again refer back to the mittens.

In as much as mittens are primarily informal in nature, since they are usually made of sturdy materials and are intended for sports wear, the design also should be of an informal nature and not too delicate, but of bold and simple character. This implies *harmony of idea.* Further consideration should be given to the relationship of the textures used in combination. Yarn is an obvious selection in this case, since it is by nature adapted to use on woolen fabrics and is of a *harmonious texture.* Shetland yarn is an excellent choice with regard to its scale or size, which is in harmony with the fabric on which it is used, and because it manipulates easily.

The next step in planning a design concerns itself with *shape harmony.* The shape or contour of the design should complement the structure which it decorates and should lead the eye pleasingly over the surface of the object. The shape of the design should be so pleasing on the surface to which it is applied that the design becomes an integral part of the whole.

To return to the mittens, one can easily see that there are three major places where design might be placed so as to complement their structure: namely, the cuff, the back of the hand, and the thumb. The entire surface may be covered with a quiet design, or unit designs might be planned for any of these structural points. Since a mitten is normally longer than it is wide, a design applied to the back of the hand naturally takes a lengthwise direction instead of cutting across from side to side. Should the design be applied to the cuff which encircles the wrist, it would likewise lead the eye in a corresponding direction. This reasoning applies to the decoration planned to enhance any structure.

If unit designs are used, they should be planned with regard to their size in relation to the particular part of the mitten they are to decorate: that is, they shall be neither too small nor too large for that area. This *harmony of consistent sizes* is closely related to the principle of *proportion*. The term *scale* is used to cover this phase of design.

The fifth and last feature of *harmony* is that of *color*. This implies coördination of the color with the design, the texture, and the purpose of the object. In the mittens, the fabric selected decides the basic color and is a determining factor in the selection of the colors to be used in its decoration. Of course, this basic color is first selected with regard to the other colors with which it is to be worn. The colors selected should also be suited to the type of design used and to the purpose for which the mittens are intended. One would not expect to use colors that are usually most suited to sheer, summery fabrics for the heavy wool used in the body of the mitten. The color as applied to the design of any surface should be so distributed as to produce pleasing *balance*. This implies that the arrangement of the design parts has already been well balanced.

The Greek standard for good *proportion* might aid in planning pleasing space relationships. This is based on the *golden oblong,* which is two units of measurements on one side to three units on the other. This standard of good proportion may be used both for the units of the design and for the proportion of the design in relation to the mitten. However, any standard of this sort should be used with imagination since too rigid an adherence to a formula is apt to deaden the design.

Scale is also an aspect of the principle of proportion. It is a consideration whenever shapes or objects are combined, and refers to the appropriateness of the combination of objects of various dimensions. Scale must be thought of with regard to the area allotted to the decorative design as compared to the entire area on which the design is placed. The units within the design itself must also be in pleasing proportion with one another, leaf to flower, line to dot, and so forth.

Balance is obtained by having an equal amount of interest on either side of an imaginary center line. There are three types of balance:

Symmetrical balance: the normal human figure as seen from the front, each side being identical with the other. Symmetrical balance is always formal, but:

Formal balance is not always symmetrical; for example, two objects or units will balance each other formally if they attract the same amount of attention, yet the objects need not be identical. A leaf and a flower may balance one another formally in a design if they are both the same size and if they are both in the same position on either side of the imaginary center line.

Informal balance is achieved when the larger of two objects is placed near the center line and the smaller of the two objects is placed proportionately farther away from the axis of the arrangement.

Rhythm is that quality within a design which leads the eye from one unit to another. This may be an easy flowing movement established by continuous lines or an accented movement achieved through repetition of like units. Another form of movement may be obtained through the use of a broken line which so strongly suggests direction that the eye bridges the gaps between each section. The rhythm within a design should be in accordance with the structure on which the design is placed, or the design will not seem to belong to that particular structure. This implies that rhythm is a contributing factor to shape harmony. By shape harmony is meant the comfort one experiences when looking at a horizontal area enhanced by a horizontal design, in contrast to the confusion resulting from the conflict of line direction when verticals and horizontals of equal attraction are combined.

If all parts of a design are of equal interest, the eye involuntarily jumps from one of the units to another in quick succession. This results in confusion. In order to avoid such a feeling of restlessness, certain areas within a design should be of greater importance than other areas. This is the principle of *emphasis* or *subordination.* The type of units used in planning a design will suggest which part of the design should receive the greatest emphasis. A design, the parts of which are successfully emphasized and subordinated, will produce a feeling of rest or repose; a feeling which is also a by-product of good balance.

When all of the foregoing factors have been considered in the application of a design to an object, the result should produce a satisfactory whole; *an object of beauty suitable to its use,* an expression of *ORDER.*

Nothing New Under the Sun

Up to this time the abstract qualities of structural and decorative design have been treated without consideration for the concrete problem of planning an actual design for a given purpose. Before one can enter into the methods of designing, it is necessary to point out the two categories into which most designing falls.

The ideal way of working is one of absolute originality. The original designer is so familiar with the techniques of breaking up spaces into pleasing shapes, and is so sensitive to such divisions and their possibilities that he is not forced, nor does he wish, to lean upon the work of others. Ideas seem to flow from the end of his pencil and bear no semblance to designs previously created. Unfortunately this facility demands a great deal of native ability or much training and experience in the field of creative effort. Few of us possess this ability or have been able to provide ourselves with such thorough background experiences.

There is another method. This is one which is more easily learned and is suited to the average individual who has not been able to avail himself of any or much art training. This method permits the adapting of designs already in existence to a particular purpose. It does not infer outright copying, but rather involves the alteration and adjustment of a motif to another shape or character. For example, a small, subordinate unit from a complex design might be enlarged and made the dominant factor in a new setting. Thus the unit might not be original, but through adaptation it has been given new personality. Similarly, a number of small units, each taken from a separate source, might be combined to form a handsome new design. Thus one's lack of originality need not prove a hindrance to the designing and execution of fine craftwork. The beginner will feel a certain awkwardness when first trying out these expedients, but with a few practice attempts he should be able to design with ease, confidence, and competence.

The act of adapting a design, even though cleverly done, is no guarantee of quality. The ability to select good source material is of as much importance as the adapting of that design to a particular purpose. It is wise to be ever on the alert for motifs which would lend themselves to decorative adaptation. A file of such source material goes far in stimulating the imagination. Currently popular and faddish designs are frequently of dubious quality and are best avoided. They are intended to catch the fancy of an insensitive public; and are often imitative to the extreme and wholly without decorative quality.

Photographs or actual examples of craft products from the Old World, such as needlework, wood carving, and ceramics, provide a wealth of good, sound material for the purposes of adaptation. *The Index of American Design,* as compiled by the WPA, much of which has been reproduced in magazines from time to time, is a treasure trove for inspiration. Numerous examples of this nature will be discovered by the observant person. The wise and interested craftsman will collect these as they come to his attention. For the person who has no such files, a bibliography of source materials will be found in this book.

The Process of Adapting a Design

In order to make the process of adapting a design more understandable, a brief outline giving the steps involved will be found helpful. If the points in the outline are conscientiously kept in mind, a design is much more apt to be successful than if the form is carelessly followed.

The points to be remembered are:

1. Cognizance of the size and shape of the object to be decorated.
2. Realization of the ultimate purpose of the object.
3. Consideration of the material involved in the process of the construction and decoration of the object.
4. Selection of source material most suited to the idea, materials, and process.
5. Analysis of the source material to determine the motif best suited to the problems involved.
6. Adjustment of the motif to the areas to be enriched by design.
7. Formulation of the idea on paper.
8. Careful checking of the design for adherence to the principles of design and good taste.
9. Completion of the drawing of the design.
10. Planning the color combination and distribution.
11. Application to the object in the chosen medium.

To further clarify the above steps, the same points have been followed and diagramed for the design used on the woolen mittens shown.

This foregoing material has dealt exclusively with a mitten. However, the same method should be followed carefully in planning a design for any craft product whether the plan is for a more elaborate decorative design, or a more simple one; these steps are always the same.

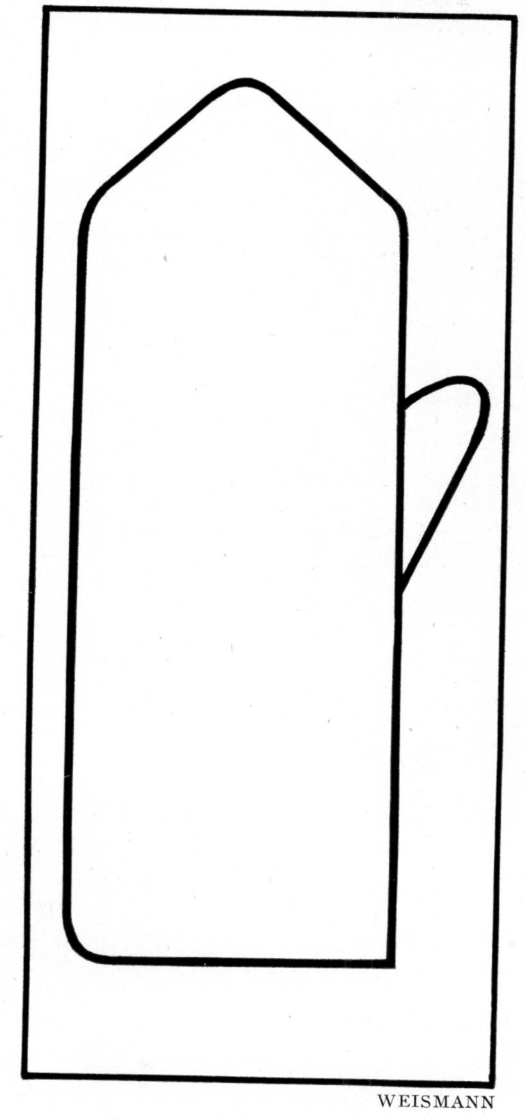

Step 1. Size and Shape

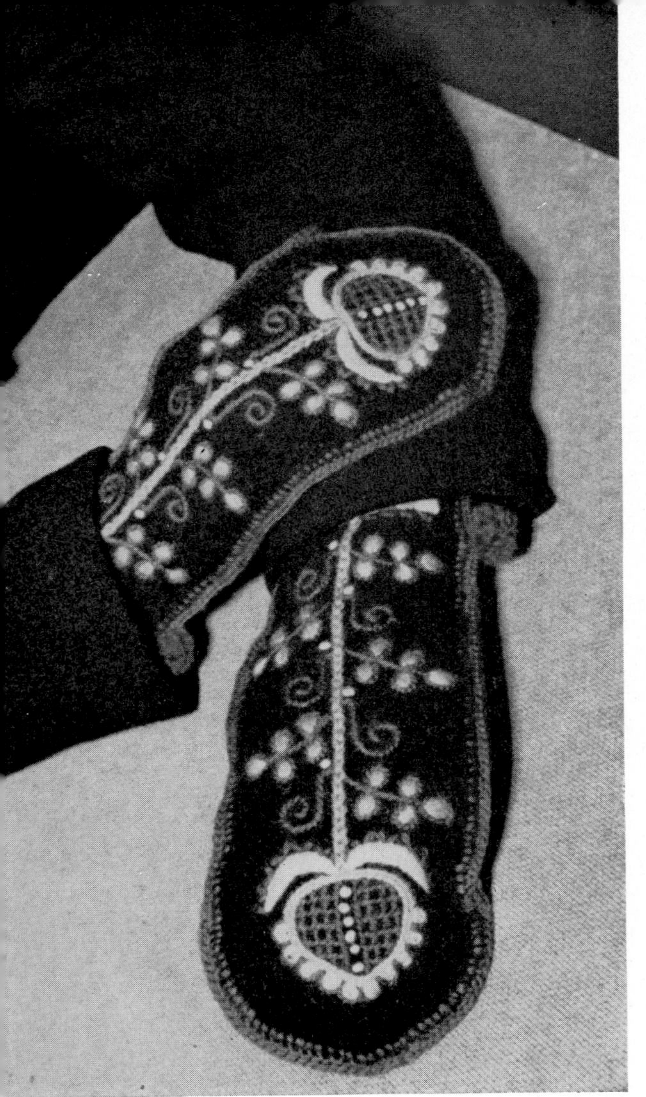

THOMAS

Step 2. Purpose of the Object

THOMAS

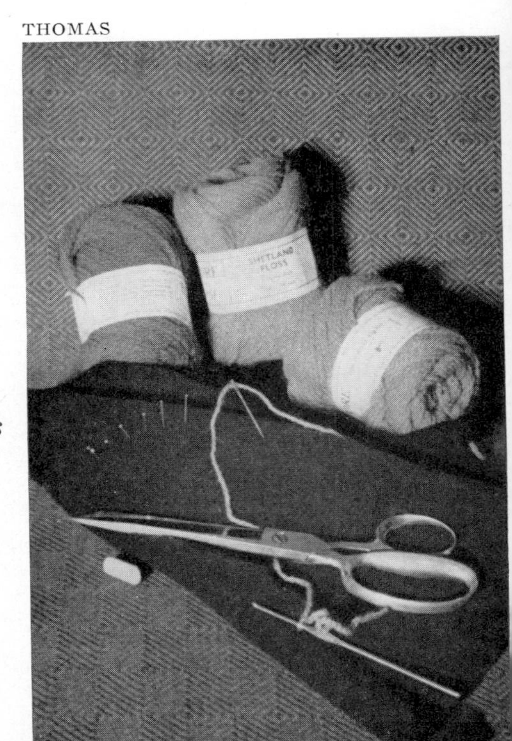

Step 3. Materials

Step 4. Inspiration for Design

Step 5. Motifs Selected for Use in Design

WEISMANN

Step 6. Motifs and Shape

WEISMANN

Step 7. Trial Drawing

Step 9. Corrected Design

Step 10. Design in Value

Chapter III

The Rainbow, Not the Gold

MANY AND LONG ARE THE TREATISES WRITTEN ON THE SUBJECT of color. A thorough understanding of the theories involved in the subject of color is highly desirable, but not absolutely necessary since a feeling for the use of color can be developed with the aid of just a few very important principles. Should a more technical knowledge of color theory be desired than is offered here, any library or encyclopedia will provide such information. We are purposely omitting technical discussion here, since it is often apt to confuse and discourage the inexperienced.

Theory Is Easy

There are three distinguishing elements of color with which even the beginner must familiarize himself. The most readily understood of these is the property of *hue*. It is the *name* of the color and simply designates the family to which the color belongs: i.e., red, blue, blue-green, green, etc. When dealing with pigments or dyes there exist only three fundamental colors, excluding black and white, which we will not here recognize as color. These basic or *primary* colors are red, yellow, and blue. A further division results from combining any two of these colors in *equal* amounts. These are known as *secondary* colors and include orange, green, and violet (purple). *Intermediate* colors such as blue-green, red-orange, and blue-violet are obtained by mixing any two of the primary colors in *unequal* amounts. This permits one of the colors to predominate. It is the predominating or outstanding color which gives the intermediate color its name. Another way of obtaining intermediate colors is through the combining of a primary color and its adjacent secondary color; i.e., blue, a primary, and a larger amount of its adjacent color green, a secondary, when combined, will produce blue-green. Reference to a color wheel will aid in the understanding of hue. An appreciation of the fact that an almost unlimited number of hues exist, will develop the potential ability of the beginner in his use of color.

The position of the hues on the color wheel is an important factor when changing hue and intensity of color. A color may be thought of in relation to its *adjacent* colors, the colors which successively follow one another around the color wheel; or it may be thought of in relation to its *complementary* color, the color which is found directly opposite to it on the color wheel. These positions are important to know when one is mixing colors to create new colors of full intensity, as yellow and blue to produce green; or when mixing colors to neutralize them, as blue and orange to produce brown.

Colors may be thought of in two groups; those that tend to be *cool* and those which are *warm*. In the first group would fall the greens, blues, and violets, and in the second group, the red, orange, and yellow hues. Intermediate colors which contain a mixture of a warm and a cool color will fall into the warm or the cool group according to the proportions of the warm or cool colors used in producing that hue.

Value is the second property of color. To many designers

this is the most important quality a color possesses. It is the *lightness* or *darkness* of a color. This is determined by the variation of a color from *normal* toward pure white or black. The normal value of a color is that value it assumes in its pure state as seen on the color wheel. It is obvious from reference to a color wheel that the normal value of colors is not constant. Yellow has the lightest normal value, and purple the darkest. Values which are lighter than normal are referred to as *tints*. When using paint or dye, tints are obtained by the addition of white pigment or water to the pure color, depending upon the medium with which one is working. Values darker than normal are known as *shades* and are obtained by the addition of black pigment to the normal value.

Intensity, the third property of color, is often confused with value. It is the *brightness* or *dullness* of a color. A simple example may lead to better understanding of this difference. Early morning, full daylight, and night may be thought of as three different values —middle value, light, and dark. But day, itself, has varying qualities of brightness; for example, sunshine with its brilliant color, and rain with its dull, subdued color, give a typical range of intensities. A color which does not have its fullest intensity is called a grayed color. Other terms which are frequently used but which have the same meaning are *neutralized, subdued,* and *dulled.* A color of full intensity is a pure color. It may be neutralized by adding some of its complementary color: i.e., add green to bright red to make a dull or neutralized red. The amount of the complementary color added will determine the extent to which the color has been grayed. If approximately equal amounts of both colors are mixed, the result will be a neutral gray. If the amount of warm color used is larger than the amount of cool color used, the result will be a warm gray or brown. If the amount varies the other way, the neutralized color will assume a cool tone such as is found in a steel gray.

Whether or not one is conscious of color combinations when using color, there are existing schemes which tend to act as suggestions, the knowledge of which will give the beginner greater confidence in color selection. These color schemes are rigid, rather mechanical patterns and should not be adhered to in all applications of color.

The first and probably the most simple of these color schemes is the *monochromatic* or one color scheme. It consists of the use of one color in various values. In order to create an interesting effect when using this scheme, the values must differ considerably or the design will appear very bland and unsatisfactory. A color scheme which uses black, white, and gray, plus one color is also known as monochromatic and is frequently more successful than a scheme built entirely around values of one color.

A second color plan is the *analogous* scheme, sometimes called an *adjacent* scheme. This involves the use of colors that are related to one another by their position on the color wheel. The relationship of such adjacent colors is strengthened by the fact that any two neighboring colors on the wheel always share a common hue: i.e., blue and blue-green have blue as a common color. Again, when this scheme is used, value is an important consideration. Failure to observe an interesting value pattern will make a color scheme lose all of its personality. This and the monochromatic scheme are known as *related* color schemes.

The third and perhaps the most difficult scheme to use is the *complementary* color scheme. This plan consists in the use of a color and its opposite on the color wheel. Interesting variations of the complementary scheme which are easier and more satisfying to use are: the *adjacent complementary* scheme, in which the color, its adjacent color, and its complementary color are used; the *split complementary* scheme, in which a color and the immediate neighbors of its complement are used. In this scheme, however, the complement itself is not used. This color scheme is usually more subtle than a straight complementary color plan. The third variation is termed the *double complementary* color scheme, and consists of the use of two complementary color schemes in the same design.

Frequently when complementary colors of the same value are used in juxtaposition, an illusion of movement or vibration appears which may be very disturbing. This is one of the factors which make a complementary scheme difficult to use. Such colors also often produce a harsh, jarring effect which tends to cheapen a design.

Not only is it important to have a good range of values in a scheme, but it is also helpful to vary the intensities of the colors. Often two colors which do not ordinarily appear well together may be used very successfully if one or both of the colors are grayed. Red and green might serve as an example in this instance.

The last important classification is the *triad* color scheme. It is composed of three colors equidistant from one another on the color wheel. The three primary colors, red, yellow, and blue, belong to this scheme. A triad scheme in its pure state is very difficult to use, but if one of the colors is somewhat neutralized, the scheme may be very pleasing. The triad scheme and all phases of the complementary scheme are known as *contrasting* color schemes.

Many people are so sensitive to the possibilities of color that they create what may be called color harmonies. These may be differentiated from color schemes in that they involve a more individual color pattern and do not strictly conform to the color schemes as listed above. This freer use of color is a mark of individuality and should be cultivated by constant association with fine examples of color usage.

Rainbows Within Reach

It is a fallacy to believe that the monetary value of an article is an assurance of good taste in the use of color or design. Simple, everyday things often have color harmonies superior to those found in more costly objects. One need only turn to nature for captivating suggestions for the selection of color. Such things as flowers, autumn leaves, birds with their colorful feathers, the soft subdued colors found in the furs of animals, the rainbow colors of fish, and the jewel-like colors of insects provide endless inspiration. If one cannot study the actual object itself, the *National Geographic* or *Audubon prints* will furnish reliable source material. The reader will doubtless be familiar with other publications of like nature.

Nature does not provide the only source for color suggestions. Many examples of good craft work from other countries as well as from our own country will offer stimulation. Fabrics, both printed and embroidered, will furnish further ideas. Other possibilities are ceramics with their colorful glazes.

An especially rich field for color suggestion is that of paintings of good quality. Usually there will be more colors in the painting than one would choose to use in a design, but by careful selection one can select an interesting scheme. To insure a truly satisfactory color harmony when using this source of inspiration, the painting should be analyzed to determine the relative proportions of the colors used. Failure to do this often results in a color harmony apparently completely different from the original source. Aside from offering a suggestion for a complete color harmony, a painting will sometimes suggest just one beautiful color to an appreciative student. This color the designer may select and combine with other colors of his own choosing.

Since it is not always possible to have these source materials at hand, one may build a file of good color suggestions clipped from magazine illustrations, advertisements, or covers. An expedient method to use in choosing the particular areas of the color reproductions is that of using a finder which eliminates undesirable portions of the picture. This method also removes the distraction of subject matter. A finder may be made of a four by six inch filing card which has a two inch square cut from its center. This "window" or frame may be moved over the surface of the illustration until the most satisfying combination of colors is found. That area may then be clipped and mounted on a filing card for future reference. A single illustration or advertisement often provides several different and interesting combinations.

Color at Work

The same principles which apply to the making of a design, apply equally to the use of color in that design. Probably the most important of these is *color proportion.* A successful color plan for a design maintains a pleasing relationship of the areas allotted to each color. The color areas should be so proportioned as to permit the dominance of one of the colors. The color covering the largest amount of space in a design determines the general color impression given by that design. There may be few or many subordinate colors depending upon the nature of the design and these should likewise be beautifully proportioned to one another.

When planning the distribution of color areas, one must also consider the *balance* of the design as it is affected by color. Size alone does not determine balance, but intensity and value are also important factors. A spot of intense color may be used to balance a large area of a dull color, since the attention focuses more quickly on the brighter area. Likewise a small amount of black in a light design will catch the eye quickly and will balance a large, light shape in the design. It is necessary to maintain a good color balance not only for the design itself but also to preserve the structural quality of the object which that design decorates.

The principle of balance in color overlaps that of *color emphasis,* which deals with the power of attraction of any unit of a design. Thoughtful arrangement of size, shape, placement, and color will determine the center of interest in a design. Color is important here because of its power to gather attention to itself and hence to the most important part of the design.

Since the principle of *rhythm* is that of movement, the eye may be led from one part of a design to another through the use of color gradations both in hue and value and/or repeated color. This rhythm may be very pleasing and musiclike or it may be so active as to be distracting and out of tune with the design.

If one mistrusts one's own judgment, a thoughtful study of fine examples of the use of color will aid in the development of an understanding and a feeling for these principles as applied to color.

Chapter IV

A Good Judge of Character

WHETHER SELECTING A DESIGN FOR ADAPTATION OR CREATING an original design, one must consider the quality of that design. Frequently a person who cannot himself draw feels that any unit reasonably resembling an object in actuality must be a good design. This is wholly untrue. Were it so, the camera would be used as a universal substitute for the hands and the head of the artist. The differences between a photograph of an object and an artistic drawing of the same object are many. The drawing usually represents a simplified version, a minimized detail here, an emphasized detail there; in short, an individualized interpretation of the unit in question. How well the arranging of details is done rests with the ability of the artist to select the salient characteristics of the actual object as he needs them for the particular effects he desires to achieve.

Consider, for the moment, the many designs used in printed textiles. Probably the most common unit used is the daisy. There are over fifty thousand copyrighted designs registered in Washington which make use of this motif. Many of them are excellent, many commonplace. One should learn to distinguish between the designs exhibiting definite character and those which are merely weak attempts at a photographic reproduction of the flower [or object] used as the predominating unit around which the design is based.

One of the prime factors in the evaluation of a design is the quality of its drawing—the care used in recording the individual interpretation of the unit onto the paper when the preliminary planning is done. This is not entirely a matter of skill or facility with the pencil or brush but rests often upon the patience and intellectual action of the person creating the design. The line of a stem or the curve of the edge of a leaf may first be put down as it is seen and then carefully corrected so that it becomes a graceful easy curve over which the eye travels smoothly. By way of demonstration, the reader might draw a simple spiral line. Look at it thoughtfully and try to determine whether the eye follows the line easily and freely or whether it must move around squared corners and clumsy curves which tend to give a sensation akin to that of riding over a bumpy country road. Now redraw the same spiral, endeavoring to correct any errors uncovered in the preliminary study of the original drawing. When the spiral is finally completed as perfectly as is possible with the freehand method, one can better appreciate the meaning of the term "good drawing."

Whether a person is a fount of originality, or one of the average group who finds it necessary to search for inspiration, the design being worked upon may fall far short of beauty and personality if it lacks this quality of good drawing. The term does not apply to photographic accuracy, speed, or the ease with which it was done. It pertains to that extra care necessary to the fineness in character of a design. A dozen people may use the same floral form in a design, yet the results will be varied and of numerous degrees of quality. One person will record every detail of line, every serration of petal and leaf, every tiny section of the flower itself; in short, he will attempt to draw everything he sees. By dint of much hard and painstaking work he may achieve a drawing which is startling in its accuracy of reproduction. However, as he labored to do what the camera could do more easily in but a fraction of a second, he has been entirely unaware of the principles of design which, like sign posts on a highway, would have guided him to a more fortunate result. Another person might incorporate a simplified silhouette of the flower into a stunning allover pattern; while yet another might find inspiration in the serrated line of a petal tip and the star-shaped stamens for a bold striped design of zigzag lines punctuated with starlike units. Good drawing requires more than good sight. It demands a consciousness and sensitivity to the purpose of the design being drawn; to the intelligent use of the principles of design; and an awareness of the possibilities of the material at hand and of one's own abilities. More than that, good drawing implies care and craftsmanship in the planning of a design; it does not tolerate sloppy workmanship.

The foregoing material applies to designing even though one's abilities may be limited to the extent that it seems necessary to trace part of a design from the work of another. While the authors recognize this as a minor larceny, they cannot overlook the fact that it is a crime committed daily by many people who would not be participating in any form of art work were this crutch removed. Even in the tracing of units, the same accuracy is essential, for the very character of the design being traced may depend on minor, seemingly insignificant, details for its charm. And for the person who leans thus upon the work of another, the foregoing discussion will be an aid to the selection of well planned designs from which to work.

Good drawing has further implications. The human eye is repulsed by impossibilities or clumsy distortions. For example, a horse may be carved from wood in the simplest manner with no attention paid to leg joints, nostrils, and so on. It might be made even less like a horse by being painted a brilliant orange; and to remove it further from actuality, be decorated with a few bright colored flowers painted on its back. The peasants of Sweden are skilled at producing these simple toys. They are completely satisfying in design, but if leg joints were indicated and done incorrectly the character of the toy would be destroyed; the human instincts would be repulsed.

Many people find that the use of flowers in a design is somewhat difficult. Perhaps it is because flowers are familiar to everyone and the designer becomes confused in his drawing through knowing too much about them. Photographic accuracy, as stated before, is not the answer; neither are abstractions or conventionalizations if done without a feeling for the fundamental principles of design. The attractive peasant flowers most of us admire are certainly unlike the real flowers themselves; yet, as flowers, they are still possible and quite recognizable. The petals radiate from a given point; often the stamens are represented, the serrations of a petal, sometimes thorns on the stems, sometimes seedpods, even though the flower is still in full bloom. Some of these things are not likely in nature but they do not offend our sensibilities because they show intelligent organization and drawing on the part of the artist. It might be said that the artist seeks to symbolize, to reduce to simple terms or lines, the flower as we know it in nature. To some extent this might be compared to the drawing of children. The child, in reproducing a figure, or an animal, or flower will do so by putting on the paper only the parts of the object which, in his limited observations, he deems important. A human figure may be reduced to a creature with a large head, straight arms and legs, and very little in the way of body. We have all seen drawings like that; we all recognize them for attempts at drawing the figure. These drawings are in reality symbolized versions of the child's ideas of the human form. His limited knowledge has not yet been confused with the addition of details of anatomy. On the other hand, the adult, knowing much more of how things really appear, frequently cannot bring himself to the point where he can simplify or cast aside detail in order to achieve the symbolic representation of the object or figure that he is using in a design. The problem must be approached with intelligence, observation, and experimentation. When the preliminary drawing is made one should study it and then seek to simplify, correct, and/or eliminate nonessential lines and forms. This should be done with all consideration for the principles of design as previously explained, and the final result is quite bound to bear the characteristics of a well drawn, well planned design.

Whether or not a design is original to the individual making the craft project, that person is bound to inject his knowledge and personality into the arrangement of the units within the design or into the use to which the design is put. Perhaps the most inclusive generalization one might make concerning character in design is that there is virtue and strength in simplicity and weakness in complexity and hazy overstatement. This does not imply that any design made of a few simple lines will be a strong, sincere artistic expression, for it may be a monotonous repetition of dull uninteresting shapes. However, the most effective patterns usually incorporate strong rhythmic lines forming contrasting shapes which are interesting without being overly complex. A design should be so planned that to remove any one part of it would be to rob it of its effectiveness. While preparing a design for some particular purpose, it is often advisable to remove uncertain shapes and lines until the final result bears not one irrelevant detail or form. This will insure a solid, well knit unit which in line and proportion will carry the stamp of sincere and vital character. With such scrupulous care one can create or select a design which will always be interesting and which will not lean upon some sentimental interpretation to hold attention.

The selection of units or motifs for a particular problem involves the consideration of harmonious kinship with their component parts and with the intended use of the article itself. The underlying quality which creates a certain effect within a design might be labeled the *spirit of the design.* Just as certain patterns in textiles seem to reflect a dainty feminine quality while others assume a sturdy or vigorous mood, so may any design for whatsoever purpose be designated as possessing certain definite tendencies in nature or spirit. It is essential that this spirit be identified and coordinated with the craft problem. It is quite conceivable that an excellent design will lose much, if not all, of its character should it be applied to an object of an alien nature. *The need for harmonious combination of design and finished product cannot be overstressed.*

Lines and areas within a design should possess this same kinship. A grouping of rather realistic floral forms with absolutely geometric or abstract shapes would tend to be distressing, while the same abstract shapes might keep pleasant company with very conventionalized flower units. A similarity of feeling between one line or shape and all of the others used within the design is part of the problem of planning that design. This harmonious adjustment of forms will allow the eye to travel over the design without being rudely stopped by some line or unit that appears not to belong with the rest. It assumes that every part of the design has been carefully gone over and checked; yet that the result is not one which looks labored, but instead is one which sparkles with an artistic life not confused by superfluities or incongruities.

Color is another important element in the character of a design. Most of us have a limited color vocabulary; we recognize and enjoy pleasing colors when we see them, but when called upon to produce an original scheme using more than one color we fail to do so imaginatively. Our thinking usually follows a stereotyped pattern of accepted and frequently seen color combinations. We are familiar, for instance, with the unquestionable but trite schemes of peach, or orchid, and green; pink and blue; turquoise and wine to name but a few. It is advisable, therefore, that one cultivate greater sensitivity to the possibilities of color and its myriad variations of value and intensity. Anyone who has tried to match a swatch of plain fabric knows that there are many blues, or reds, or browns, as the case may be. To realize this and then learn to use color intelligently and with feeling takes time and imagination. In another chapter where color is discussed more fully, some of the scientific aspects of color and its mixing have been considered in greater detail. It is suggested there that a color file of interesting schemes be kept for reference.

When adapting a design for a particular purpose, it is not unusual to find that the colors used in the original design are unsuited to its new personality or are not especially attractive at the outset. If this be the case, substitutes may be used. However, it is well to bear in mind the fact that not only the color, but the value, or dark and light quality, of the color is an important factor in the balancing of the design. Hence, in changing a color scheme, one must consider the dark and light distribution of the original colors and attempt to keep that quality, at least, in order to retain a pleasingly balanced pattern.

Color should also identify itself with the subject matter providing the foundation for the design. A unit composed of flowerlets and a delicate tracery of leaves and stems would be harmonious with a soft pastel scheme; but the robust character of a sturdy peasant design of conventionalized flowers, leaves, and perhaps figures and animals demands brighter or more earthy colors to enhance it. Because a certain combination of colors is beautiful and pleasing in one design is no indication that it may be used indiscriminately for any design with the same satisfactory results. The color used in a design should look like the design, should so complement it that its removal or change would take away some of the character of the design itself.

Unless a unit is composed entirely of abstract shapes or lines, there is some subject matter from which it has been evolved. Probably nature with its flowers, leaves, grasses, and countless other forms is the source most drawn upon. Often an event, a world situation, literature, or a period in history will be popularized commercially by manufacturers and advertisers and this will be reflected in the designs used to decorate any number of contemporary items. The designs of Mexico and South America have been appearing in one form or another since the publicized drive for inter-American solidarity saw its inception.

Sometimes the results of such a drive are worth while for they bring to light many unfamiliar and highly artistic examples of the work done by artists and craftsmen of another civilization. Frequently and unfortunately, however, the true character and qualities of the designs of the country are overlooked or supplanted by an Americanized concept of what Americans believe to be characteristic of the native design. These results are seen in biased and unaesthetic designs on china, linens, textiles, book-ends, and similar products which are dependent in no degree upon basic quality but rather upon commercial appeal. It is wise to be wary of any design which appears too often upon manufactured articles. In considering a design, try to discover whether it is the subject matter used or the use to which the subject matter is put that has the greater appeal. Interesting or unusual subject matter is no guarantee of quality in a design; it is the arrangement, the drawing, the color, and the interpretation in general which determine whether a design is good or poor.

There are a great many sources from which one may seek inspiration for a design to be used in the decorating of a craft project. Roughly, these sources might be divided into two classifications: those from which the design alone is used for inspirational purposes, and those which lend themselves completely, design and material, to the making of some object. It is primarily this latter group with which we are concerned here, for it will serve as a stepping-stone for the beginner into the realm of more creative design. A wide range of materials, already bearing some design motifs, are easily available to everyone. Much of this can be used in one way or another to enhance what might otherwise be an unadorned structural unit. Wallpapers, yard goods, ranging from dress fabrics to drapery fabrics; printed handkerchiefs, wrapping papers, decorative ribbons, and belting, to name just a few, often incorporate designs which lend themselves to use in a way quite different from that for which they were originally designed. An unusual fabric which one might not consider at all suitable for a garment could be used to cover a portfolio or book. A wallpaper of pleasing design and color might renew a marred or ugly wastebasket. Many materials such as those mentioned are limited in their use only by the scope of one's imagination and ingenuity.

Sometimes the design in a paper or fabric will be completely satisfactory for the use to which one wishes to put it. Occasionally it may seem advisable to alter the design or color in some respect in order that it take on some quality not found in the original. For example, a wallpaper of the desired background color, texture, and design that one wished to use for covering a box might harmonize more completely with other objects in a room if one of the colors in the pattern were heightened. This might be done with water color since the paper takes this medium very well. A pale yellow could be made more brilliant, or a dark outline around a group of flowers might give more sophistication to that design unit. Perhaps just part of the design in the paper would answer some particular purpose. In that case, it might be cut out and applied to the object in mind.

There are two ways for considering materials of this nature. One might, given a length of beautiful fabric or a few yards of decorative wallpaper, try to think of all the possible uses to which the material could be put. How many variations are possible in converting the fabric or paper into useful and artistic objects? Or if one wished to decorate some particular article with a certain type of design, one might search about for a suitable material. Either method is entirely practicable since, on the one hand, the material is serving to stimulate constructive imagination and on the other hand it is being used to satisfy an already prescribed need.

Whether the material should be used in either of these two ways, however, rests with the quality of the design it embodies. Every design should be judged according to the standards previously outlined, for commercial reproduction and sale on the market does not signify that it is one which is worthy of being preserved in any permanent form.

To illustrate more clearly the premise that wallpaper or fabric of good design can be used to stimulate creative and constructive imagination, a volume of wallpaper samples was secured from a co-operative dealer. From these sample sheets a variety of articles were constructed; all of them were suggested by the papers themselves. These examples are in no way intended to include everything to which this material might lend itself but are reproduced to show just a few of the possibilities.

THOMAS

NEEDED MATERIALS

Besides the containers and wallpaper, paste, and scissors, India ink and water colors are useful for accenting the designs.

THOMAS

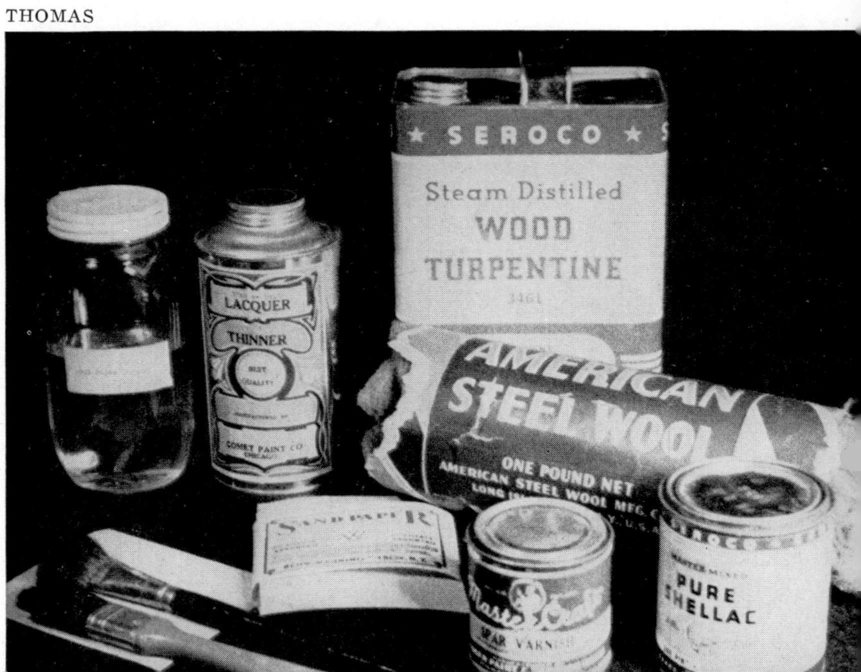

FINISHING MATERIALS

Wallpaper lacquer, spar varnish, and shellac are all useful for protecting the surfaces of various craft products. Rubbing down with number 3/0 steel wool improves the finished surface.

A LAMP SHADE OF WALLPAPER

A sheet from a sample book was large enough for a ten inch shade. The wallpaper should be mounted on heavy white paper before sewing it to the frame. Bias tape or gimp conceals the stitches.

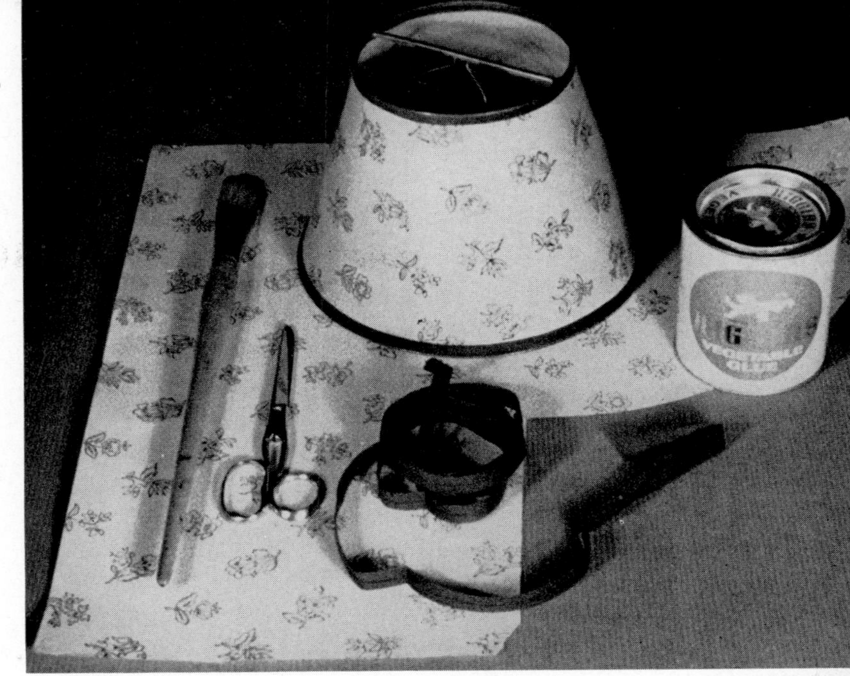

THOMAS

THOMAS

A TABLE MAT

A piece of wallpaper was mounted on cardboard, bound with bias tape applied with vegetable glue, then lacquered several times.

THOMAS

DESK SET

The motifs from a single piece of wallpaper may be used to make a matched set.

THOMAS

A SHORTENING CAN AND CLOSE RELATIVES

Two coats of enamel and wallpaper motifs saved these containers from the junk pile. A coat of shellac protects them.

EMBELLISHED BOXES

A quaint rooster camouflages a pill box.

THOMAS

THOMAS

WOODEN TILES

The square tile boasts the use of motifs cut from several different pieces of wallpaper.

Chapter V

Ways and Means

The Way Around

IT IS USUALLY EASIER FOR THE NOVICE TO BEGIN WITH A BORDER design or a unit design. This may be because a narrow bounded area is readily visualized as completed with the addition of some simple lines or forms. Actually just as soon as a top and a bottom boundary line have been drawn, the design might be considered as finished for it already answers its primary purpose, i.e., an edge or margin. However, for most purposes a border is used to add a decorative note. Consequently it is essential to know just what the possibilities and limitations of this type of design are.

Most border designs are composed of a unit or series of units or lines repeated at intervals over the length of the enclosed area. With this in mind, it can be seen that a design used as a border should be one which permits the eye to travel its length easily without serious interruption. Any line, form, or color which breaks this rhythmic movement does not rightly belong in a border design. Sometimes a design which does not seem to lead the eye easily over its length would be very successful if the units used within it were brought together more closely. Spacing the units forming a border too widely necessitates a jump in vision from one to another rather than suggesting a well planned, transitional movement.

Frequently the rhythmic effect is achieved through the use of an unbroken, though not always straight, line running the length of the border. The line may be unbroken or it may be so cut at regular intervals that the eye automatically bridges the gaps and sees it as a continuous line. It is important that this continuous rhythm be felt within a border design even though it may not be there as a definite line. It is well to take cognizance of the fact that the eye travels normally from left to right; recognition of this fact will lead the wise designer to plan a line movement in that direction. In so doing, the natural movement of the eye is facilitated. However, it is not essential that every line or object within the prescribed area lead in the direction indicated. While the main movement may be from left to right, minor lines or units may move in the opposite direction. Sometimes this is necessary, especially if the dominant movement is very strong and directs the eye too quickly down its length.

For one who has never designed a border there are numerous expedient tricks which will be of help. First, of course, the width should be decided upon and this in view of the particular area to which the border is to be applied. Since a border is a running design made up of repeated units, the length is not quite so important a consideration. Draw the top and bottom boundary lines the desired distance apart. Between these two lines at regular intervals (the distance should be proportioned to the height of the border and may be arbitrarily decided upon for this purpose) draw vertical or slightly diagonal lines to connect the boundary lines. Already there exists a somewhat more complicated design than that created by the first lines drawn; already there is a certain movement created by the repetition of these lines. Through the center and down the length of the border draw another line preferably not continuously straight but wavy, zigzag, scalloped, or broken. Between the first set

WEISMANN

of verticals and above the center line draw some simple geometric unit: a circle, triangle, or square. Between the adjoining verticals draw the same unit below the center line; the next above, then below, and so on. While the border is still quite simple, it has taken on new interest with each addition. Further additions may be made at will, but these additions should be so placed as to give dominance to either the vertical movement in the repetition or to the horizontal movement.

This same method with a few variations can lay the groundwork for any number of original border designs. The central line might be raised above dead center or placed somewhat lower on the band, or omitted entirely. The vertical lines might be curved in various ways, or they could be zigzagged, or scalloped. The vertical lines might be omitted and the center line given greater importance and interest. The abstract forms need not retain their abstract qualities entirely but might be turned into conventionalized flowers, leaves, or animals. If the border is a compact and complete unit the upper and lower boundary lines may be omitted entirely.

Another method which may be followed successfully to produce an attractive border design is equally simple. From colored paper cut a number of geometric forms of various sizes. Several units of each form are necessary, and it is well to cut each form from a different color of paper. One might, for example, cut six red triangles, six yellow circles somewhat smaller than the triangles, and six dark green squares either larger than the triangles or smaller than the circles. By arranging these or similar units on a piece of paper cut to the width desired for a border an interesting effect may be achieved. One will find that there are many variations possible in the arranging and rearranging of the shapes being used. When the design is interesting and satisfies the requirements for a good border, the cut pieces should be pasted to the paper to be used as a pattern for the final border if it is to be transferred to some particular object. Here again the shapes need not retain their abstract personalities but may be converted into recognizable forms. A triangle could become a leaf, a circle, a flower.

Line and form are not the only elements which establish the rhythm of a border design. Judicious use of color will also define or increase the rhythmic quality. Since color has several characteristics —hue, darkness and lightness, brightness and dullness—these should be used with an understanding of the effects they produce. A good border will be predominantly dark or light in value, and the light and dark arrangement will give strength to the movement within the design. An equal amount of dark and light color would make the border monotonous or broken owing to the lack of emphasis on any one part. The value which catches the eye first is the one to be used in playing up the important movement of line or form within the design. If the border is predominantly dark, probably the lightest value will command the attention first. This, then, would be the one to use in singling out the essential rhythmic quality of the border.

Since a bright color has the power to focus attention upon itself more readily than a dull color, the rhythmic order of a design may be further strengthened through the proper application of such color. A small area of brilliant color may become more powerful in a design than a larger area of a dull color. The eye will move over the design from one such bright spot to the next, and these spots or areas should be so placed as to complement the intended movement within the border. As with the apportionment of the amounts of light and dark used in the design, so should unequal amounts of bright and dull color be used in order that a disorganized or monotonous effect be avoided.

When one is planning a border which is to go around a square or rectangular area such as might occur in a tablecloth or wall hanging, certain problems arise where the design is to turn the corner. There are a number of methods for solving such problems which are as much a part of designing the border as is the border itself. One method which has been proved very satisfactory is that of placing a small mirror upright on the border and across it at a forty-five degree angle. It will reflect the design at right angles to itself, and by moving the mirror slowly back and forth one can discover the most effective treatment for the drawing of the design at that angle. While the mirror is held in position, a small sketch should be made of the corner design as reflected in it; when the mirror is removed, the design can be worked out in detail with the remainder of the border. Or if desired, a light pencil line can be drawn along the edge of the mirror as it rests on the border. A tracing of the first half can then be made, the tracing paper folded at the center edge of the tracing (the line upon which the mirror rested) and the complete unit drawn by going over the pencil lines seen through the thin paper.

Some border designs lend themselves to quite another treatment wherein an entirely separate but related unit is designed to fit into the corner square. The border design will lead up to this unit on either side. Such a method when used may be so planned as to give emphasis to the corner itself. This is sometimes desirable in certain designs. It should always be remembered, however, that the corner unit should be kept in harmony with the other portions of the border. There should be some existing relationship between the lines, forms, and colors used in that motif which will cause it to appear as part of the rest of the design and not as a wholly alien unit.

Not all border designs need special care at the corner area. If a design is repeated regularly within a square area, then it will fit naturally into the square formed at the corner. Or if the design is composed simply with the lines which run the length of the border, the lines will almost of themselves turn at the designated place. It is only with the more complex designs that the corner area presents any particular problem, but since this problem is so easily solved by either one of the two methods described, one need have no fear when planning such a design.

Repeat with Reason

An allover design is one which is composed of a unit or series of units repeated according to some definite method whereby the entire surface of a given area is decoratively covered. In certain respects this type of design may seem somewhat more difficult to produce than a border design, since it involves an area not necessarily bounded on any particular side. Because allover designs range from the exceedingly simple to the very complex, and because there exist certain prescribed methods with which the repeat plan of the motif can be worked out, the beginner need have no more qualms over this phase of design than over that of border design.

Before attempting to create an allover pattern, it is essential that the characteristics of a good design of this sort be understood. If the purpose of an allover design is to cover a surface with a repeated unit, that repeated unit should make a pattern which will decorate but not destroy the surface that it covers. In other words, the structural base to which the design is applied should be optically preserved. A flat surface should remain a flat surface; a nicely shaped wooden bowl, if covered with an allover design, should still retain its beauty of contour. Any design which gives the illusion of depth within itself will tend to destroy the structure to which it is applied. In view of this, a flower drawn too realistically or a series of objects shown in all the accuracy of perspective are generally considered poor choices for surface patterns. While it is not necessary to dispense with forms based upon nature when selecting subject matter for a design, it is advisable that those forms be treated in a flat, decorative manner.

Occasionally a design composed entirely of abstract lines or shapes brings such lines or shapes together in a way which gives a three-dimensional quality quite unintentionally. This is the result of optical illusion and should be remedied either through changes made in the design itself or in the colors or values used, since often the last named are the elements producing the unwanted effect.

A successful surface design is one which is seen as a pleasing whole without a spotty or broken appearance. Whether the design is quiet or dramatic in its entirety, it should be one over which the eye can move rhythmically and easily without uncomfortable interruption. Lines and forms used in the pattern should adhere to the principles of good design; should be harmoniously related in scale and spirit. A loose, bold, free treatment of one portion of a design would scarcely harmonize with a small, detailed, and carefully drawn companion motif.

The ultimate use to which the design is to be put also has considerable bearing upon its nature. If the area it is to cover is small, the motifs and spacing of units within the design should be scaled to that area. A large design would lose much of its charac-

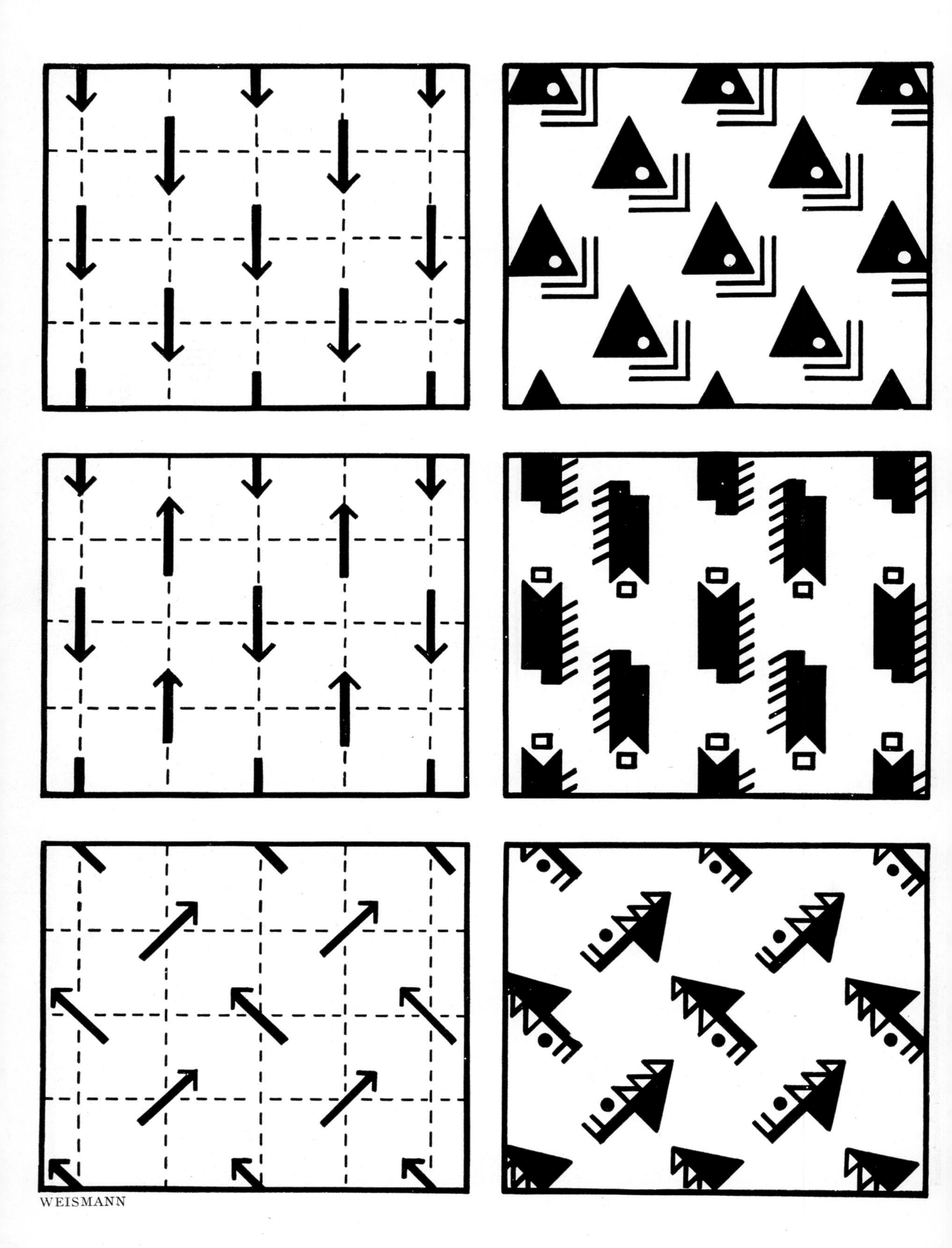
WEISMANN

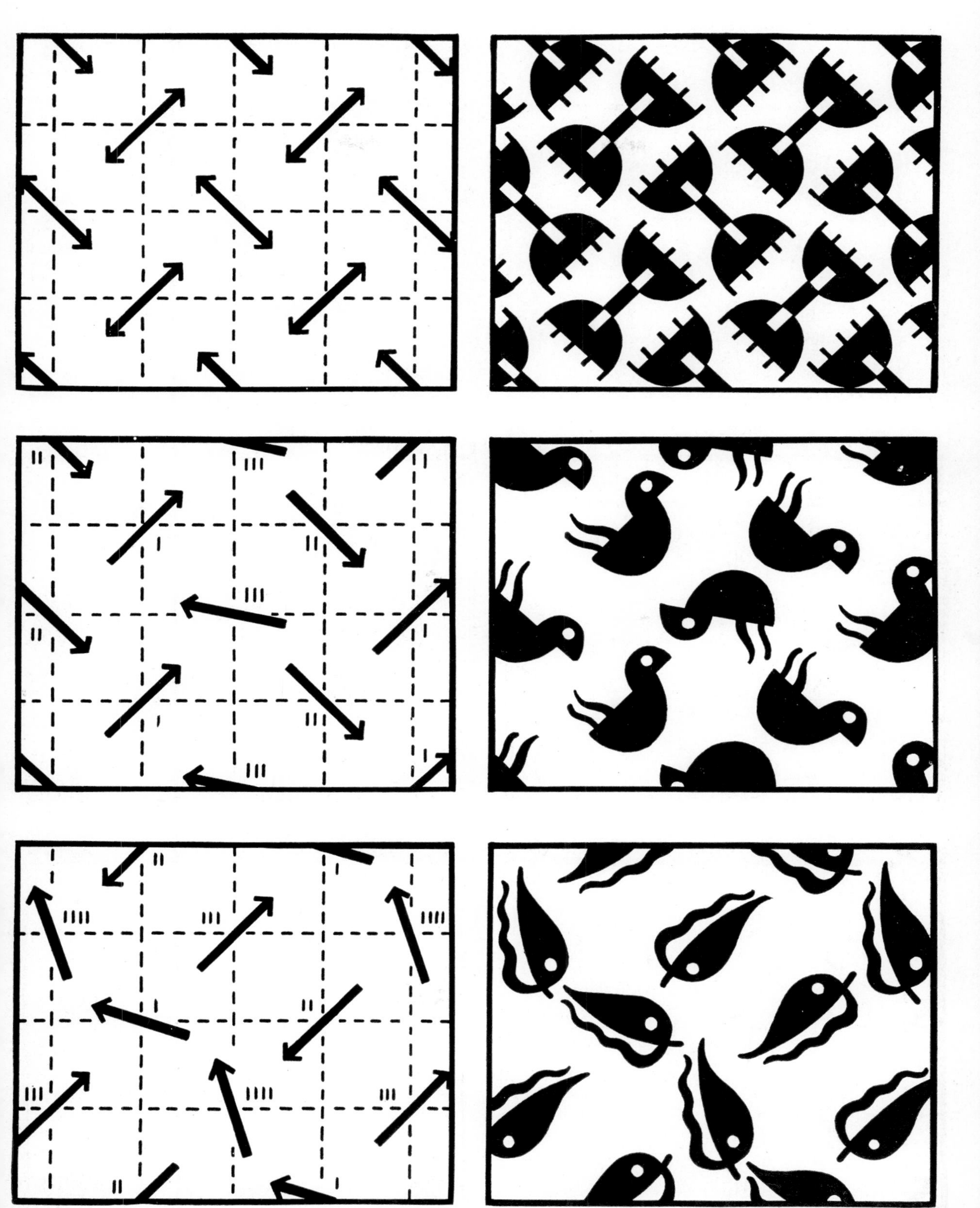
WEISMANN

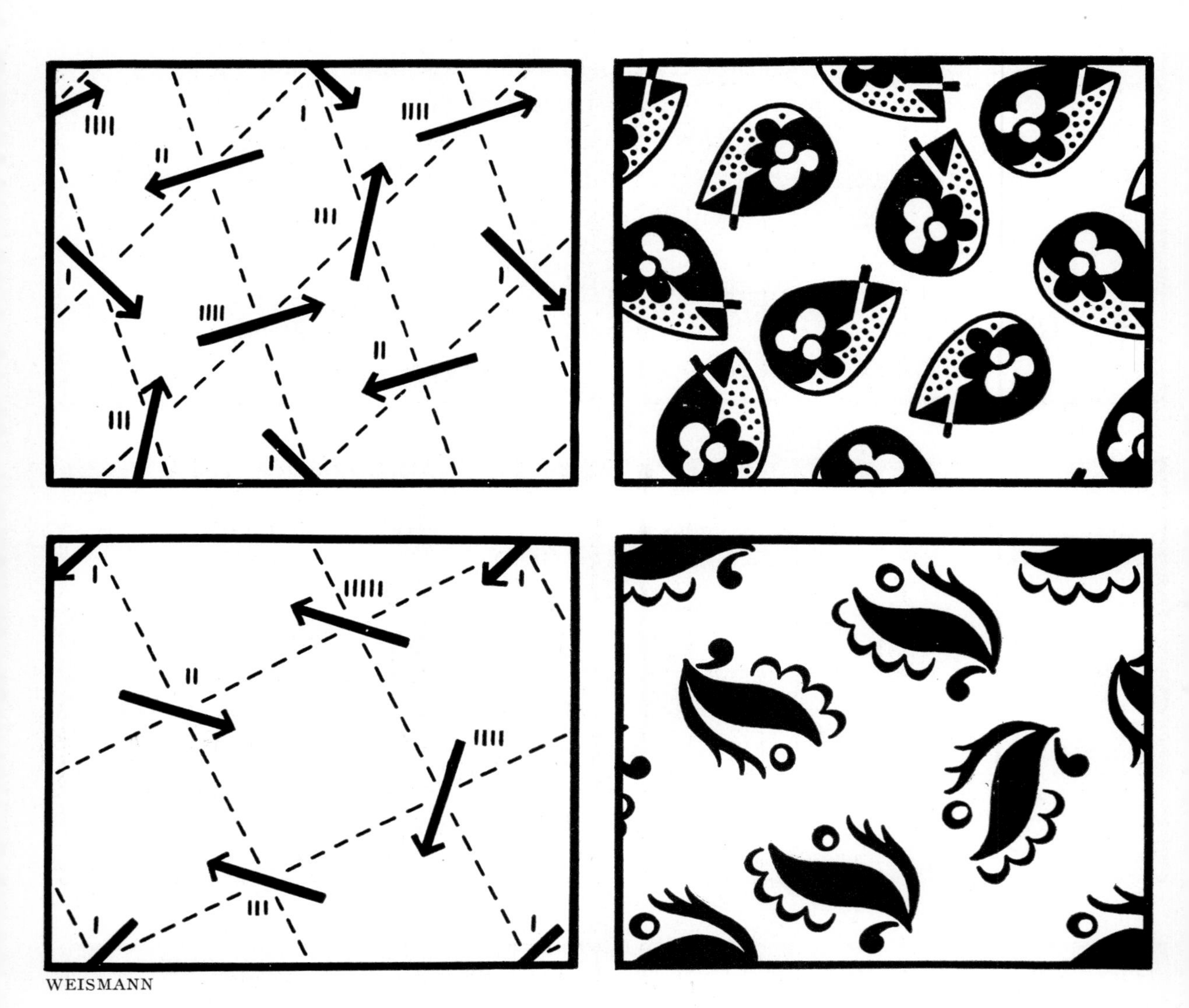

WEISMANN

BASIC REPEAT PATTERNS

The diagrams to the left in the preceding designs are shown to indicate the patterns into which the designs fall. They may be used as guides in creating new designs. Often a unit will appear to greater advantage in some other arrangement than that in which it is first tried. Thus it would be wise to become familiar with all the methods shown here.

ter and charm when applied to a small surface. Scale is not the only consideration, for the nature or spirit of the design has equal bearing upon its final purpose. A delicately feminine allover pattern would not be at all suitable for the lamp shade of a sturdy pottery lamp used in a masculine room. Thus harmony of idea is another primary factor in the success of an allover pattern.

The nature of the design and the technique used in its drawing will do much to determine the kind of colors to be used. A bold handling of line and form will often gain added strength with an equally bold use of color; whereas a small, dainty pattern will usually seem to suggest a soft, feminine color scheme. The color is also controlled somewhat by the texture of the surface to which the design is applied. It would not be advisable to put a tiny tracery of design in pastel color onto a coarse heavy fabric.

The colors should be carried through a design in order to preserve the intended rhythmic pattern rather than to break it into spotty, disorganized points of interest. One is reminded again of the fact that color has two important properties, value and intensity, and that both of these will produce certain definite effects when the color is applied to the desired areas.

One may begin an allover design in several different ways. The most simple method and the one which is advisable for a beginner, is that of first designing a unit which can be repeated in the final design. By carefully working out a single unit, both in design and in color, and then tracing it according to the repeat pattern desired, the final effect is usually satisfactory. Occasionally when the unit is seen as a repeated pattern, it may seem necessary to adjust or omit some of its details in order to increase the rhythmic pattern or to bring it into closer organization. The beginner will keep his first motif simple in color and design, but as his knowl-

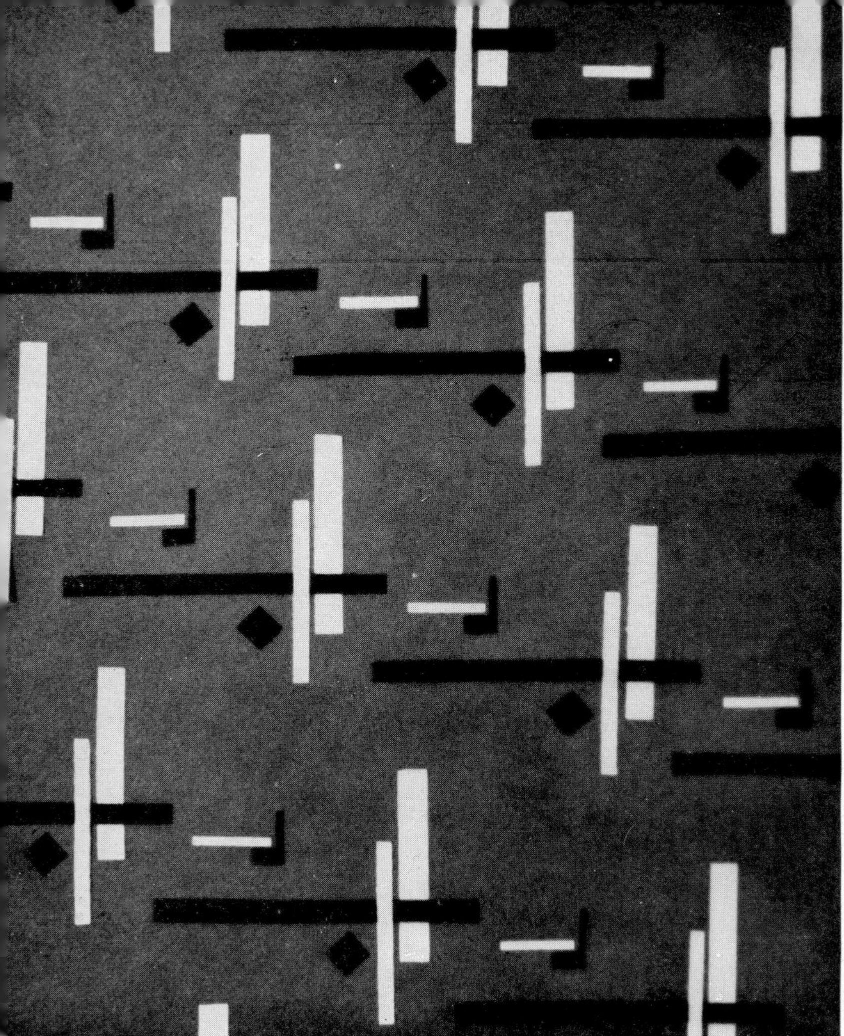

THOMAS

ABSTRACT ALLOVER DESIGN

by Esther Otte

Cut paper is an expedient method by which to work out designs.

edge increases, more complex patterns may be worked out. Frequently a unit repeated according to one of the simpler methods given will produce an altogether different effect than when it is repeated according to one of the more complicated methods.

Another means of designing an allover pattern is much like that discussed for border designs. Numerous units of varying shapes and sizes may be cut from colored paper and adjusted into an allover design. A piece of ruled or graph paper will serve as an ade-

CUT PAPER ALL-OVER DESIGN
by Josephine Brownlow

Designs of this type are excellent to use for block printing or stenciling.

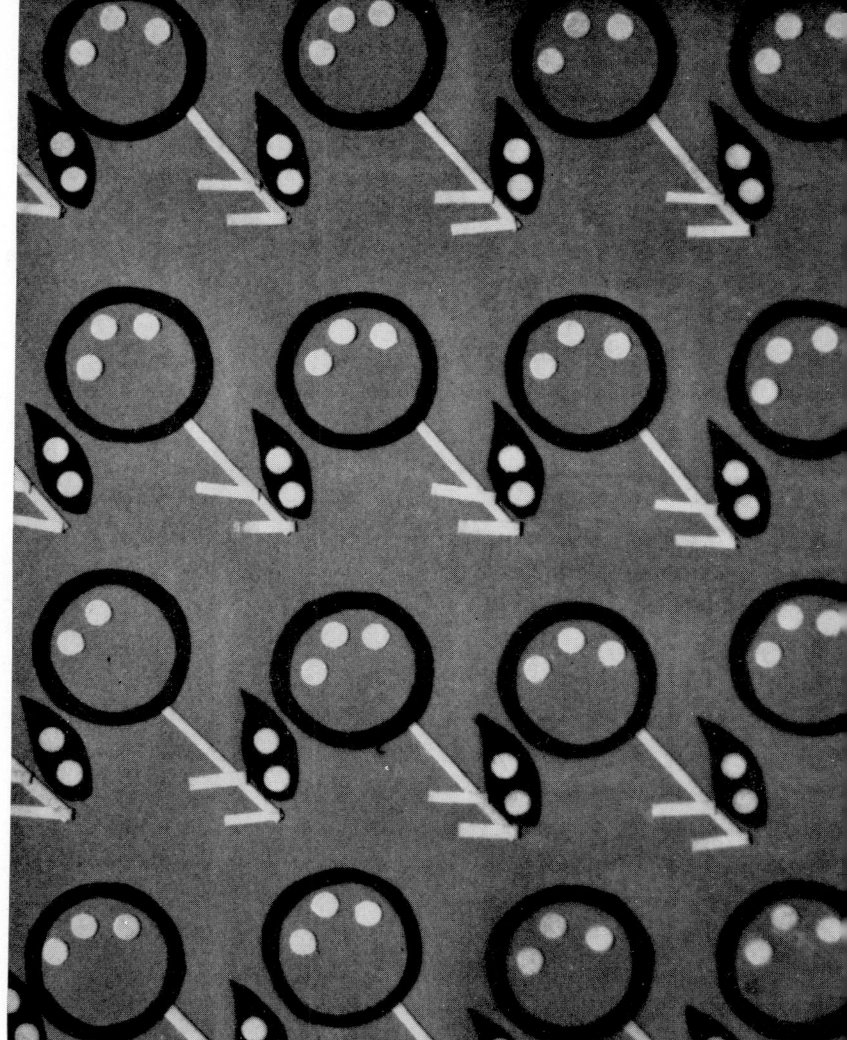

THOMAS

quate background and will facilitate the regular placing of the units. This piece of work, then, may be used as a preliminary plan for the final design which may be worked out in another medium. It should be remembered that while the colored paper units will probably be essentially geometric, the final design may incorporate such shapes and cast them into more realistic or more recognizable forms. For example, a circle might become a flower. Free, totally abstract forms can be cut or torn from paper just as well if one is inventive. It is said that one of our foremost textile designers lays out many of her designs in this way.

The foregoing material has dealt chiefly with allover designs consisting of definite units. It must be remembered that striped and/or plaid designs also fall into the classification of allover designs. In both of these types, the point of primary importance is the interest created by the variation in width and color of the background spaces as well as the lines which make the design. A design composed of stripes of equal width is quite apt to be monotonous, whereas one of stripes of unequal but pleasingly related widths will be interesting.

Unusual Units

When a design is being planned to decorate the surface of some particular object and it seems desirable to keep it as a single unit, the problem presents complications not encountered in the planning of an allover or border design. The first factor to be considered is the shape of the surface to be decorated. Whether it is round, square, or rectangular, the design should be so planned as to conform to, and become a part of, that shape. A unit planned for the top of a round box would not appear to advantage on a box with a rectangular cover. One might say that a good unit design, though not necessarily bordered by a definite line, so suggests the shape it is being planned for that when seen apart from it, the shape would still be felt strongly. To accomplish this successfully, any lines or forms which are so forceful as to break the given space into unharmonious shapes should be scrupulously avoided. A square broken into two triangles by the use of a definite diagonal line moving from one corner to the opposite corner would not be as useful a foundation for a design as would be a like square divided into

A symmetrical unit of design is one which is arranged in perfect balance on both sides of the center. It is a formal design arrangement.

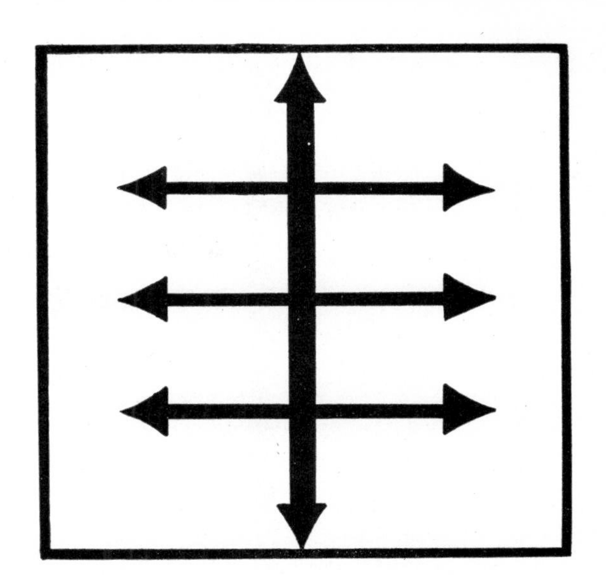

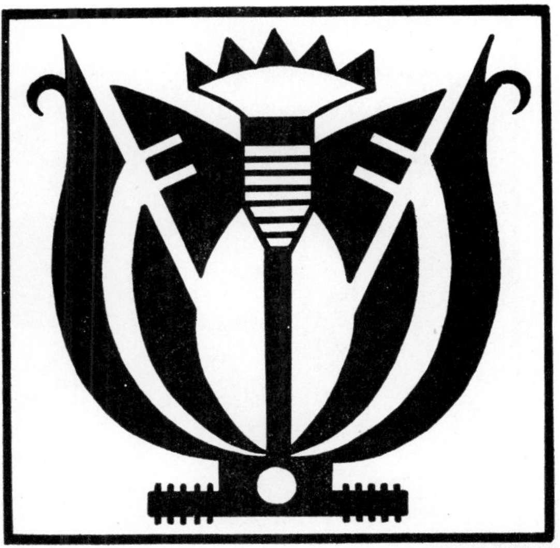

WEISMANN

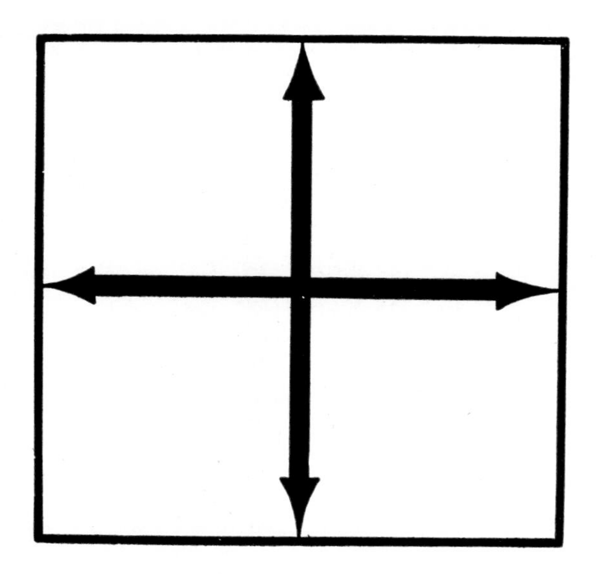

A bisymmetric unit of design is one which is arranged in perfect balance on all of its sides. It is a formal design arrangement.

WEISMANN

An asymmetric unit of design is one which differs on all sides but which still retains a balanced arrangement. It is an informal design arrangement.

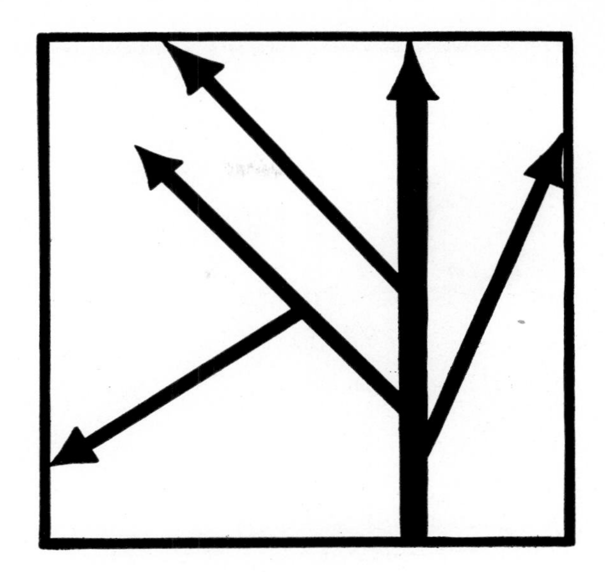

WEISMANN

THOMAS

ABSTRACT DESIGN

by Marilyn Sincox

This cut paper design might very well be used for a patchwork pillow top.

four triangles through the use of two diagonal lines. In the second case, one line would tend to nullify the other since it moved in the opposite direction; and the attention would be drawn to the intersection of the two lines. Thus the center of interest remains within the unit rather than being drawn away from it, as would happen in the first example.

The designing of a unit for some particular shape means simply that the shape in question is broken up interestingly with lines and forms integrated into a pleasing relationship. These lines and forms may be very abstract with no representational qualities, or they may resolve themselves into conventionalized realistic objects such as flowers, leaves, animals, or figures. Usually, when working with abstract or geometric forms, it is well to use line and shape contrasts. A design composed entirely of straight lines is apt to

STYLIZED FLOWER
by Audrey White

Strength is gained by omitting realistic details.

THOMAS

look sharp and brittle, whereas the introduction of some relief in the form of curved lines will soften the design and afford pleasing contrasts. If realistic objects are desired within the unit, they should be selected and composed with every thought given to the design itself. It is usually the tendency for the beginner to become so involved with accurate representation as to overlook the quality of the form as it relates itself to the design. This can be avoided somewhat if the designer can coach himself to forget the actual flower, bird, or other object which he may first have had in mind. Then he may use a combination of geometric forms which, when assembled into a design unit, suggest an object of nature, without being so specific as to portray an exact type at the expense of good design. Too often a beginner will allow himself to be so strongly held by an idea that it becomes very difficult to give full play to the imagination. Good designing needs an imaginative approach.

No matter what comprises a unit design, it will follow one of several basic layouts. These layouts apply to a unit design intended for almost any shape, and a working knowledge of them will greatly aid the beginner when he first plans such a design. As has been suggested previously in another section, after the preliminary pattern has been decided upon, colored paper cut into various shapes might be used and arranged against a background of the correct dimensions until a satisfactory combination of foundation forms is arrived at. This arrangement could then serve its turn as an outline for a complete and detailed drawing of the design as it was first visualized or as it grew in the mind of the designer during the preliminary experimenting. The same principles of design that were described in more detail at the beginning of this chapter must be applied to any unit design. Contrasts in line, form, and value are essential to the well planned design in order that its nature will be one which will hold the interest over a long period of time. Such contrasts should be organized, of course, with care being devoted to the relationships of curved and straight lines, large and small forms, and dark and light values. The association of the unit of design and the shape onto which it is to be placed should not be forgotten at any time; each should and must complement the other.

Chapter VI

Figure Flattery

WOMAN, THY NAME IS VANITY IS PROVED EACH DAY THAT ONE lies abed in the morning suffering from wardrobe boredom. This may be just an excuse to stay in bed a little longer, but too often it's the truth. Perhaps one's closet does contain more costumes than the average; or perhaps it contains just one or two which must do duty day after day, and for every sort of occasion. Whichever the case, the psychological reaction is the same since everyone tires of the clothes he wears.

A wardrobe may be compared to a meal which lacks the proper variety or seasoning. Just as spices can stimulate an appetite, so can accessories lift a wardrobe from the commonplace, and add to a general feeling of well-being.

Not only is one's mental setup important to the way he starts the day, but it is important to the effect he makes upon others. Many do not admit dressing to impress others, but can it be denied? Refusal to admit this would mean that one took no precautions as to appearance before superiors, that one never gave a shiny nose an extra dusting of powder before going to a tea. The social responsibility of neatness and grooming is well understood, and since it is not the province of this book to instruct in that direction, this section will deal explicitly with the adjuncts of the wardrobe.

Most budgets cannot stand the strain of high style, though hearts may yearn for the newest expression of some creative stylist. Many take refuge behind a "don't care anyway" attitude which is expressed by complete disregard for the matter of wardrobe planning in any respect. Should consideration be given the economic factors here involved, it would be realized that no matter what talents one may possess, or how much of a success one may have achieved, ultimate attainments are often dependent upon the impression made upon others.

Frequently one hears of otherwise successful women who are kept from advancement or who lose their positions because of poor taste in personal clothing selection. Good taste does not mean an absolute acceptance of current style, but, rather, wise selections from the garments and accessories available at the time. This involves understanding of personal figure problems, personality, and financial standing.

Even though one may be cognizant of his particular problems, he may give the impression of being correctly but unimaginatively clothed. Why not strive for individualism? It takes so little time, effort, and ability to achieve distinction after one has the knack for selecting and combining accouterments with imagination. Do not bend over backward to be different; do not try to be conspicuous in a bizarre way! Such attempts usually bespeak poor taste and may mark one as an individual but not as an individual that one would wish to meet. Do not be sensational! To freshen up that wardrobe, or to add an unusual note, try a decorative accessory.

What is an accessory? It is something which is added to the wardrobe but which is not essentially a part of it. It is designed to heighten the effect of the wardrobe. One has often noticed how the effect of a basically plain dress is intensified by a beautiful clip or by some unusual buttons. In like manner, two or three different belts may be used to make one frock appear to be several. Embroidery might be added to a year-old dress to beguile one's friends into believing that there has been a new addition to the wardrobe.

Doubtless all will agree that accessories are valuable additions to any wardrobe, but perhaps many are already computing the cost of these articles as it would figure in their personal budgets. Consider making them. One may have a preconceived notion that making his own accessories would take a great deal of talent, or that if one did make them that they would look "home made." A little patience, very little money, visualization of the many possibilities, and a few spare moments will teach one that this is a fallacy. The following pages are filled with suggestions and directions for accessories which will add fillip to everyday existence. With these for suggestions plus a little personal imagination, countless other ideas will present themselves to the creative thinker.

As the Indians Did It

Fashion recurrently selects belts as her favorite point of emphasis, and the fashion-wise woman is ever alert to suggestions which will enable her to add to her own collection. Whether a wide belt or a narrow belt is the more becoming to one's own figure, it may be a distinctive note in a wardrobe. A belt need not be of leather or of the same material as one's dress or skirt to be attractive. There are any number of methods and materials suitable to the making of an unusual and interesting belt.

Because there has been a great deal of material published on the art of leather tooling, it is being purposely omitted in this chapter. We mention it only as a possibility and as a suggestion to those

who might be interested in this craft. Less familiar techniques will be discussed here. Not only are these techniques less familiar, and therefore more unusual, but they also require less equipment and less expensive material.

FINGER WEAVING is a technique, really a many strand braiding process, that was developed by the North American Indians. Many tribes are credited with its development and preservation, but research has shown that similar techniques have been used from north to south on the American continent.

Originally this craft was probably done with leather thongs and it may still be so done. However, for the purposes of adaptability and convenience, yarn has proved itself very satisfactory. Heavy weights of yarn are best. Germantown, knitting worsted, tapestry, and peasant yarns may all be used. Fast color cotton yarns, such as moss yarn, the lighter weight rug fillers, and perle cottons, sizes three or five, are also suitable and attractive.

For the beginner, two of the more simple of the possible variations of this technique are most easily comprehended. One produces a chevron stripe if more than one color is used; the other, a diagonal stripe moving from one side of the belt to the other. The number of colors used is left to the discretion of the weaver. It should be borne in mind when selecting the colors that they be harmonious in combination and pleasing with the dress with which the belt is to be worn. One way of insuring this is through the use of one color that repeats

FINGER WOVEN BELT

by Barbara Bentson

Chevron stripe.

that of the dress. Both the hue and the value of the color are very important. The design of the belt will be most pleasing if there is an adequate value contrast.

The greatest problem in designing a belt of this kind is that of determining the relative width of the stripes. Each area or color should be considered as an individual stripe, so that both the dark and the light areas have pleasing variation. The relative proportions of the stripes are set by the number of strands of yarn used for each stripe; for example, if three times as many strands are used for one stripe as are used for another, the first stripe will be three times as wide as the other. When planning the sizes of the stripes the principles for obtaining good proportions should be applied.

One of the characteristic qualities of a belt of this kind is its flexibility, a factor which permits looping or tying into a soft knot. Calculation of the length of the strands of yarn to be cut for weaving involves consideration of the following: the woven length, which includes the waist measurement; the amount needed for the knot; and the length desired for sash ends; the sum of which must be doubled, because about that much is taken up in the process of weaving. To this add the length desired for fringe on each end of the belt.

Cut the desired number of strands of each color to the necessary length. The greater the number of strands used, the wider will be the belt. Sixty-two lengths of knitting worsted will produce a braid approximately three inches wide.

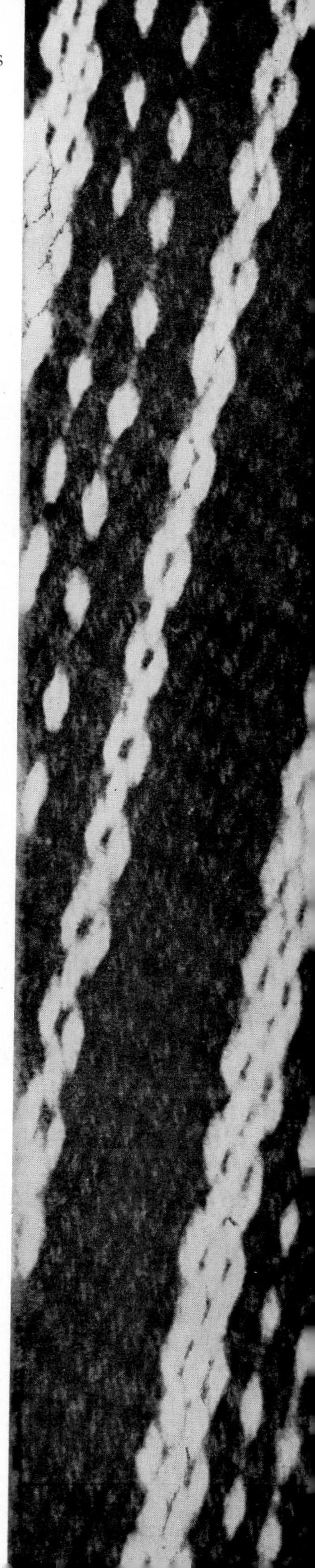

FINGER WEAVING

Diagonal stripe.

THE CHEVRON PATTERN

Arrange the same number of strands of each color on either side of the center in the same relative positions. In other words, duplicate one side of the center in reverse on the other. There should be not only an equal number on each side of the center, but also an even number on each side, such as ten and ten, twelve and twelve, twenty and twenty, etc. Thus your plan might read from the left, six brown, nine green, five tan, center, five tan, nine green, six brown. Starting at the left, wrap each thread in its proper order once around a pencil or short stick. Permit a length of yarn extending beyond the pencil in one direction to equal the length allowed for the fringe on one end of the belt. This divides the original length of yarn into long and short parts. After each yarn has been looped about the pencil in its correct position, the short or fringe end of the yarns should be tied together in one knot close to the pencil or stick.

Take a short piece of scrap yarn, about 18 inches long, double it and put the first left-hand strand of yarn in the loop thus formed. Twist this short length of yarn once, and place the second strand of yarn between the short ends against the twist. Twist the short piece again in the same direction as before, and place the third strand up against this twist. Repeat until all the strands of yarn are held firmly in place, one next to the other, and in their proper positions. This *stay* should be put as close to the pencil as possible.

The material is now ready for weaving. Tie the fringe end securely to some stable object at a height convenient for working. Divide the group of yarns in the center. *It is essential that this center division be constantly maintained.* Grasp one group firmly in each hand. Take the first thread from the center of the left-hand

PREPARING YARN FOR FINGERWEAVING

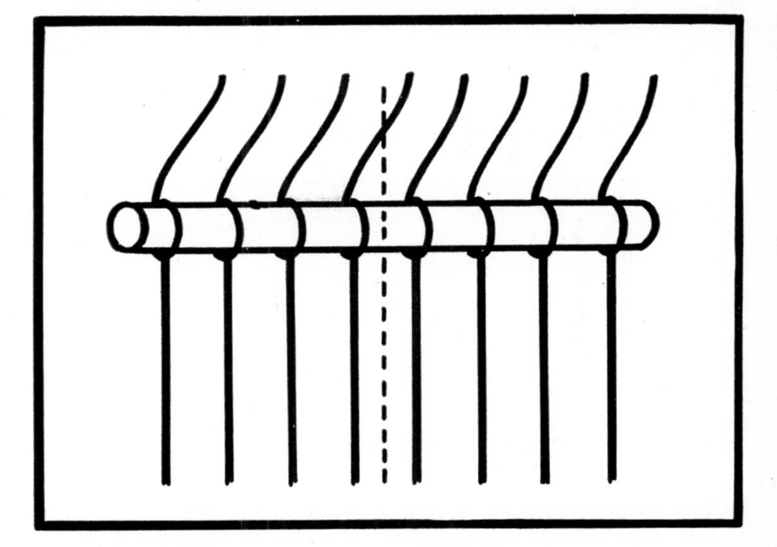

Wrap each strand firmly around a small stick or pencil allowing sufficient yarn above the stick to form a fringe of the desired length.

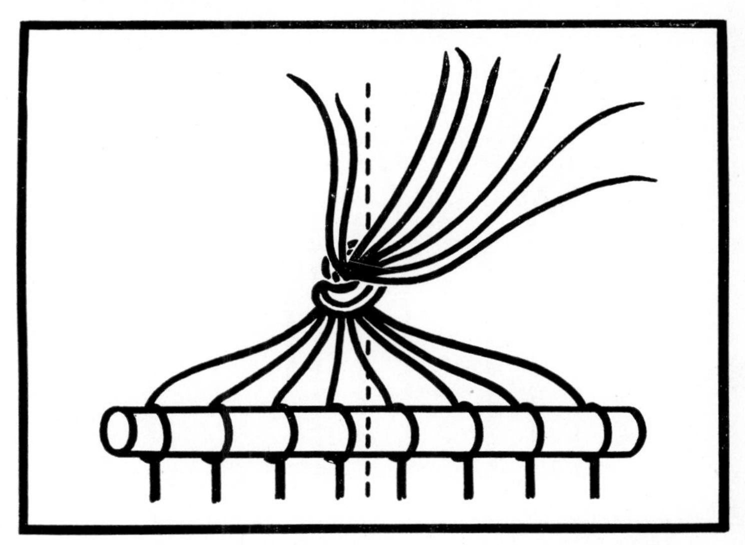

Tie the fringe end in a knot and fasten this knot to some secure object such as the back of a chair.

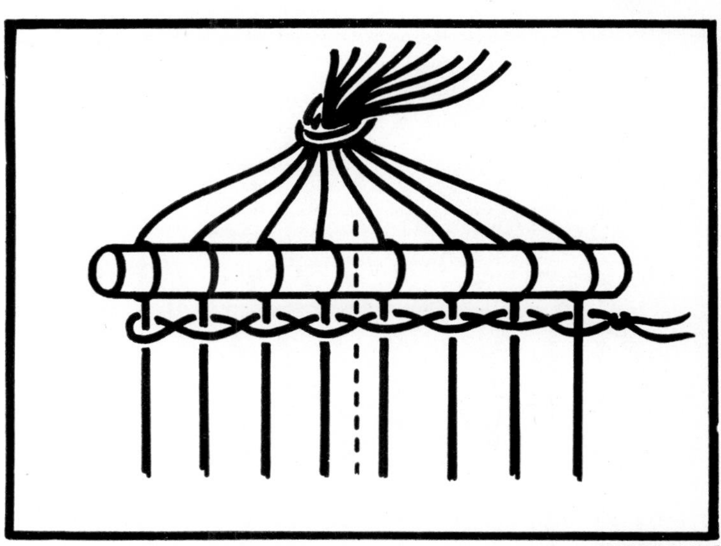

Secure the order of the yarn by twisting an extra length of yarn between and around each strand. The material is now ready for weaving.

WEISMANN

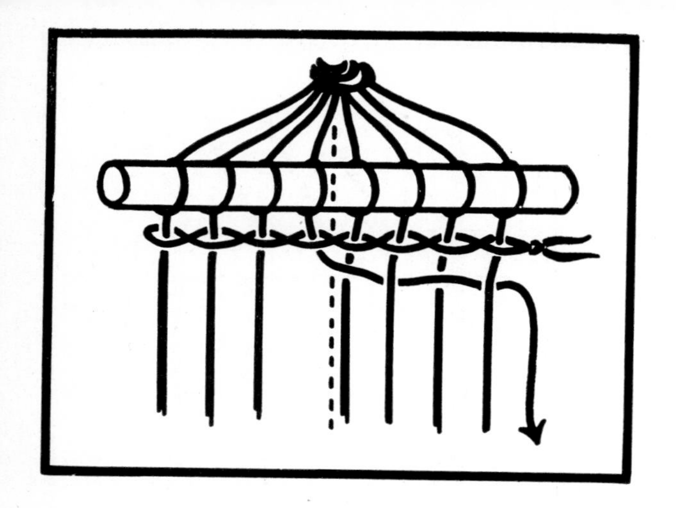

FINGER WEAVING

The chevron design.

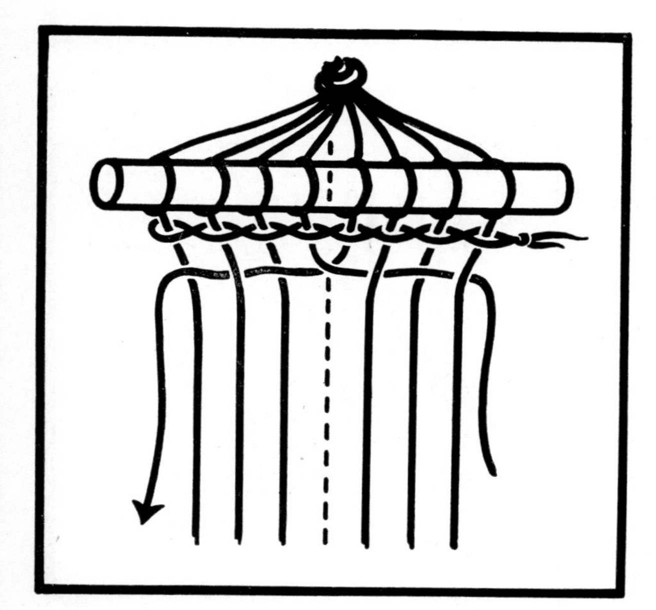

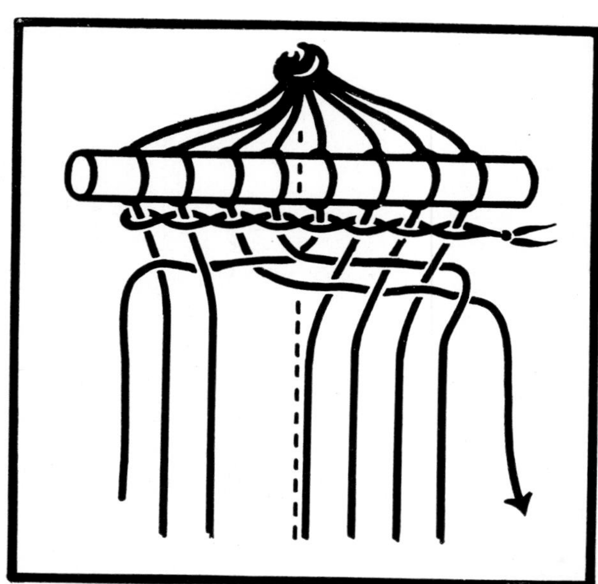

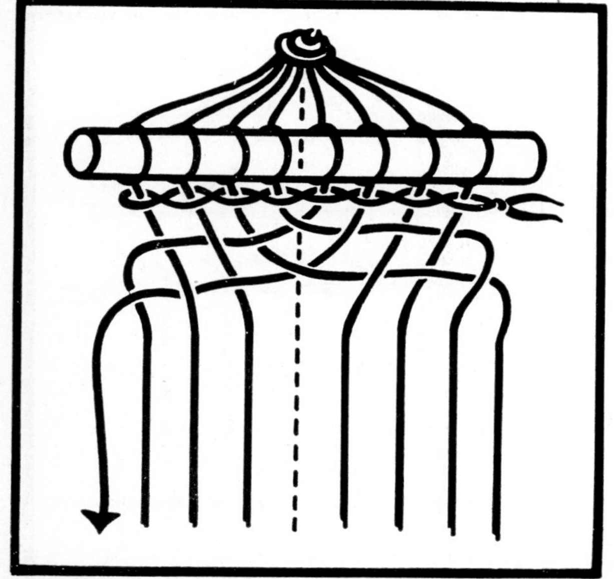

WEISMANN

FINGER WEAVING

The diagonal stripe.

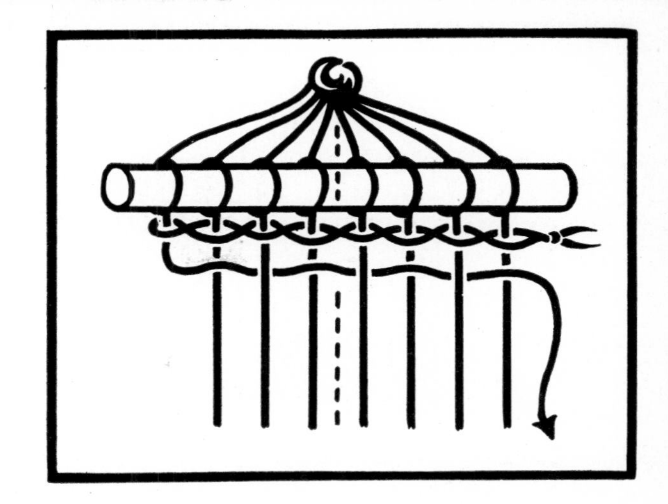

WEISMANN

group and pass it over the first thread from the center of the right-hand group, under the second, over the third, under the fourth, etc., until it emerges at the opposite side of the group from where it started. Permit this thread to dangle free. Start again at the center with the first thread to the right of the center. Weave to the left until this thread emerges at the outside edge to the left; permit it to dangle free. Start again at the left-center and weave to the right as before. Bring the first dangling yarn into the group and weave over or under it as though it were a part of the group. This process is basically like that of any simple weaving; i.e., the weft thread passes alternately over and under the warp threads. Repeat the process, again using the right-center yarn and weaving left, being sure to include the dangling yarn on this side. Always leave the yarn last woven dangling free on the side until a new strand replaces it. Continue in this manner, left and right, until the desired length of fabric has been woven. The tension of the yarn and the width of the belt are controlled by adjusting the dangling thread as it is finally taken into the group of threads when it is replaced. Good technique is a necessity to the belt's beauty.

The Diagonal Stripe Pattern

The length of yarns to be used is figured in the same way as for the chevron pattern but the weaving process differs slightly. Tie the yarn to the pencil in an arrangement that forms a pleasing striped pattern. It does not have to be arranged the same on both sides of the center. For weaving, instead of beginning at the center and weaving alternately right and left, begin with the first thread at the extreme left (or right) and, beginning over the first yarn, weave over and under across the entire group of yarns. Leave this yarn dangling as before. Start at the original side with the second yarn and weave it across the entire group. When the new weaver emerges at the far side, be sure to include in the group the old one left dangling before. Continue weaving, always from the same side, always alternately over and under, until a sufficient length of woven fabric has been obtained.

From the Egyptians

CARD WEAVING, a method developed centuries ago by the Egyptians, is another process by which belts, hat bands, purses (strips sewed together), suspenders, and dress trimming, as well as braids for household purposes, can be made. The cards with which the weaving is done really comprise a simple loom; hence the fabric that results is actually woven, in contrast to finger weaving, which is basically a braiding technique.

The materials required for card weaving are simple. A number of cards two and one-half to three inches square, cut from stiff, smooth cardboard which does not fray easily, are needed. Trunk board, heavy poster board, or the cardboard used for bookbinding is excellent. Each card should have a hole one-eighth to one-fourth inch in diameter punched in each corner. These must be very accurately placed about one-half inch from the corner, exactly in the same positions on each card.

The holes should be labeled *A*, *B*, *C*, and *D* respectively in clockwise fashion. Corners *A* should be marked in some way so as to be easily observed when looking at the cards from the side. Clipping the corner or coloring it with a crayon or ink are suggested methods. Number each card successively 1, 2, 3, etc.

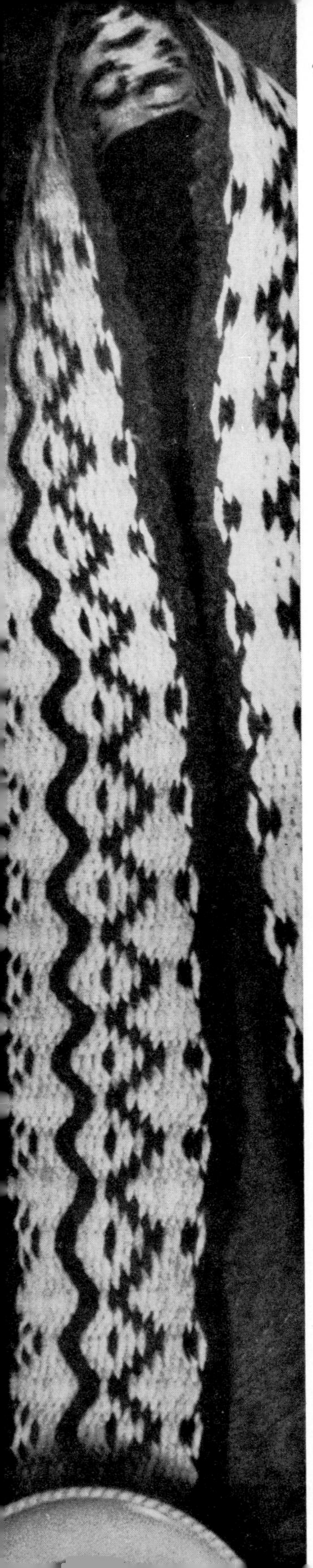

The number of cards needed depends upon the width of the fabric desired. Twenty cards will be sufficient to make a piece of material approximately one and one-half inches wide if woven with Shetland yarn. Narrower or wider widths may be made by using fewer or more cards. Germantown or knitting worsted will make a wider belt per number of cards than will the Shetland yarn. The use of carpet warp results in material of approximately the same width as that produced by Shetland yarn.

Warp and weft threads are needed for this craft. The warp threads may be of a good quality Shetland yarn, Germantown or knitting worsted, carpet warp, string or perle cotton in sizes three or five. The weft thread may be the same as the warp thread and is less conspicuous when chosen in the same color as that of the outside warp threads.

The warp threads will need to be considerably longer than the length desired for the finished woven band. Thirty-one inches of warp works up into about twenty-seven inches of woven material. This does not allow for fringing, finishing, or for the play of the cards when weaving. An extra eighteen inches of warp should be ample unless long fringe is desired. All warp threads must be exactly the same length.

The procedure followed when designing the pattern will be more easily understood if the accompanying diagrams are studied carefully. If there is no squared paper at hand, rule off a piece of paper so that there are four rows of squares, one above another. The number

CARD WOVEN BELT

by Virginia Nelson

The cards were threaded from one direction only. The cards were reversed every fourth step.

of squares in each row should be identical with the number of cards prepared for use. There are four rows of these squares, each row representing a corner of the cards; label them at one side of the diagram: *A*, *B*, *C*, and *D*. Above each square in the top row place a number beginning with 1 above the left-hand square and continuing in order until the right-hand square receives the same number that appears on the last card to be used in the weaving.

Decide how many colors are going to be used for the belt. As many or as few colors as one wishes may be used. Moderation, however, is always a good rule. A pleasing value contrast is helpful in bringing out a clean cut pattern. A colored pencil or crayon to indicate the color of each warp thread to be used will facilitate the designing of the pattern.

Study the group of squares to visualize the many possibilities obtainable if the squares were filled in solidly with the various crayons to form simple mosaiclike designs. Very young children often amuse themselves in this manner for hours at a time and many adults still find it a fascinating bit of seatwork. Try a number of the best ideas by actually filling in the squares. The proportion of each color used and the distribution of each should be checked carefully. The designs need not be symmetrical, but simple designs made up of fairly large areas usually weave up into the most attractive patterns. It may help to remember that each colored block represents only one "stitch," and appears very small indeed in the finished product.

CARD WOVEN BELT
by Edith Nelson

The cards were threaded from one direction only. The cards were turned in one direction.

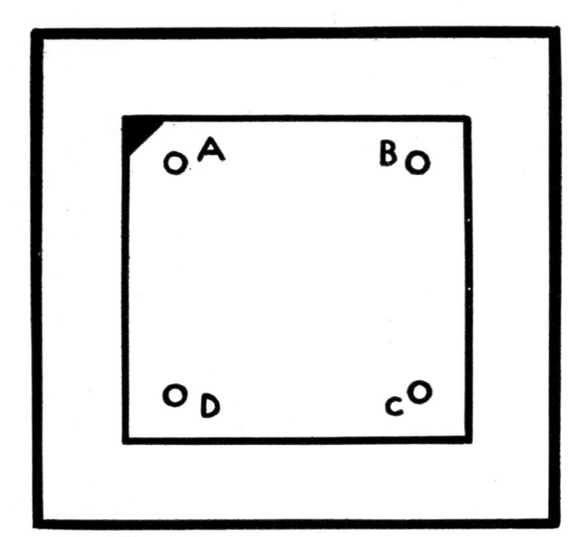

Card for weaving.

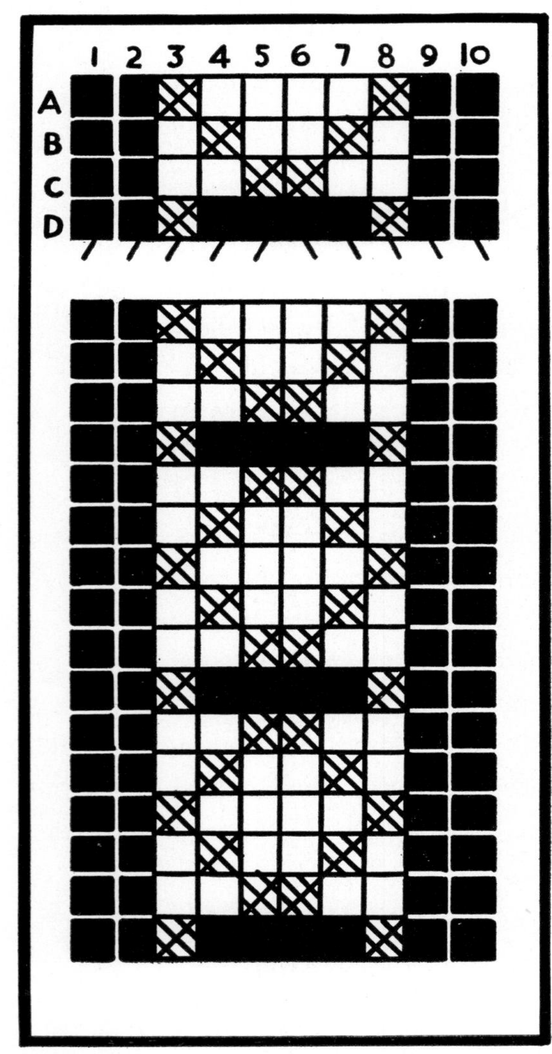

Preparing the design.

WEISMANN

Choose the best of the paper patterns. This pattern represents the design across the entire width of the belt to be woven, but only four weft threads of its length. This colored chart merely shows the areas in which the various colors will appear. The actual design takes on interest brought about by the direction the threads twist as the material is being woven, and by the manipulation as controlled by the craftsman.

The cards are warped according to the pattern chosen. This is a simple process if one always bears in mind the fact that each letter on the diagram represents a hole in the card and that each number represents a single card. To warp cards for the design shown in the accompanying diagram, the following order is indicated:

Card 1—*A* black, *B* black, *C* black, *D* black
Card 2—*A* black, *B* black, *C* black, *D* black
Card 3—*A* gray, *B* white, *C* white, *D* gray
Card 4—*A* white, *B* gray, *C* white, *D* black
Card 5—*A* white, *B* white, *C* gray, *D* black
Card 6—*A* white, *B* white, *C* gray, *D* black
Card 7—*A* white, *B* gray, *C* white, *D* black
Card 8—*A* gray, *B* white, *C* white, *D* gray
Card 9—*A* black, *B* black, *C* black, *D* black
Card 10—*A* black, *B* black, *C* black, *D* black

It will be seen from a study of this chart that in order to weave this pattern forty strands of yarn are needed—four for each card. Of these forty strands, twenty are black, eight are gray, and twelve are white. Each strand of yarn is drawn through its proper hole, with care being taken that the strands are all drawn through the proper side of the card. At the bottom of the pattern diagram or draft are small lines slanting up or down to indicate whether the threads are to be put through the holes in the cards from face

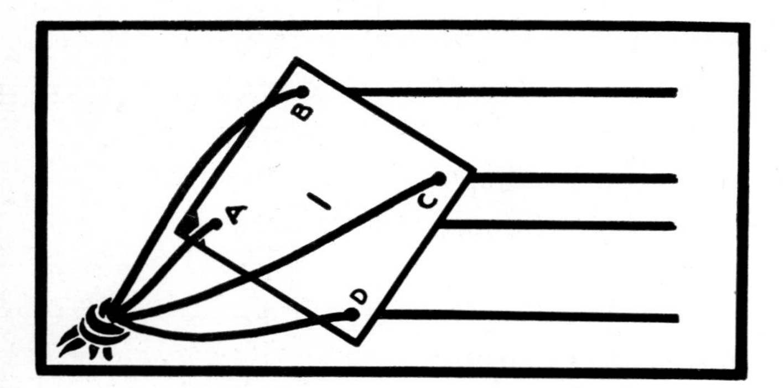

Warping the cards.

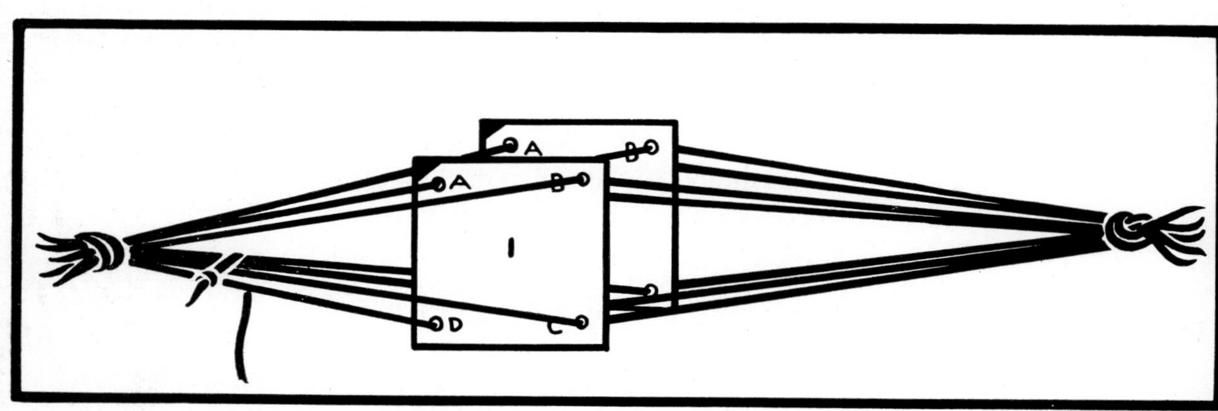

WEISMANN

Preparing the warped cards for weaving.

to back or from back to face. Usually the direction of threading changes at the center of the pattern. Many patterns may be threaded all in one direction without destroying the design; in fact, the twisting of the threads is responsible for some interesting variations. The accompanying photographs show the effect of the two methods of threading. After each card is warped, it is well to tie the ends of the four strands into a loose knot to prevent their slipping free of the card.

The directions for weaving are as follows: Gather together all the warp ends from holes *A*, *B*, *C*, and *D* on one side of the cards, which have been stacked one upon the other in order of number, corresponding corners one over the other. Tie these ends securely into a knot. Fasten the knot firmly to some stationary object. This is important. Straighten out the warp from the other end and tie another knot about twenty-four inches from the first knot, keeping the cards between the two knots. Tie this knot to a chair (or to one's waist) so that the tension may be kept steady. After pulling the threads fairly taut, grasp the cards firmly in both hands and turn so that the lettered sides are perpendicular to the floor, with corner *A* closest to the weaver.

Push the cards along the warp threads toward the body so that one may grasp them comfortably without arm strain. It will be noticed that the threads have divided themselves into two groups forming a shed. Slip a one-fourth inch strip of thin cardboard into the shed nearest one's body. Turn the cards away from their original position in a counterclockwise direction so that the corner

CARD WOVEN SAMPLER

The cards were threaded both ways; the change of direction was made in the center.

lettered *B* takes the position just held by letter A. Put another strip of cardboard through this shed, pushing this cardboard close to the first piece. Continue turning the cards in this fashion until corner A is again in its original position. Using cardboard strips or a one-inch strip of rag for the first few turns instead of a regular weft thread gives a firm foundation for the rest of the weaving.

The regular weft thread is usually the same as the warp thread, and preferably the same color as the outside warp threads. Cut a piece a little less than two yards long and insert it in the new shed. Have an equal length extend on each side. Turn the cards again, and through the shed formed insert both ends of the weft thread, pulling them firmly but not tightly to the opposite sides of the warp from which they were first placed. The use of a double weft such as this produces a firm web, and it is easier to keep the edges of the belt even and free from loops. The weft threads should be pushed into place with the side of the hand, a ruler, or any other contrivance the weaver finds handy. Continue weaving until the warp on the other side of the cards is twisted so tightly that weaving is difficult. Then one may do one of two things: either start turning the cards in the opposite direction, which automatically unwinds the warp, or untie the warp end and untwist it by hand. Tie the warp into position again and continue weaving as before, turning the cards counterclockwise.

Pattern changes are obtained by changing the direction in which the cards are turned at regular intervals. For example, if the cards are turned four times counterclockwise, then four times clockwise a symmetrical unit is formed. It is fun to experiment with this procedure, for many original effects can be obtained. The edges of

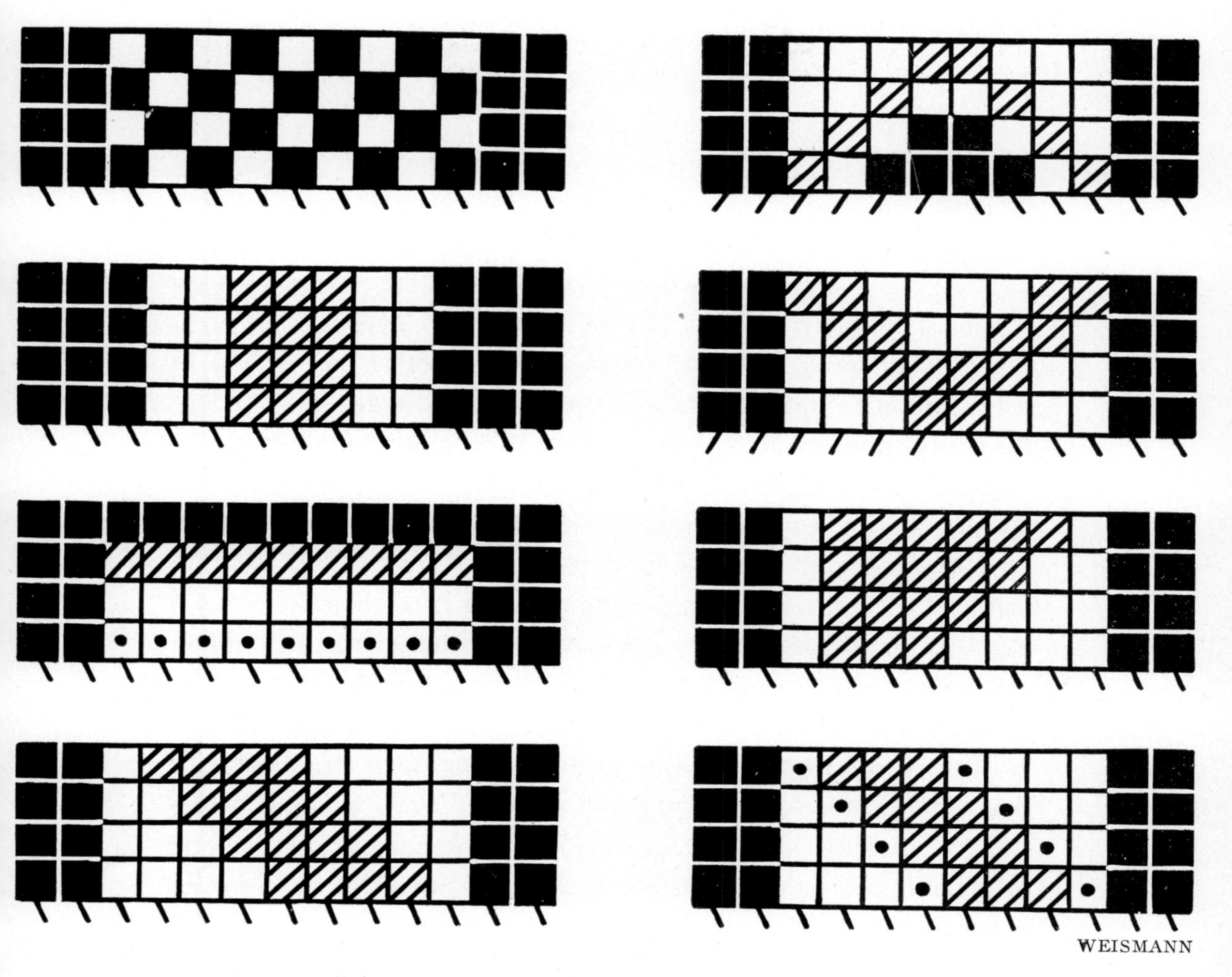

PATTERNS FOR CARD WEAVING

the woven material are more difficult to keep even when the cards are turned in opposite directions.

It is wise to jot down on a piece of paper exactly what the next turn will be when leaving one's work even for a short time. It is difficult to correct an error, especially if wool warp is being used. Slipping rubber bands around the pack of cards whenever the weaving is put aside is a great help as well.

When the weft thread has come to an end a new piece may be added by placing the new length in the next shed. The short ends of the old weft may be cut off close to the fabric when the weaving has progressed an inch or so. The nature of the weaving will hold the ends in place without danger of raveling.

The bibliography will suggest references if one wishes to delve into the more complicated forms of card weaving.

Ingenuity will suggest many ways to finish the ends of the braid. A few suggestions will surely bring to mind others. The ends of the braid may be stitched several times by machine to prevent raveling and then the raw edges bound with cloth or thin leather (the tops of kid gloves or leathers of similar weight are usable). The loose ends of yarn may be knotted close to the braid and cut evenly to form fringe of the desired length; or a heavier fringe may be made by twisting two strands of yarn separately, then twisting them together. Other than these finishes are the braids made from three or four strands. Four-strand braid fringe is exceptionally attractive. It is a rare occasion when a commercial plastic or metal buckle forms a suitable addition to any of the hand-woven belts.

Grandmother Did This

Occasionally a design which uses greater freedom in line, motif, or repetition than that found in a pattern produced by card or finger weaving will be better suited to a particular dress. Sometimes too, the fabric from which the dress is made will be a more satisfactory background for a decorative belt than will another ma-

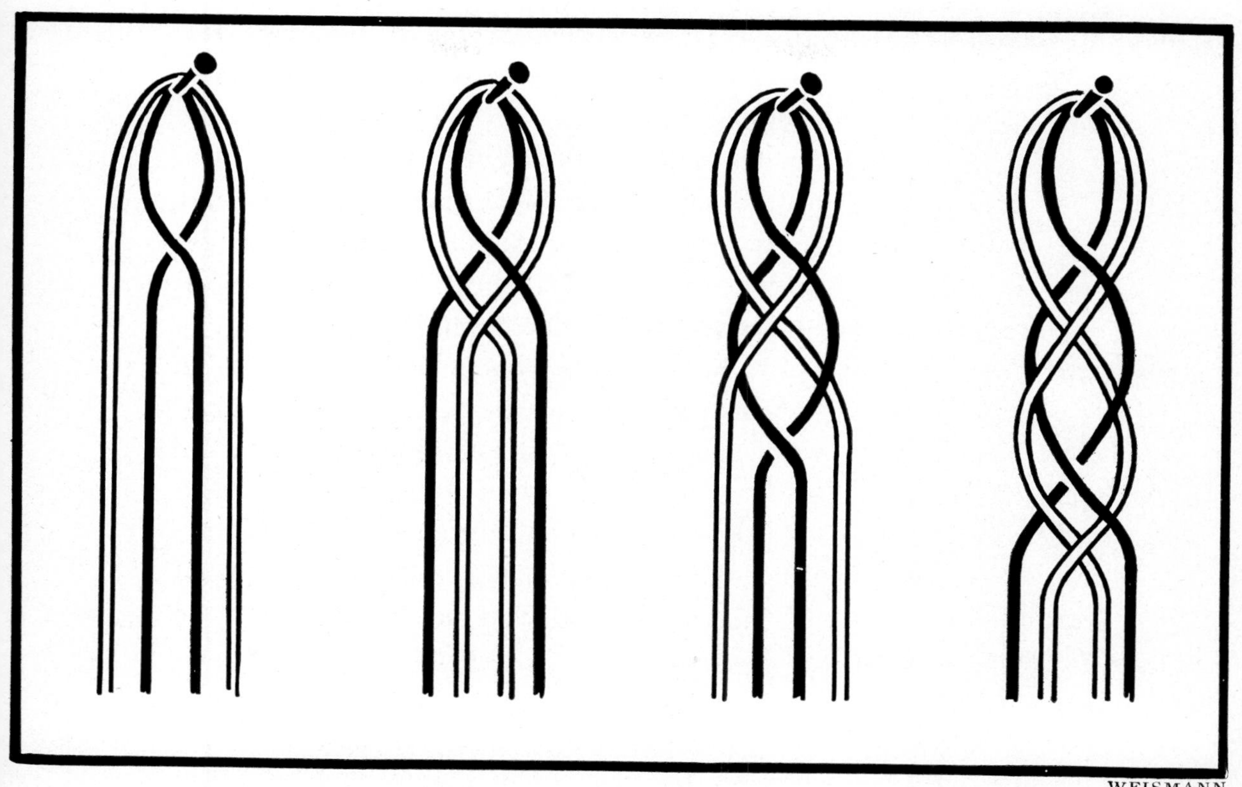

FOUR-STRAND BRAIDING

terial. Stitchery is one means for producing unlimited freedom of expression in the interpretation of a design and at the same time may be done on a piece of the dress fabric itself. It is not always, of course, necessary to do the stitchery on the dress material; other materials may be equally attractive as a basis for a well designed, decorative belt.

Needlework is something that the present day miss usually concedes to her grandmother. Do not for a minute imagine that

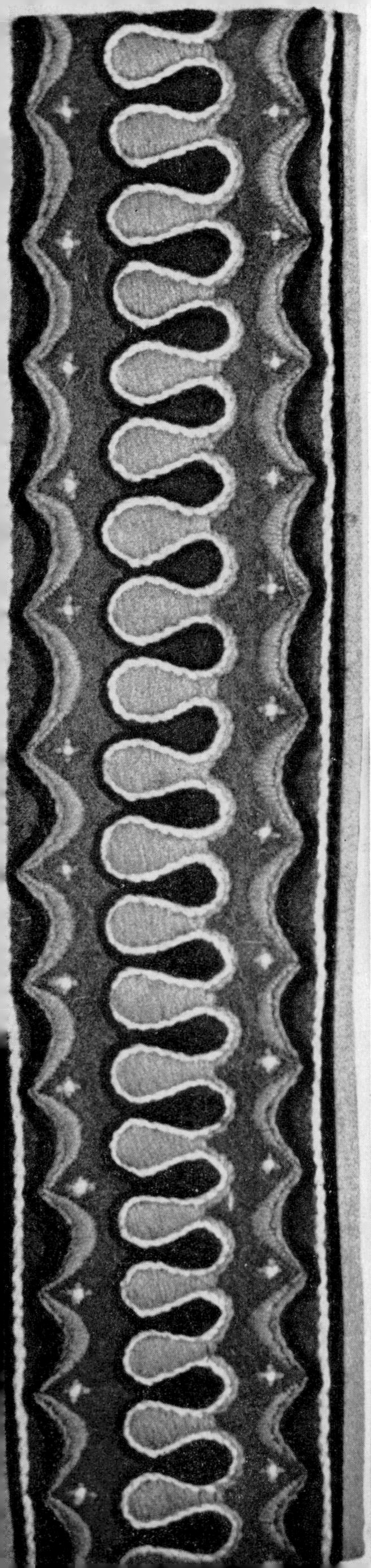

this is a lost art buried under the mass production of our machine age. It takes to revival like a duck to water and it pays dividends for the time and effort it may take.

Two variations of technique not frequently used in making a belt will be considered in more detail here. It is to be understood, as we have mentioned before, that these are just suggestions presented with the hope that they may open the way to further experimentation on the part of the reader.

Yarn on Felt (or Wool)

After the fabric selection has been made, decide upon the length and width of the finished belt. Cut the belt to the desired shape, allowing sufficient material for seaming and fastening. Plan the design for the area to be decorated. This design may be a border following the length of the belt, or it may be a surface design consisting of small, repeated motifs. Draw the design on paper to actual size. To transfer the design to the fabric, pin the paper to the cloth and run small basting stitches along the lines of the design, taking care to go through the fabric at the same time. Then the paper may be torn away and the basting threads used as guide lines for the yarn embroidery. Another method may be followed.

EMBROIDERED BELT
by Barbara Weismann

The paper design may be pierced along the lines of the design either by pricking with a pin or by using a seam marker. This perforated pattern should then be securely pinned to the fabric and powdered chalk pounced through the holes with a piece of cotton. If this method is used, it is essential to re-mark the transferred design on the fabric with a basting stitch, since the chalk guide lines will rub off during the process of embroidery. If one has confidence in his own ability, time may be saved by drawing directly on to the material with chalk.

In view of the fact that the design must be planned with an idea of some of the stitches that will be used in its execution, directions have been included for a few of the most usable and most quickly done stitches. With a small amount of practice, sufficient skill will be developed to produce a finished looking piece of work. While practicing these stitches, think of their possibilities in an actual design; they will suggest many original uses.

Often people beginning work of this sort have difficulty in selecting materials appropriate for use in combination. For convenience a table of suggestions has been prepared. (See page 90.)

NEEDLE-POINT BELT

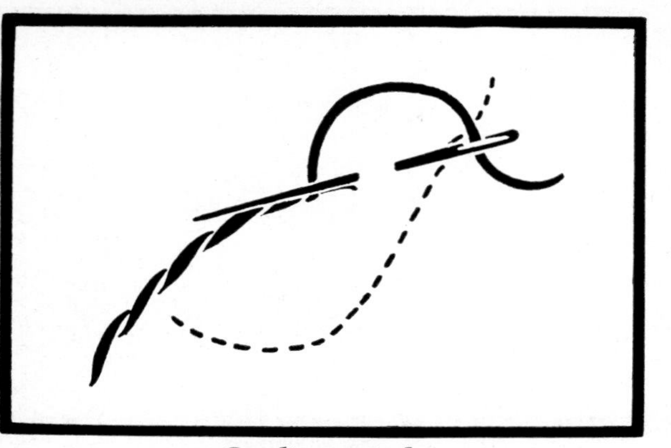

Outline stitch.

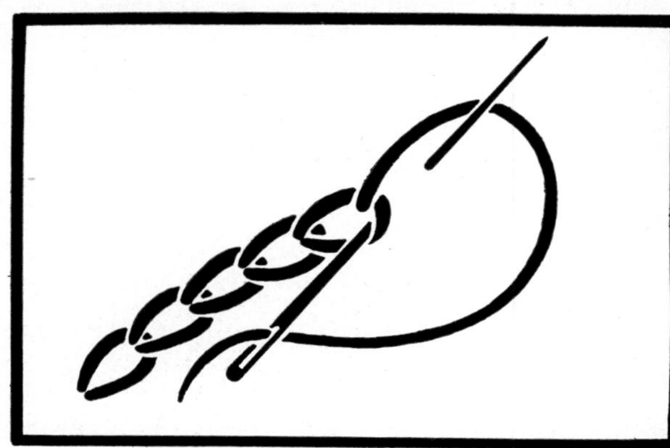

Chain stitch.

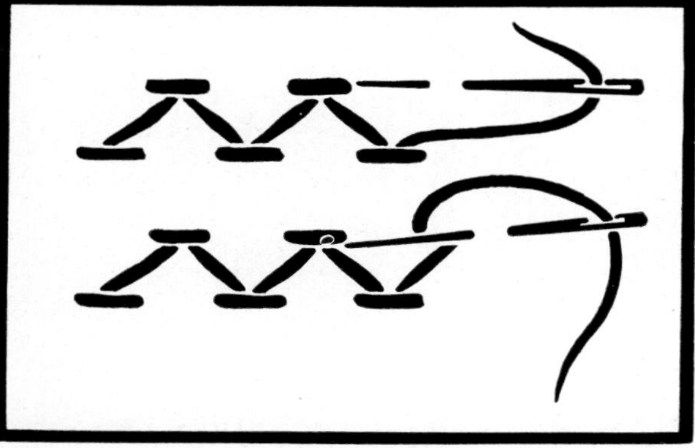

Chevron stitch.

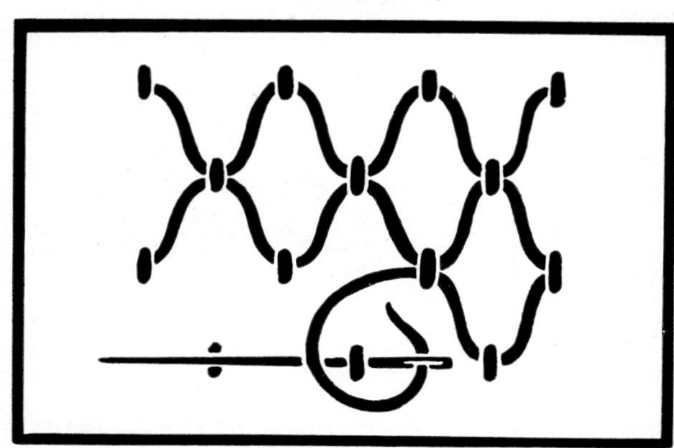

Mexican stitch.

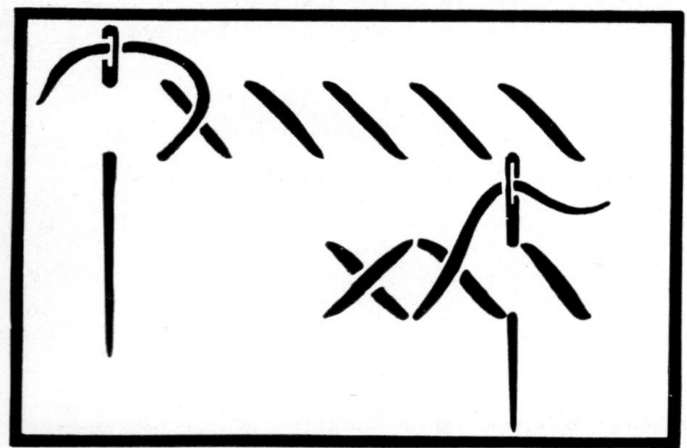

Cross stitch.

Lazy daisy stitch.

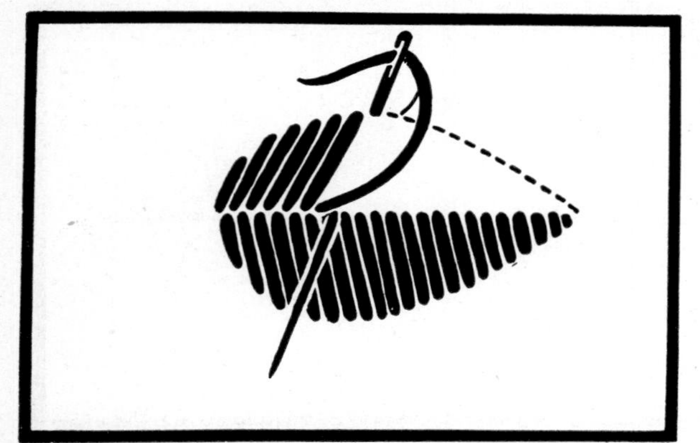

WEISMANN

Satin stitch.

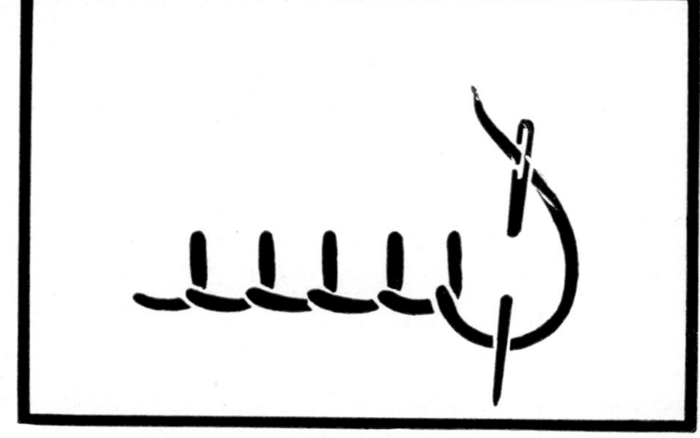

Blanket stitch.

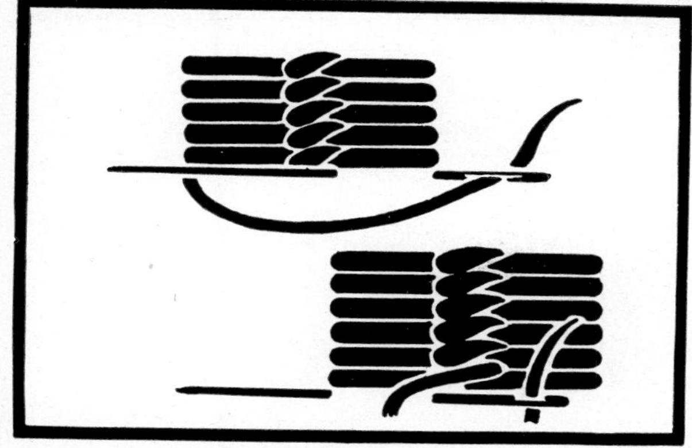

Roumanian stitch.

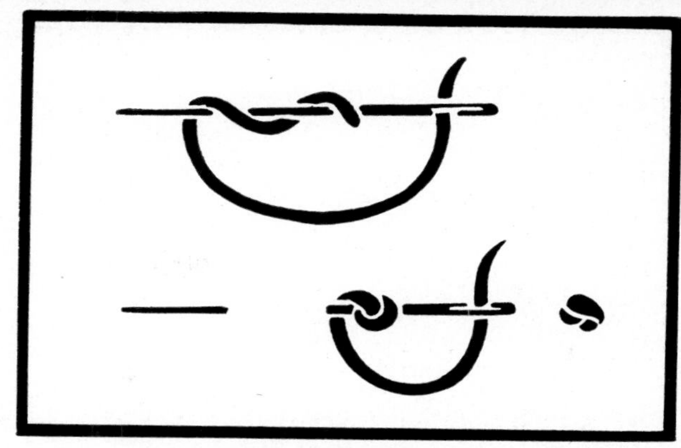

French knot.

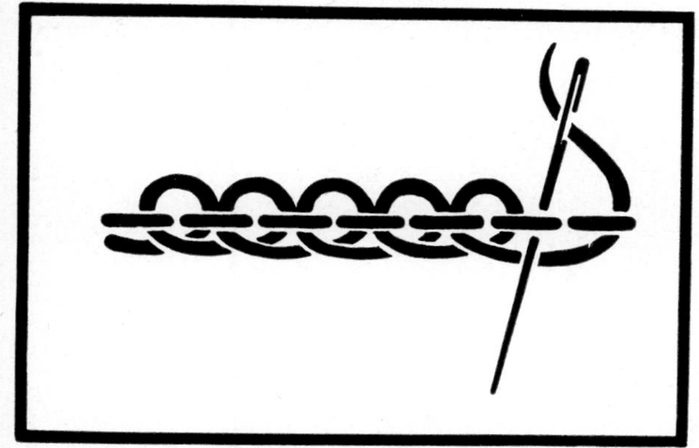

Pekinese stitch.

Loop stitch.

Feather stitch.

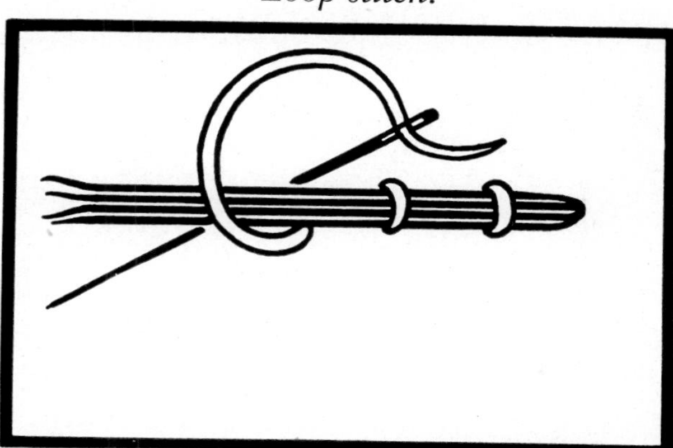

Couching.

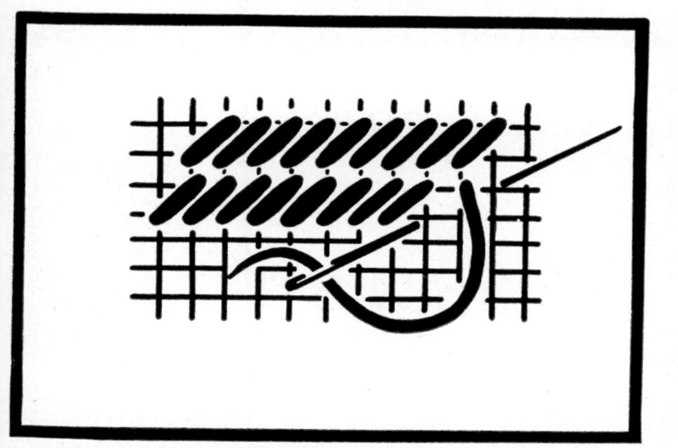

Needle point.

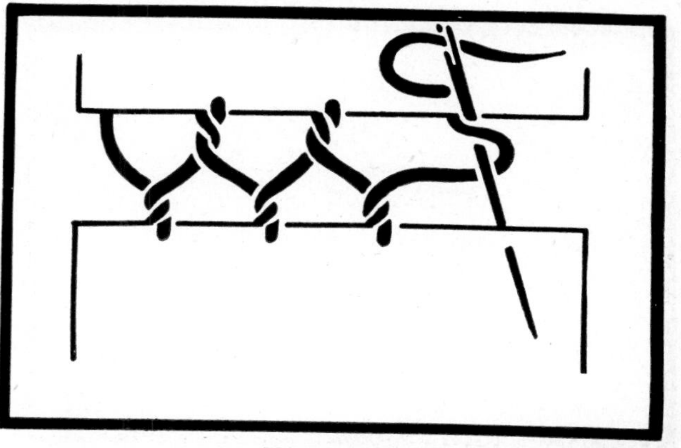

Faggoting.

WEISMANN

On heavy or coarse textures:	Use one of these:
Wool suiting	Shetland floss
Felt	Tapestry or peasant yarns
Monk's cloth	Germantown or knitting worsted
Burlap, etc.	Cotton moss yarn
On medium textures:	**Use:**
Linen	Linen thread
Cotton	Linen or six-strand embroidery floss (dull floss is usually in best taste)
Wool crepe	Shetland floss or Shetland chiffon yarn
On fine textures:	**Use:**
Sheer wool	Shetland chiffon
Silks and velvets	Silk rope or floss
Sheer cotton	Six-strand embroidery floss

With the stitchery planned, the design transferred to the material, and the proper weight of yarn or embroidery floss selected, the actual embroidery may begin. Care must be taken to keep the stitches evenly and neatly placed and the tension of the thread correct so that the material will not be pulled out of shape. Do not plan a design which calls for carrying a long unsecured thread over the surface of the material, as it will be pushed out of position when used and may snag or catch on such things as furniture or buttons. A floating thread should be no longer than one-half inch.

The method of fastening the belt should be determined when the original idea is conceived. There are many methods which may be used, each one of them calling for certain allowances to be made when the fabric is first cut. One of the photographs will give a clear picture of one of the more simple means that may be chosen. It consists merely of a continuation of the lining fabric rolled back on itself to form a sufficiently large, decorative cylinder at either end of the belt. The lining was rolled around a fringed strip of the background material cut slightly wider than the width of the belt. Hooks and eyes were sewed to the under side of the cylinders to close the belt. This fringed extension was not necessary and might well be omitted in this type of closing.

Other methods for closing or fastening a belt are:

TYING: In this case the belt must be planned for additional length to be taken up by the knot.

LACES: In this method the belt is not planned to overlap. The ends may just meet or they may be separated slightly. Eyelets for laces may be punched and embroidered or they may be put in by a shoemaker. Plastic lacing hooks or rings may be obtained at the notion counters in most department stores. Cords may be made of strips of the basic fabric, the lining material, or of the yarn or floss used in the embroidery. If the laces are made of yarn or floss, a number of strands should be twisted or braided to make a firm cord.

BUTTONS: Any button of appropriate texture, size, and color would be suitable, but most attractive "buttons" can be made of wooden beads, cylinders made by rolling up strips of leather, or fabric, bits of dowel rod plus a small screw eye, and so on ad infinitum.

ZIPPER: When using this, be certain to get a zipper that opens at both ends.

BUCKLES: Generally speaking, an ordinary "store-bought" buckle does not look appropriate on a handmade belt. If the buckle is covered with yarn or with the fabric used in the belt, it seems to belong to it. However, one method which has proved successful uses several small buckles. These may be sewed to small strips of the fabric which in turn are sewed to the wider belt. Two or three may be used, depending upon the width of the belt.

The methods for closing belts which appear in the accompanying diagram have all been found to be satisfactory. Where leather is suggested as a likely material, the top of an old glove may be used. Sometimes it is possible to purchase leather scraps of assorted colors and weights at a leather supply house. Such scraps are usually sold by the pound and may be obtained at a reasonable cost.

Remember that ingenuity and inventiveness are as important items in the workbasket as the needles and yarns and flosses that are used for these crafts.

Appliquéd Belt

Numerous materials may be used for appliqué. Probably the most usable of the many which might suggest themselves is felt, since that fabric, when cut into shapes and applied to the foundation, has no raw edges to turn under and hem down. The entire design could be cut from colored pieces of felt and arranged pleasingly on the basic material with due consideration for the shape of the belt. The pieces which compose the design might be further elaborated with the addition of decorative embroidery. If this method is used, the design should be simple, with all of its parts well scaled to one another. Obviously, the success of the final product depends to a considerable extent on the care used in the selection and arrangement of the units within the design. If these various units are so detailed as to be difficult to cut from the felt and difficult to apply, the quality of the final effect is jeopardized. The

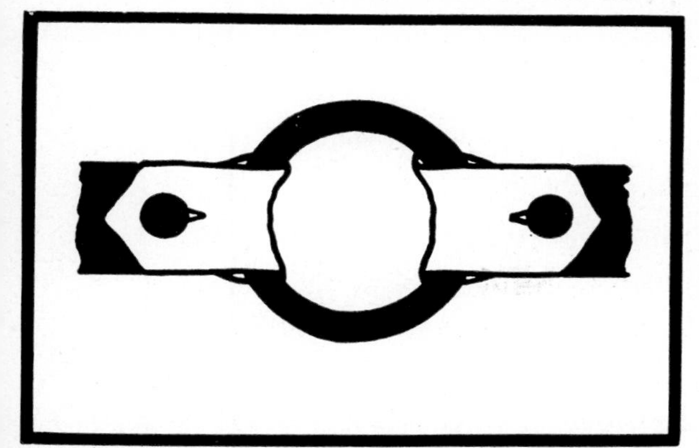

Wooden curtain ring and buttons.

Buttons and loops.

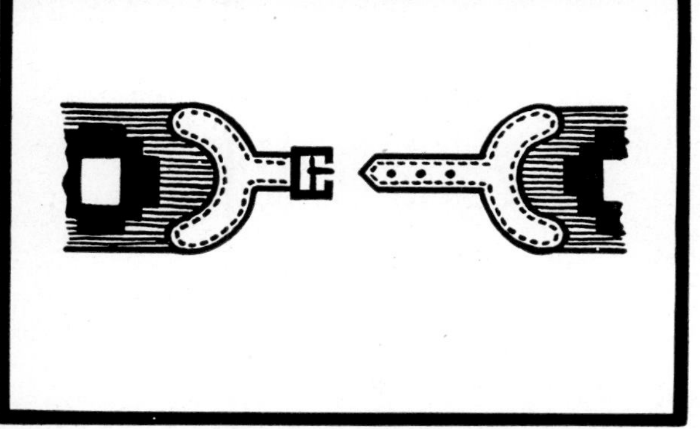

Leather over buckram.

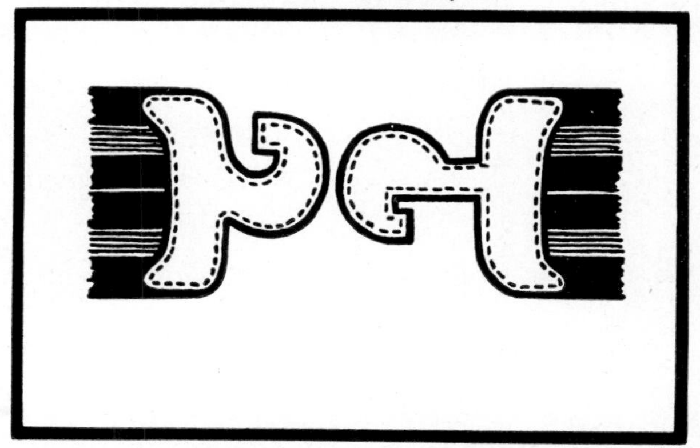

Leather or fabric over buckram.

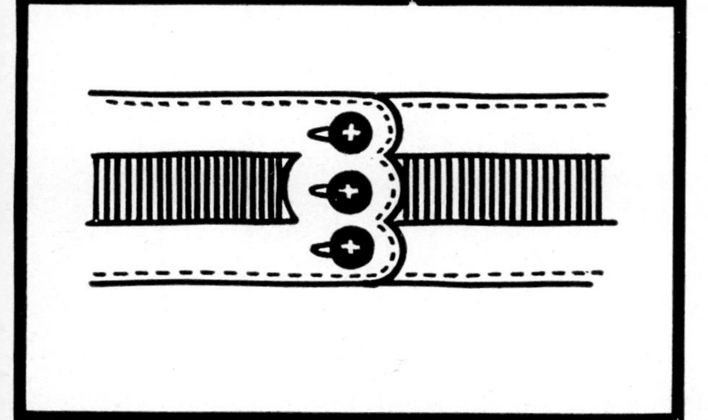

Buttons and scallops.

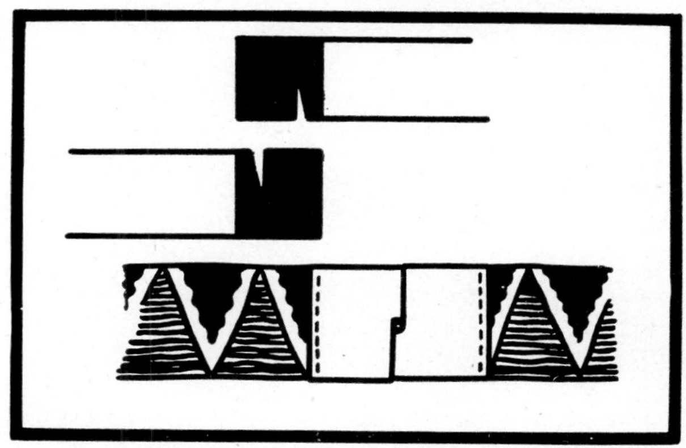

Leather or fabric over buckram.

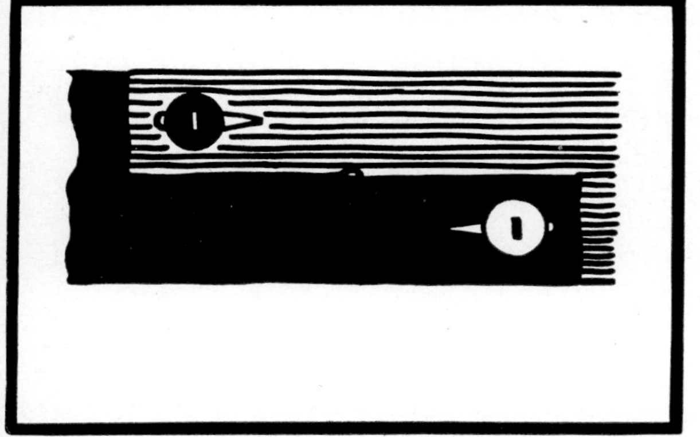

Lapped ends with buttons.

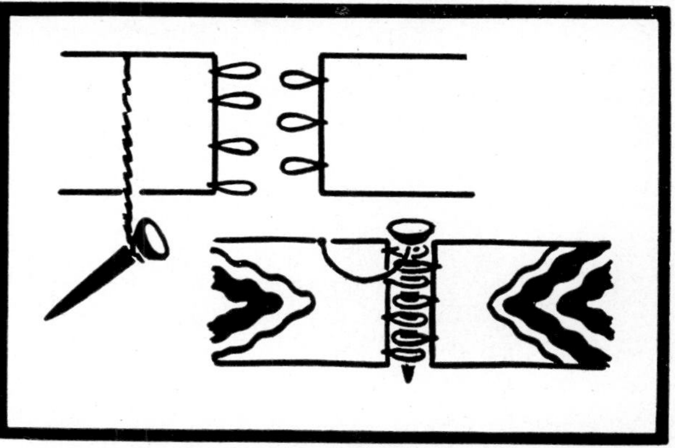

Golf tee or wooden peg.

WEISMANN

design units may be slip stitched to the foundation material or held in place with a mending tissue now on the market for simple patching. It is usually sold at notion counters.

When planning the design, it is best to think of the belt as a border design and to plan an easily followed rhythmic border. This may be achieved through the repetition of one or more units or by the use of a continuous or an easily connected line such as a simple wavy or zigzag line. When selecting the units to use in the pattern, every consideration should be given the principles governing good design. Simplified, conventionalized units (not naturalistic copies) will be best suited to this type of work. The units and the final design should be considered in relation to the dress or ensemble with which the belt is to be worn. Delicate, small flowers, however well conventionalized, on a belt to be worn with a heavy tweed suit would be extremely inappropriate. The final effect should also be considered in relation to the type of figure on which the belt is to be worn. A heavy figure would not be flattered by a wide belt with a great deal of value contrast and a horizontal movement in the design.

If stitchery is combined with felt units, as in an appliqué belt, it may be given the most prominence in the design or it may serve as secondary decoration. Whichever it is to be, the yarn or floss used should be harmonious in texture with the felt as well as with the type of design being used. Simple stitches can be assembled to produce a very decorative effect with econ-

FRINGE FROM AN INDIAN BELT

omy of both time and energy. One advantage gained by the use of embroidery is that it permits a more flexible variation in scale because small stitches can be used in contrast to larger appliquéd units. Embroidery may also serve to tie isolated units of appliqué together into one well integrated design.

When selecting the colors to be used for either of these types of belts, the colors should be chosen with the design, the fabric, and the ensemble in mind. A simplified color scheme, as well as a simplified design, is usually the most satisfactory.

Needle-Point Belts

The advantages to be found in a belt made with needle point are numerous. In general, a belt made this way is definitely of a dressier type than most of those made with other methods. The design may be made up of fine units and intricate detail, and color may be used to produce an almost jewel-like effect. The technique results in a firm belt which may be a simple, straight, decorative band or may be shaped to repeat some curved or pointed line in the dress itself. Needle-point or cross-stitch canvas or a firm scrim makes an excellent foundation for the stitchery, which should be planned to cover the canvas completely. Sometimes a course but evenly woven material such as linen crash may be used advantageously.

APPLIQUÉ BELT

Petit point is not suggested for this purpose since it is too fine and would be too tedious a method for any but the most patient.

Yarns suitable to needle point should have a high twist in order that the design stand out clearly. Tapestry yarns are a very good choice and come in a beautiful range of colors. Peasant yarns are equally usable and frequently are found to be brighter in color than the soft neutralized tones of the former yarn.

Finishing the Belts

As embroidered belts do not look well on the back after the stitchery has been done, nor do they show to the best advantage if they are crushed out of their original shape, it is usually necessary to stiffen and line them.

Belt stiffening may be bought by the yard or crinoline may be used. In some cases the belt will not need much stiffening and a lining of grosgrain ribbon will give enough body to the embroidered fabric. Other lining materials are silks, taffeta, sateen, or the fabric on which the stitchery was done originally.

The stiffening should be cut to the desired width and length of the belt. Fold the edges of the embroidered fabric down over the stiffening and tack into place. The lining fabric should be cut about half an inch wider than the belt itself. The edges of the lining should be folded to the wrong side, then slip stitched to the belt securely so as to cover the material used for stiffening. This is a concealed lining or facing. However, the lining may form an important part of the design. By cutting the lining wider than the belt itself, sewing it to the belt with the right sides to the inside, and then turning right side out, the lining will extend over the edges of the belt to form a binding. This may be of a contrasting color,

Photograph by Photographic Service, Iowa State College.

WHITE EMBROIDERED JACKET

by Helen S. Petersen

Contemporary design uses strong, simplified motifs. The hand loomed fabric is a perfect foil for cross stitch.

value, or even fabric. This method was used in finishing the belt shown in the accompanying photograph.

Stitchery for Style

A well known fashion commentator has said that embroidery should never be used on a dress as it is apt to mark the dress as being "homemade." This seems too inclusive a statement, because it does not take into account many costumes which have been given added distinction by a smart note of decorative stitchery. It is true that often a dress has looked "homemade" as a result of *poorly designed* and *poorly executed* decoration. Sometimes it is the result of decoration which has been used to conceal basically poor structure in the dress itself. Occasionally it is the result of poorly selected yarns used in the stitchery or lack of consideration for the position of the decoration on the garment.

On the other hand, well planned stitchery may set the keynote of a very distinctive costume. A well chosen bit of such decoration will give individuality to an otherwise commonplace garment, and insures one against the possibility of seeing one's neighbor wearing a duplicate costume.

One need not make the basic dress. This may be encouraging to those who lack confidence in themselves as dressmakers. A first problem might be the injection of new life into an old dress. The present collar on the dress might be removed and replaced by a band of embroidery which could also be repeated at the cuffs: or if not there, on the belt. If the dress boasts pockets, those might receive the emphasis; or the sleeves, the yoke, or the blouse front; whichever seems to compliment the dress the most.

Should one buy a dress as the foundation for decorative needlework, be sure to select the garment with an eye for all the possibilities mentioned. Of course, all of the areas suggested should not be utilized for decoration on the same garment. Remember that restraint is a mark of individuality.

Some fabrics lend themselves to stitchery much more readily than others. Fabrics of coarse, but firm, texture are usually found more suitable and are more easily embroidered since they have more body. Among the summer fabrics that might be used are heavy linen, salyna, hopsacking, and crash; in the winter fabric group, flannel, wool crepe or rep, light weight, but firm, tweeds, broadcloth, velveteen, and others of similar quality are usable. If silk is used as a foundation for decorative needlework, very fine delicate stitches as well as suitable yarn or floss must be chosen in order to be in harmony with the texture of the fabric.

For the heavier materials Shetland floss of the regular or chiffon weight, or for a dressier garment angora, are most appropriate. A yarn having many twists to the inch is more difficult to use for embroidery, as each stitch seems to remain on the surface of the material rather than become a part of it. If the material is a wash fabric, the embroidery floss should also be selected for its washable qualities. Six-strand floss is usable with wash fabrics.

The stitches previously suggested in this section may be used singly or in combination to produce interesting decorative effects. Diagrams and directions for the working of more complicated stitches may be found in books devoted to the art of needlework.

Many articles in our wardrobes other than just belts and dresses can be used as a basis for attractive handiwork. Some lend themselves to a more formal and reserved type of design, others to a gay informality. Briefly they are:

Sweaters

These may be decorated with an allover design of some small, evenly spaced unit, or the decoration may be confined to some structural point on the garment, such as the opening, the neck line, the pockets, or the sleeves. An informal note may be struck by the selection of the motif for the stitchery. Peasant designs may be the source of many fine inspirations.

Other Informal Garments

In planning designs for the decoration of any of these garments—suspenders, belts, jerkins, house coats, smocks, aprons, blouses, jackets—the same principles should be considered as were outlined in the discussion of embroidery for dresses and sweaters. Some of the garments mentioned in the list above need not necessarily be informal in nature. For example, a jacket could be one suitable for beach wear, or through the use of a different selection of style, fabric, and design, be suitable for formal evening wear.

Chapter VII

Traveling Companions

VERY OFTEN A SIMPLE, BUT UNUSUAL ENSEMBLE OWES ITS INdividuality to the decorative quality of the purse carried with it. Many of us cannot afford a great variety of purses at the usual department store prices, since genuine leather (and who wants imitation leather?) is not inexpensive. To overcome this handicap, one may devise any number of simple, easily made bags or purses that will successfully point up the costume.

All sorts of fabrics, according to season, lend themselves to this purpose; as, for example, felt, wool coating, velvet, heavy silks and satins, velveteen, linen, and heavy cottons. Fabrics like these may be used in such a way that the structural design of the purse adequately augments the ensemble without the addition of decorative design. Sometimes this is preferable, especially when there is already a great deal of pattern used elsewhere in the ensemble, as in the case of a dress made of printed material. If the bag is to be the outstanding decorative note, its surface can be enhanced by embroidery, quilting, cording, or the combination of several materials to give texture and color interest.

When considering either the purchase or the making of a purse or bag, the type of costume with which it is to be carried and the use to which it is to be put are of prime importance in both the selection of the shape and the materials. Normally bags and purses fall into four groups. The first and most used group would be made up of all those bags suitable for business, school, and street wear. These are usually sturdy, capacious, and simple. Most often, too, these purses are designed to go with the coat or suit, rather than any dress, that might be worn for those occasions.

Group two would include bags suitable for dressy afternoon or date wear. These may be designed to harmonize with a certain dress, and are frequently of a decided color rather than of the more neutral basic colors usually selected as the background for one's wardrobe. They may be more elaborate in shape and more decorative than the practical daytime purse.

The third group consists of the formal bags. These are small, since they are intended to hold only the indispensable lipstick and powder, keys, and, perhaps, a little "mad money." Their character may be practically conservative, or highly frivolous and decorative.

Group four contains the special purpose bags, utilitarian down to their core. Such would be beach bags, knitting bags, and kindred types.

In newspaper parlance the term "morgue" has a very useful definition. It is the name given to a collection of ideas and clippings garnered from here, there, and everywhere. Why not give this idea a place in one's own life? Build a personal file or notebook morgue. Seldom does one go into a shop, look at a magazine, or attend a social gathering without being struck by some new and clever ideas. Clip or sketch the idea before it slips from memory. It may not be used today, tomorrow, or perhaps ever; but sometime it may be fuel for a new addition to one's wardrobe. The use of a morgue does not imply slavish copying but rather a source of

A STENCILED BEACH BAG

by Mary Ellen Hustad

Stenciling is discussed under Fanciful Fabrics. This bag is made of white duck, lined with waterproof silk.

Photograph by Helen Ludwig.

inspiration. The shape of the bag one sees in a clipping of an exclusive model may suggest just what is needed to set off one's own ensemble. The design may be executed in entirely different materials from the original. In similar fashion, handles, closings, manipulation of material, and methods of decoration will bring new ideas to the observant individual.

Since this book concerns itself with decorative accessories, an embroidered bag from each of the first three groups will be illus-

Photograph by Lloyd Matterson

KNITTING BAG
by Roberta Burbeck

The care with which a design is executed is responsible for much of the character of the finished product.

trated here. Since the fourth group includes such a wide range of types, and since the construction and decoration of each of these types varies completely with the nature of the bag, they will not be discussed in this book. Instead, it will be left to one's ingenuity to fashion variations suitable to specific needs.

Strictly Business

Since it is of the utmost importance to have a large tailored bag and one which closes securely, a simple envelope style consisting of two large compartments closed with zippers has been selected.

The Structural Design and Execution

First, the size must be decided upon. This must be thought of in relation to the individual's build and proportions (a very little lady with a very big bag looks as though she were going on a trip).

TAILORED BAG

The simple design embroidered in a very limited color scheme—two grays and bright red on black—gives distinction to this purse.

THOMAS

After the general size has been determined, the relationship of the length to the width is an important factor. Here one may follow the standards as exemplified by the Greek Oblong, 2:3, or a pleasing deviation from this ratio.

The interior of the purse should be planned in keeping with personal requirements. This would include the number of pockets, size of the change purse, and devices for securing cosmetics, cigarettes, and pencils. It is well to plan at the outset to fasten the change purse to the interior of the bag by a short length of hat elastic. This permits freedom of handling and at the same time insures safety when using the smaller purse.

The material for a daytime bag might be either felt or firmly woven wool coating of a color that fits into the wardrobe.

Directions for Construction

Make a paper pattern that measures twice the depth but the same width as the size previously decided upon. Allow for half-inch seams on each of the two long sides of the pattern, and a full inch at each end. Cut two of these strips from the material. Linings may be cut at the same time, and to the same measurements with the exception of the top and bottom, where only a half inch need be allowed for hems. Two lining strips will be needed. Cut the pieces to make the desired pockets from the scraps of the lining fabric, which might be sateen, silk crepe, or rayon taffeta. Unless the outer fabric has a great deal of body or stiffness of its own, stiffening will be necessary. This may be buckram, crinoline, or muslin, depending upon the amount of additional stiffening required. If stiffening is used two strips should be cut without the seam and hem allowances. A piece of sheet wadding placed directly underneath the embroidered surface during the finishing of the bag plumps its sides with a professional touch.

Since the divisions of the purse are formed by stitching the material across from the center of one long edge to the center of the opposite edge and then folding on that line of stitching so that the short sides come together, it is necessary to place the pockets in the lining with this construction in mind. Remember that the open sides of pockets are at the top and not at the bottom. If one is not careful he may find his bag more individual than efficient!

If the outer surface is to be decorated with embroidery or by any other method, the piece which will be on the outside of the finished bag must be decorated before the purse can be sewed together. Detailed suggestions for embroidery and other methods of decoration will follow these directions for the construction of the purse.

Place the right sides of the two strips of the outer material

CONSTRUCTION OF THE TWO-SECTION ENVELOPE BAG

Cut and stitch outside fabric, right sides together, to within one inch of either end.

Cut, set in pockets, and stitch lining fabric.

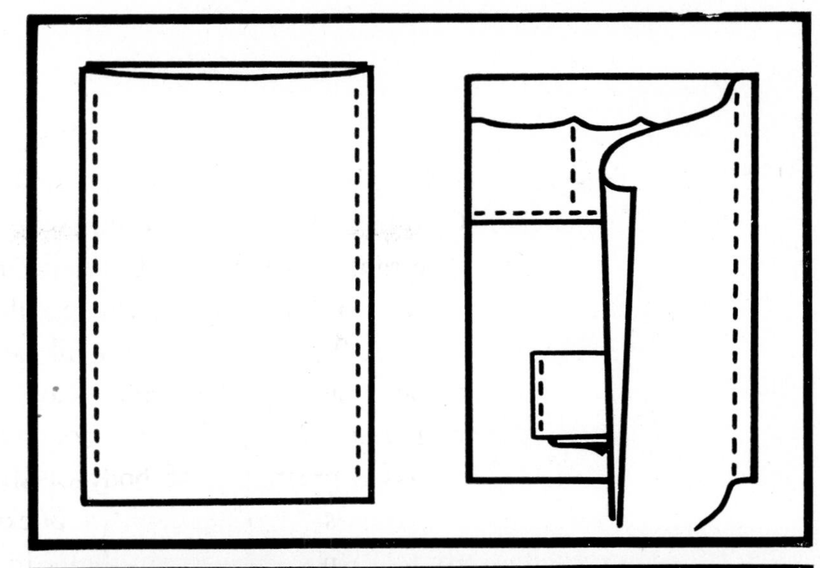

Sew zipper closings to open ends of outer sections. Keep face of zipper toward inside and ends in line with the seams on outer section. Open zippers and turn section right side out, press. Push zippers into position to form headings; stitch.

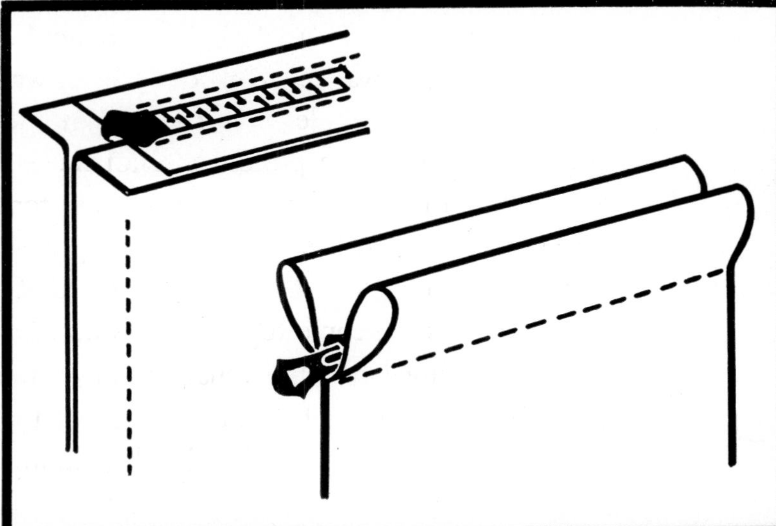

Insert lining and stiffening, pull into position, and stitch through all fabrics through the center. Slip stitch lining to zipper tapes.

Fold on center line, slip stitch ends together.

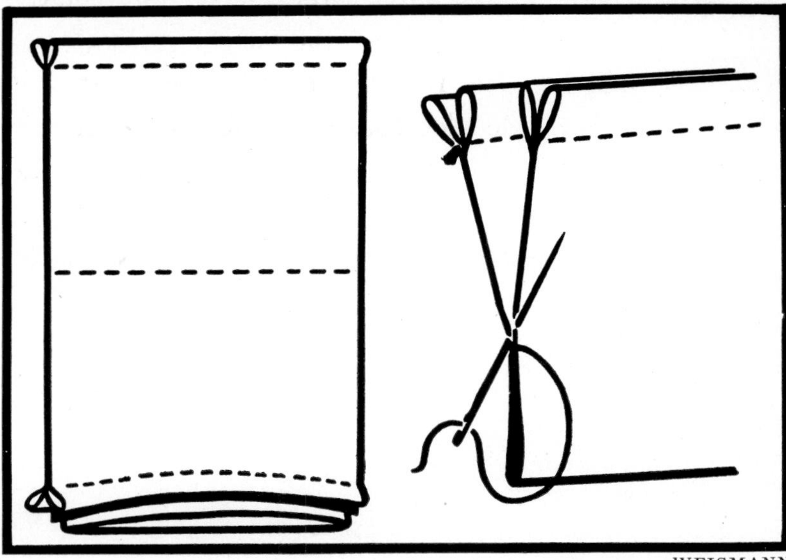

WEISMANN

together and down the long sides only, stitch one-half inch from the edges to within one inch of the ends.

Sew the zippers to the open ends of the outer fabric. Keep the face of the zipper toward the inside and the ends of the zipper in line with the seams on the sides of the outer section; the edges of the zipper tape coinciding with the edges of the fabric. Open the zippers and turn the fabric inside out. Press the seams. Push the zippers down toward the center of the bag until the heading has been formed. Secure the headings with concealed stitches.

Put the two right sides of the lining sections together and stitch them one-half inch from the edge down the long sides. Do not turn inside out, but slip this section into the tube formed by the outer fabric. Slip the strips of stiffening between the lining and the outer fabric. If buckram is used for stiffening only one piece of it is necessary and it should be inserted between the decorated or outside fabric and the lining nearest to it. Use a piece of muslin for the stiffening between the inner layer of fabric and the lining. Pad the design with cotton wadding if desired. Baste or pin these layers of material together to prevent slipping. Be sure that all edges coincide; give especial attention to matching the design motifs at the sides of the purse. Find the point halfway between the open ends. Mark across from side to side with a chalk line or a basting. Stitch along this line either by hand or machine. If the stitching is done by hand, be sure to go through all thicknesses of the material. Fold the purse on this stitched line, pin in place, and slip-stitch the envelope sides together. If just the sides are sewed together, and not the zippered edges, there will be an extra pocket between the two sections. This may prove handy for a handkerchief or gloves. The decorative design may be of such a nature that the seam joining the two envelopes may be made a decorative feature by emphasizing it with appropriate stitchery and color, or by outlining it with cord.

To finish the lining process, open the zippers, pull the lining into place so that it fits without wrinkling. Fasten in place with pins or a basting. Fold under the raw edge of the lining to bring it within one-eighth of an inch from the metal or plastic edge of the zipper. This distance from the zipper will prevent the lining from catching when the zipper is opened or closed. Slip stitch or catch stitch into place.

For convenience, and also for a decorative touch, pulls may be added to the zipper ends. Any number of things will suggest themselves. The possibilities include tassels of yarn or of the fabric, wooden or composition beads, and commercial pulls purchasable at any notion counter. Small pulls, such as those listed, are especially effective if the zippers have been attached so as to open in opposite directions. This would give a balanced effect when both zippers are closed. Tassels or pulls of different colors help one to quickly identify the two pockets of the purse.

Bracelet pulls might be made of wooden curtain rings, plastic bracelets from the ten-cent store, or a large shaped fold of the material itself. If such a large pull is selected, one only should be used. A bracelet handle as described above is frequently more satisfactory if attached to the purse itself, rather than to the small zipper pull.

The Decorative Design and Its Application

Since the ultimate purpose of a daytime purse is that it be carried when one is wearing a suit or simple street costume, the design must also be considered from that point of view. Normally most ensembles planned for street wear are conservative in line and color; the decorative design on the bag should harmonize in idea. A simple geometric design lends itself best to such an interpretation. It offers a maximum in effect for a minimum of effort. The personality of the person for whom the bag is intended must be considered when planning the design. However, neither strikingly bizarre nor sentimentally feminine lines should be used for a daytime bag; they are more appropriate for sports or formal wear. Careful planning in this matter will produce a bag which can be carried over a long period of time; one which will not become tiresome or "dated."

A specific design will be formulated here. It must be remembered that this design will not be one suited to every type of individual. It is intended for a suggestion only, and as a point of departure for creative effort on the part of the reader. This plan follows the outline given in Chapter II for adapting a design.

1. Cognizance of the size and shape of the object to be decorated.

The original paper pattern used will be helpful in planning the decorative design for the already established size and shape of the bag. In order that it be accurate, fold in the seam allowance, and fold the paper, as one will the material, to form the center division. This will produce a simple rectangle of a given proportion.

2. Realization of the ultimate purpose of the object.

The bag is to be a tailored, roomy, serviceable bag to be carried with tailored ensembles. For that reason the design should be planned so as to be conservative, fairly neutral in color, and simple in line. If planned in this way, it will fit more readily into the daytime wardrobe.

3. CONSIDERATION OF THE MATERIAL INVOLVED IN THE PROCESS OF THE CONSTRUCTION AND THE DECORATION OF THE OBJECT.

Black wool broadcloth has been selected for this purse. It is a sturdy, easily worked fabric which tailors well and is harmonious in texture with the average wardrobe. It is particularly adapted to the construction outlined above. However, some other fabrics would be equally suitable.

For the stitchery itself, wool yarn harmonizes best with the texture of the wool broadcloth. Three-ply Shetland floss or the somewhat more expensive tapestry and peasant yarns may be used. The last two mentioned are of better quality and produce a far richer effect. For the beginner, Shetland yarn is satisfactory and can be used very effectively. If one is fortunate enough to have yarn left over from some previous work, experiment with it on a scrap of the fabric or felt being used to determine its usableness. It may be every bit as good as the yarns mentioned.

4. THE SELECTION OF SOURCE MATERIAL SUITED TO THE IDEA, MATERIALS, AND PROCESS.

From a portfolio of designs, reproductions of craftwork done by the natives of New Guinea, an interesting, conventionalized flower motif, treated very geometrically, has been used for the bag illustrated here. The unit in itself has a great deal of character and yet is simple enough to be appropriate. In the unit are lines which repeat and thus strengthen the rectilinear form of the bag. Though the motif is fundamentally geometric, its scale suggests an appropriate feminine quality. Likewise it is suitable to the background fabric and the stitchery to be used. Because of the nature of this design, very few colors are necessary to produce an effective product.

A knowledge of only a few essential stitches is needed to reproduce the design onto the fabric. The flower may be done in satin stitch, and the stem in two or three rows of outline stitch placed closely enough to appear as a solid unit. The straight-line

WEISMANN

NEW GUINEA–NATIVE DESIGN

leaves may be done in a single row of chain stitch. These three stitches not only produce a nice variation in texture but they also harmonize with the nature of the design. The directions for making these stitches appear earlier in this section.

5. Analysis of source material to determine the motif best suited to the problems involved.

From the original New Guinea design the flower, stem, and leaf units have been selected.

6. Adjustment of the motif to the areas to be enriched by design.

The units have been arranged to produce a surface pattern composed of stripes. The scale of the original native design is in a great measure responsible for the character of the design. In order to preserve this quality, the same fine scale should be used in the adapted design. The size of the purse being constructed suggested the use of three rows or stripes of the flower unit separated by rows of the stem and leaf unit. From the photograph one can observe that the relative proportions of the two stripes of the design are subtle and pleasing, and not monotonous as they would have been had they been equal in width.

The background areas as seen in the original design have been omitted, and the leaves have been joined so as to produce a herringbone effect. By moving the petals close to one another, the design created by them produces an interesting rhythmic pattern. A simple, straight line of several rows of outline stitch marks off the top and bottom of the design.

7. Formulation of the idea on paper.

It is well to think through the foregoing steps thoroughly before beginning to formulate the design on the paper pattern. This will save a great amount of time and energy and will insure a more satisfactory result. With the plan already in mind, the de-

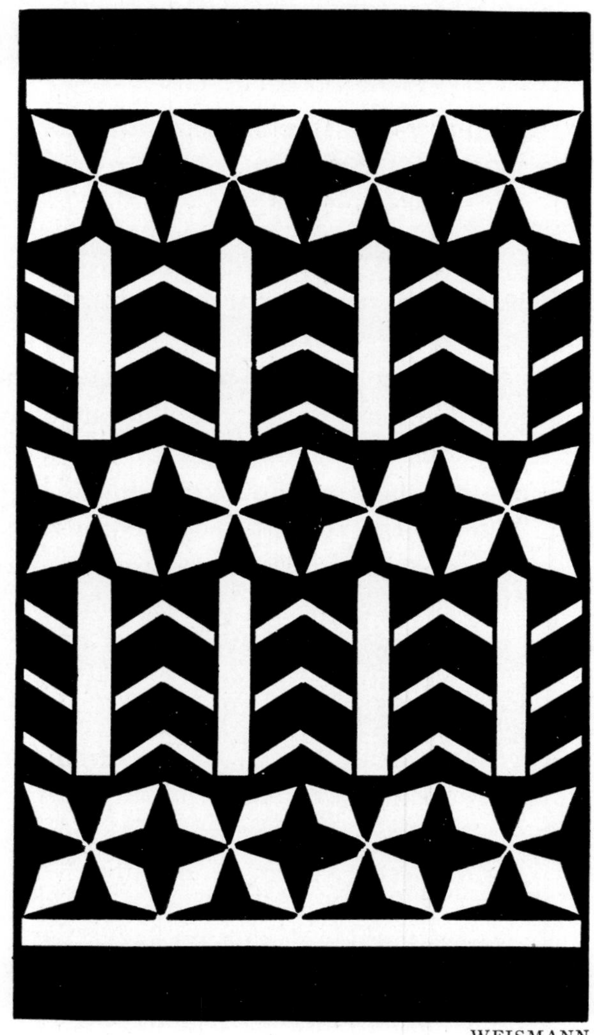

WEISMANN

ADAPTED DESIGN

sign may be drawn to the exact proportions in which it is to appear on the finished product.

8. Careful checking of the design for adherence to the principles of design and good taste.

Refer to Chapter II. *Harmonious Integration of the Principles of Design.*

9. Completion of the drawing of the design.

Make any necessary changes in the design and adjust it for accuracy and clarity of drawing. Carelessness at this point is often responsible for inferior workmanship.

10. Planning the color combination and distribution.

For the purse shown in the photograph, black wool broadcloth was used for the foundation. It was planned to be used with a wardrobe built around black as a basic color. Two tones of gray, one quite dark, and the other light, were combined with a red of middle value. These were selected because they gave a good value range and the red gave a good color accent. Other colors might be used. Those chosen are conservative and harmonize readily with almost any other wardrobe color. They also seem suitable to the character of the design. Since red was the only true color used, it might have seemed spotty if placed at widely spaced intervals. For this reason it was used for the flowers which form an almost solid band of color. For the same reason the light gray was used for the leaves, which form an almost continuous line movement across the bag. The dark gray was reserved for the stem unit. This unit is spaced at the greatest interval, and would not have been appropriate in either of the other two colors. This second gray is really a transitional value between the light gray and the black of the broadcloth. It interrupts the strong rhythmic movement of the herringbone design without breaking it entirely, and in this way it forms a pleasant accent without being spotty.

11. Application to the object in the chosen medium.

In order to insure the greatest amount of accuracy in transferring the design to the cloth, the original paper pattern should be pricked along the lines of the design, then fastened securely to the fabric to be used for the purse. Powdered chalk or whiting should be pounced through the tiny holes pricked in the design. Remove the paper pattern carefully and run a basting thread along the dotted lines. This will serve as a guide for the stitchery. If the object being made is large, it may be more satisfactory to transfer one line of the design at a time to the fabric. This will prevent the rubbing off of the chalk dots before the basting has been completed.

Embroider the design neatly and carefully in the chosen stitches. After this has been done, the basting threads should be removed, and the fabric pressed on the wrong side, using a damp cloth and a moderately hot iron. A sufficiently thick pad beneath the embroidered surface should be used to prevent any flattening of the stitches.

The procedure followed for the construction and decoration of this specific bag is an example of the method to be used for the construction and decoration of any other object, whether it be for the wardrobe or for the home.

Conversation Piece

We are usually our most feminine selves when we dress up for a tea, a bridge party, or a date. Perhaps one puts the best foot forward only to impress women friends, or perhaps one strives to cater to some gentleman's ego. For any such occasion a bag with a fragile feminine type of design seems appropriate. The design may be very fine in scale if one is a very little, delicate lady; or it may reflect a dignified feminine quality for the more conservative personality. The design should definitely not be in the naive, informal spirit of peasant handiwork. Motifs based on finely scaled geometric or graceful floral patterns seem to adapt themselves best to afternoon bags. The size of the bag and its general structural design should also suggest the more dressy occasion. Various constructions lend themselves to this classification.

The group offering the greatest number of variations is that which includes the pouch bag. This may be made on a frame; or it may be shaped and carried by bracelet handles, shaped loops, or braided cord. Any number of shapes might be used: circular, with a cord handle traveling around the sides and the bottom and left free at the top to form the handle; triangular, square, or rectilinear.

Small envelope bags may be made in a number of ways. Experimentation with paper will give stimulus to the imagination, and various shapes and ways of making bags of this nature can be evolved. More specifically a bag made of buckram and carefully lined may be incased in a removable, washable slip cover of heavy linen decorated simply with Italian hemstitching or embroidery. In this type of bag a muslin cover is usually placed over the outside of the buckram to act as a pad for the slip cover. Colored covers might be made so that the bag could be quickly changed to harmonize with various costumes.

Envelope bags may be fastened with buttons and loops, snap fasteners, decorative frogs, or a loop or slit through which the end of the envelope flap can be slipped.

Quaint drawstring bags are decidedly feminine and help immensely to create an air of fragility. These bags are made from a circular piece of fabric cut from one piece of material or made in sections (as an umbrella) of differently colored or textured pieces. The drawstring may be run through a heading on the bag or may

THOMAS

AFTERNOON BAG

This might be one way to add fillip to a black afternoon dress. Leave off the usual clip or necklace and carry a conversation-making bag instead.

be pulled through eyelets in the bag, or through loops, or rings sewed to the outside of the fabric. If any of the latter are used, there must be an even number of these to permit the cord to draw the bag shut correctly. Two cords should be run through the heading, eyelets, or loops. One of these cords is pulled to one side and one to the other to close the bag. The loops formed by the drawn cords will make handles for the little pouch.

Thinking through all of the possibilities in each one of these groups will lead one to design a bag more creatively than by simply following step by step the directions given for the one type described here. However, these directions will afford a starting point from which one may digress at will.

There is very little actual expenditure represented in the bag in the illustration. Everyone would not have the same collection of material in the scrap bag, but this list may be helpful. The fabric was left over from a linen blouse. It is lemon yellow and of fairly heavy weight. The black suède once was a jaunty streamer on a hat, and the cardboard came from the laundry in the shirts. The cardboard was thin, so three layers were pasted together to make it strong enough to be serviceable. There didn't happen to be any black soutache braid or ball fringe on hand, so that had to be purchased. Some scraps of black lining material were usable, and there's always a can of vegetable glue. It is a staple if one is craft minded. An old wooden bracelet was used for the top of the bag, but a round powder box of suitable size, with top and bottom cut out would make a sturdy foundation too.

Directions for Construction and Decoration

Cut one circular piece measuring thirteen inches in diameter from the linen and one from the lining material. There is considerable handwork necessary before the bag is finished at the top, so it is wise to prevent unnecessary raveling of the circles by machine stitching the two pieces about one-eighth inch from the edge all around.

The base of the pouch is made of a five-inch circle of heavy cardboard. Place this cardboard circle in the exact center of the yellow linen and mark its position carefully with a sharpened piece of chalk. Remove the cardboard and baste along the chalk line. Put in another line of basting stitches two inches away from the first line. Divide the space between these two concentric circles into a number of equal areas, going around the center. Five or six is good for a circle this size. Cut a paper pattern the exact size of one of these areas; upon it draw a simple double loop design that fills the area well, but in no way appears crowded. Keep the loops few in number and fairly large. After a satisfactory design has been attained pin or baste a similar-shaped piece of carbon or graphite paper to this pattern. Use this as a guide for tracing the loop design around the circle formed by the two guide lines of basting stitches on the yellow linen. Trace accurately and try to avoid pressing down upon the carbon-backed design heavily with the finger tips. The smudges resulting from too heavy a hand are almost impossible to remove.

Then sew the soutache braid over the traced design. If one has a braiding attachment for the sewing machine and finds it simple to use, that would be an expedient procedure. However, it does not take long to sew the braid on by hand. Use small stitches directly down the center of the braid on all straight lines, but catch stitch the braid invisibly on one side only when forming the loops. This combination of the two accepted ways of applying braid by hand keeps the background material free of all puckers. Be sure to begin and end each series of loops in such a way that the cut end may be hidden underneath the braid. The outer covering of soutache braid frays out easily; sew the ends into place with a number of closely placed over-and-over stitches.

The ball fringe makes an excellent accent for the braid design. Cut the fringe one-quarter of an inch on either side of the threads from which the ball is suspended. The short threads can then easily be pulled out, leaving two threads long enough to be put through the eye of a needle and be pulled through the fabric. Pull each thread through separately about one-eighth inch apart, then tie the ends securely. Fasten a ball into place between each series of loops.

Spread a very thin layer of paste over one side of the five-inch circle of cardboard; then put it, paste side down, exactly in the middle of the wrong side of the yellow linen circle which has been decorated with braid and balls. Spread paste over the exposed

CONSTRUCTION OF AFTERNOON BAG

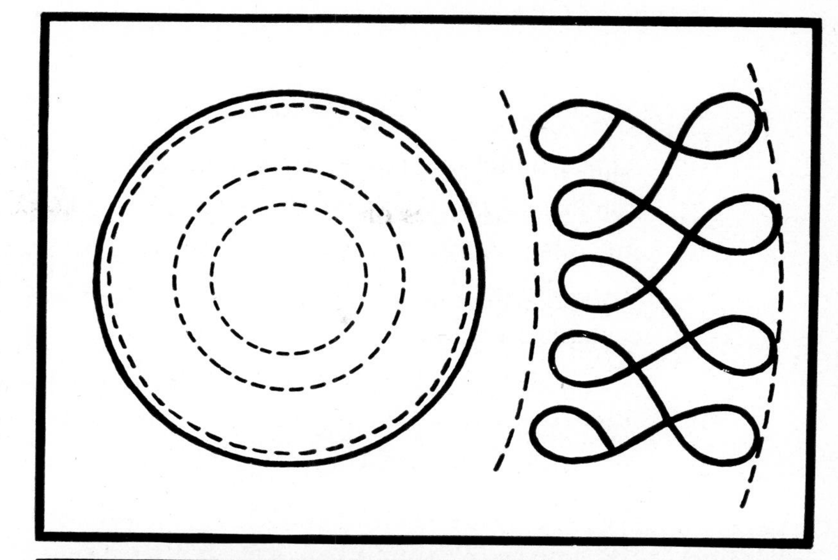

Stitch edge of outer fabric to prevent raveling. Baste guide lines to mark position of bottom circle and applied decorative border. Sew braid along traced guide lines.

Stitch inner and outer sections of top band together at upper edge. Seam to form circle. Sew lower edge or inner section to lining of pouch, keeping raw edges toward outside. Slip bracelet between inner and outer sections.

Ravel tape of ball fringe and pull raveled threads through handle fabric—knot on wrong side. Make lid according to directions. Fasten lid hinge and ends of handle under outer section of bracelet covering. Slip stitch covering to pouch.

WEISMANN

side of the cardboard and place the lining material down upon it so that the edges of the two cloth circles exactly coincide. Smooth out all wrinkles. Be sure to use the paste sparingly; it is used only to facilitate the next step. Hold the base permanently in place by stitching through both pieces of fabric as close as possible to the cardboard. If a sewing machine is being used the cording foot makes this process very simple.

The wooden bracelet makes an attractive, firm top for this gay little bag. Cut a length of suède sufficient to encircle the bracelet and wide enough to cover the outer side of the bracelet. Cut a width of lining fabric for the inside of the bracelet. Be sure to allow for seams on both pieces for the top, bottom, and ends. Sew the strips together along one edge and at the ends.

Either by hand or by machine, gather the outer edges of the circles forming the bag and the lining to the same circumference as the covering for the bracelet. Both the lining and linen may be gathered at the same time. Sew the gathered edge of the bag to the bottom of the bracelet lining. Slip the suède covering over the bracelet, but do not sew into place at this time.

There is a clever little cover on this bag. Make it by cutting a disc of heavy cardboard to the inside diameter of the bracelet. Cover this disc with yellow linen which has been decorated with braid loops and a single ball in the center of the design. It is necessary to provide a hinge and a fastener to make the lid function properly. A half-inch strip of the suède about one inch long will make a good hinge. Sew one end to the underside of the cover. Directly across from this, also on the wrong side of the cover, sew a loop of the suède made by cutting a pear-shaped hole in the center of a larger piece of suède. A piece measuring one and three-quarters inches long by three-quarters of an inch wide with the corners of one end rounded will be right. The little hinge and the fastener loop should extend beyond the edges of the cover when it is viewed from the right side. The hole in the tab used for fastening should be large enough to go over a ball cut from the fringe.

In order to make the inside of the bag as neat as the outside, cover a thin piece of cardboard, only slightly smaller than the cover, with lining material. Pin into place with the wrong sides of each disc together. Slip stitch the lining to the cover. This little procedure covers completely all the bumps and ridges that normally result when fabric is gathered.

Insert the projecting end of the hinge into the seam joining the lining and suède covering of the bracelet. Rip just a few of the stitches near the end seam to form a small opening. Sew the hinge into place securely. Directly across from the hinge, and near the lower edge of the suède band covering the bracelet, fasten a single fringe ball. This will make the button to keep the lid in place.

The handle for this bag should measure one and one-half inches wide by twelve inches long. Make it of a strip of linen for the top, and suède for the lining. Seven balls sewed at equal intervals along the center of the linen strip will make a transitional note between the decorative motifs and will give interest to the handle itself. Tuck the ends of the handle up under the suède band covering the bracelet and sew in place. The handle should form a right angle to the axis formed by hinge and fastener loop. To finish the bag slip stitch the lower edge of suède covering the bracelet to the bag itself. If these stitches are small and closely placed the leather will conform to the shape of the bracelet, concealing this last stitching almost entirely.

Glamorous Gadgets

The formal bag gives one the opportunity to indulge in a bit of whimsy. As stated before, it should be small, and it may be frivolous. For that reason a little bag of unusual character will be described here. The idea for this odd little bag came from great-grandmother's sewing basket, where it served the practical purpose of harboring the elusive thimble. Someone away back in that time had utilized the shape of a beechnut for the purpose. If one makes this interesting little gadget he is certain to surprise his friends with an imaginative choice of accessories.

Owing to the construction of this bag, it should be just large enough to hold the minimum essentials for a very gala evening. The actual size will be determined by the amount of space needed for compact, keys, and a few coins.

The bag is made of three melon-shaped pieces of cardboard or buckram sewed together to form a little three-sided, nut-shaped box. One side is left partially open. To open, the two pointed ends are pressed toward each other to force open the unsewed side. When released, the sides spring back into place, safely closing in the contents.

This type of bag and the purpose for which it is intended suggest materials rich in nature, such as brocades, velvets, taffetas, metal cloth, and satin. If one is one's own dressmaker the bag might be made from scraps of the material used for an evening dress or wrap.

Directions for Construction

From a flexible strong cardboard cut three melon-shaped pieces which measure five inches at the longest point and two and

FORMAL BAG

Just big enough for a few essentials.

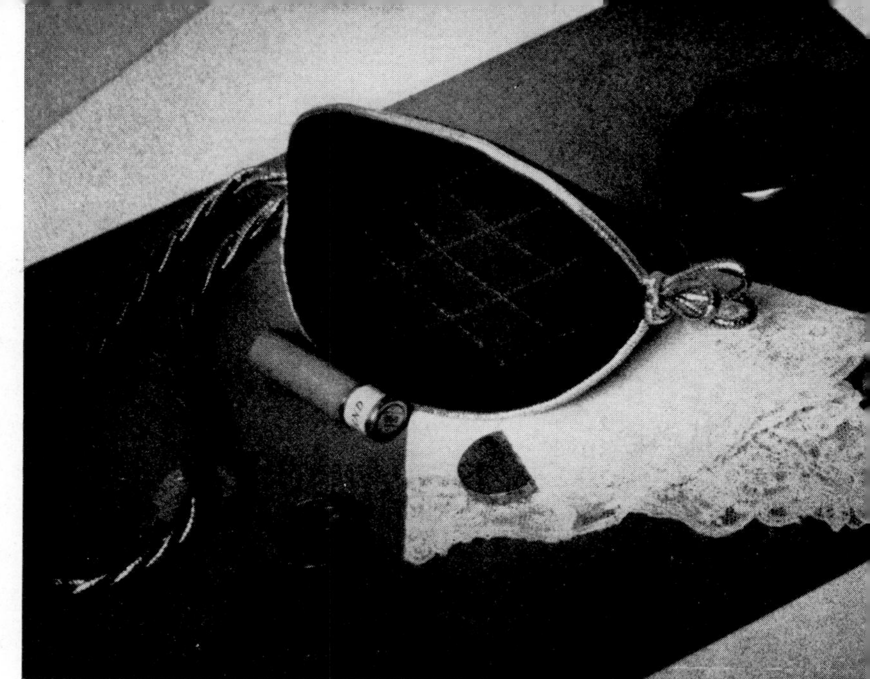

THOMAS

three-quarters inches at the widest point. Draw the form with a smooth, regular curved line from point to point. If the cardboard is thin, use it doubled, cutting six pieces of the described shape. Should buckram be substituted, six pieces will also be necessary. Paste or baste these thin pieces of cardboard or buckram together.

If the evening bag is to be covered with quilted material as is the bag shown in the photograph, the fabric must be quilted before it is cut to cover the cardboard pieces. For this process, the following materials are necessary: the outer fabric (satin was used in the photographed bag), sheet wadding, and light weight muslin. Two layers of wadding will be necessary if one desires the quilting to be quite puffy and soft. Stretching the quilted material over the cardboard forms smooths out the quilted effect considerably. Draw guide lines for the stitching on the muslin. In the photograph, the bag was quilted in a simple diamond pattern so that all the quilting could be done before the pieces were cut for the bag. However, if the quilting is to be done in a more elaborate design, the design must be planned to fit the curved, shaped surfaces of the cardboard. Baste the three materials together with the sheet wadding on the inside and the penciled guide lines showing on the muslin. It may be necessary to baste the fabrics together in only slightly separated lines to prevent the silk from slipping out of place during the stitching; sew by hand with tiny running stitches, or by machine, along the guide lines on the muslin, using a silk thread that matches or harmonizes with the satin outer fabric. Lay the three cardboard pieces on the quilted fabric, using care to place the forms in relation to the quilted design. With these shapes as patterns, cut the fabric, allowing for a three-quarter inch seam around each of the pieces of cardboard. Put a small running stitch one-quarter inch from the outer edge around each of the sections of fabric. Place the cardboard piece in position on the fabric and pull up the running stitch, drawing the edges of the fabric tightly over the cardboard. Fasten the thread to keep the material in position. Do this with each of the three pieces.

To line these sections, cut the fabric to be used one-quarter inch larger than the cardboard. One piece of lining will be needed for each section. Turn under the edges of the lining and slip stitch to the outer quilted fabric close to the edge and over the exposed surface of the cardboard.

Baste the three covered sections together to form the box-like bag. When these are basted accurately, overcast two seam edges very tightly and firmly down their entire length. Overcast the third side only one inch from each end, leaving the center portion open. Remove the basting threads. One will find that when one presses on the top and bottom of this little box, the unsewed length will spring open enough to permit a compact and other small articles to be slipped into it. If the tips of the sections are not sewed together, the cut ends of the gold cord used for decoration may be pushed through to the inside. This greatly facilitates the finishing details.

To further embellish the bag, a decorative braid may be sewed over the seamed edges. For the bag in the illustration a gold cord of a bit more than one-eighth inch in diameter was used. This was cut in lengths sufficiently long to permit twisting (or braiding) the three strands together from where they met at the top to form a loop long enough to slip over the wrist. Enough cord was also allowed to form three small loops to finish off the bottom of the bag with a stiff little tassel. Decorative cording should be sewed along the edges with an invisible slip stitch. When selecting a finishing cording or braiding, care should be exercised to choose a trimming that is harmonious with the other fabrics used to make the bag. Do not use a cotton cord on a satin bag.

Suggestions for Decoration

Since the gold cord that was suggested has seasonal limitations, other materials may be used to enrich the box form. The side panels might be decorated with needle point, with silk embroidery, or with sequins according to the nature of the dress or wrap with which the bag is to be carried. Any embroidered decoration should be planned to fit well into the shaped panels and should be appropriate to the texture of the floss used for the stitchery. A silk floss suggests a finely scaled motif. If sequins are used, the entire surface might be covered or the sequins could be fastened to the fabric to produce a definite design.

Chapter VIII

"Rich Man, Poor Man—"

OFTEN BUTTONS ARE THE ONLY DECORATIVE NOTE ON A DRESS or suit. And just as often it is very difficult to find the right buttons for a particular purpose; or on finding them, to discover that they are beyond the means of one's pocketbook.

The following ideas have been used successfully to give the proper decorative effect to a garment without too great a cost.

Leather Buttons

Small scraps of leather, obtained by the pound in lovely colors, from some leather findings store; suède banding, purchasable in trimming departments; or pieces of leather cut from discarded belts or the tops of gloves may be used to make attractive and different buttons.

If the leather is heavy enough, similar shapes of various sizes may be built up in pyramid fashion, glued together and punched for sewing to the fabric. These leather layers may be of one color or of various colors and may be held together with rubber cement or glue. The finished button should be firm enough to hold its shape under use.

Another method, and one suited to soft pliable leathers, is that of rolling the material into tight cylinders. The strips of leather

WOODEN BUTTONS

Designed by Barbara Weismann, executed by Mark Doll

Some of these designs would make attractive clips or pins for sport clothes.

THOMAS

should be long enough to produce a cylinder well proportioned to the length that the button will be when finished. After the leather has been rolled tightly, it may be fastened by winding with a thin strip of leather of the same or a contrasting color. A small loop of this binding strip should be left at the back of the button to fasten it to the fabric. A similar button may be made from a long wedge-shaped piece of leather. The ridges formed by the narrowing width produce an interesting texture. The narrowest end may be extended to form a loop at the back of the button. A bit of glue will hold the layers of leather in place.

Wooden Buttons

These may be made in a variety of ways. The first thing that suggests itself is the wooden button mold and its attendant possibilities. The molds come in any number of sizes and may be enameled a solid color, waxed over the plain surface of the wood, or painted with some simple design with oil paint. A large brass

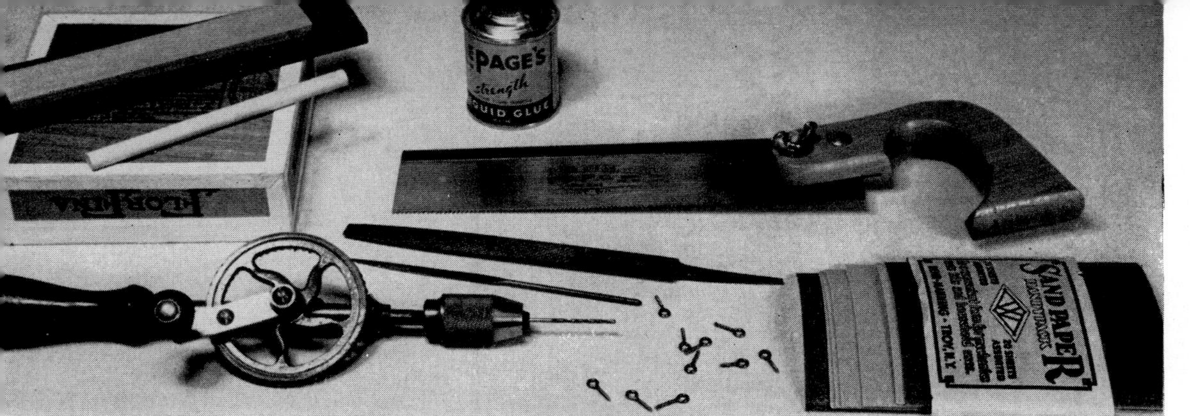

THOMAS

TO MAKE WOODEN BUTTONS

One needs these everyday supplies. Needle files are good standard equipment for craftsmen.

paper fastener may be put through the hole in the center of the mold and fastened through an eyelet in the dress. The metal top of the fastener may be enameled a color to harmonize with the dress or the button.

Careful workmanship is necessary to the success of a second type of button which may be made from such ordinary material as cigar box wood and doweling. This or any other thin wood may be sawed into simple shapes with a coping or jig saw. The top surface may be decorated with simple stripe or plaid designs made by cutting shallow grooves with the saw or a very fine file. Holes should be drilled through the button or a small screw eye inserted in the back of the button for sewing to the garment. Great emphasis must be placed upon the finishing of all edges of these buttons to insure a professional piece of work. The best method of finishing is to bevel all edges with a fine wood file, and to smooth every surface of the button with very fine sandpaper. Experimenting with both the saw and the file on a scrap piece of wood will lead one to discover endless possibilities resulting from the manipulation of the tools upon the material. Some of the effects which have been obtained and which may point the way to further developments in this technique are milled edges, as found in coins; deeply beveled edges further decorated with file cuts placed in step formation; cone shapes built up of two or more layers and held together in the sewing, or glued into place if the button is to be sewed to the garment through a screw eye.

After the wood has been thoroughly filed and sanded, various finishing methods may be followed. To preserve the natural color of the wood, apply two coats of white shellac. After it has thoroughly dried use a fine sandpaper or number 3/0 steel wool to remove the shine and any roughness. The final satin finish is obtained when a coat of floor wax is applied to the button. If the color of the wood seems undesirable, it may be altered by staining with regular wood stain, or by painting with water colors to produce colors other than browns. After the stain has dried the button should be finished in the same manner as described above.

Cork, a material which can be worked in much the same way as wood, except that it can be cut with scissors or a knife, may be purchased in sheet form at an auto supply house. Another form in which it can be used is the cylindrical bottle cork. The bottle cork variety may be cut into rounds of the desired thickness or cut lengthwise to form half log shapes. An interesting buckle may be made by placing a number of the half log shapes side by side upon a piece of fabric and sewing them securely into place. The stitches may be planned to form a decorative band of color across the top and bottom of the buckle.

Fabric Buttons

Aside from the usual fabric-covered buttons there are many other methods of handling fabric in the making of buttons. A simple cylindrical button may be made by cutting a piece of fabric the desired width, fringing the long edges just enough to produce a pleasing edge, and rolling it to the desired diameter. To secure the fabric in place, the cylinder may be bound at intervals with embroidery floss or yarn to produce an effective stripe down the length of the button. This may be done with a contrasting but harmonious color. Fastening these buttons into place is a simple matter; merely sewing them from the back is sufficient. If buttons of this type are used on a wash dress, small safety pins may prove more expedient than sewing.

Variations on this technique may be developed by rolling several colors of fabric together or one color around another. The effect of this is apparent only from the ends of the cylinder.

Should one wish to have the buttons covered commercially, the fabric may be decorated with needle point or other embroidery before it is sent to the tailor. Extreme care should be exercised in observing the proportions of the finished button when planning and executing the design on the fabric. It is also necessary to send the fabric to a reliable tailor to insure accuracy in the making of the buttons. The entire effect can be destroyed if the design is pulled out of shape or placed off center when the button is covered.

Felt is another fabric that lends itself to further manipulation for this purpose. It may be rolled and bound as suggested for the fabric buttons, or built up in layers as suggested for the leather buttons, embroidered, or appliquéd.

Metal Buttons

If one has access to a few more tools, i.e., a pair of metal shears, a drill, a ball peen hammer, metal files, pliers, a block of

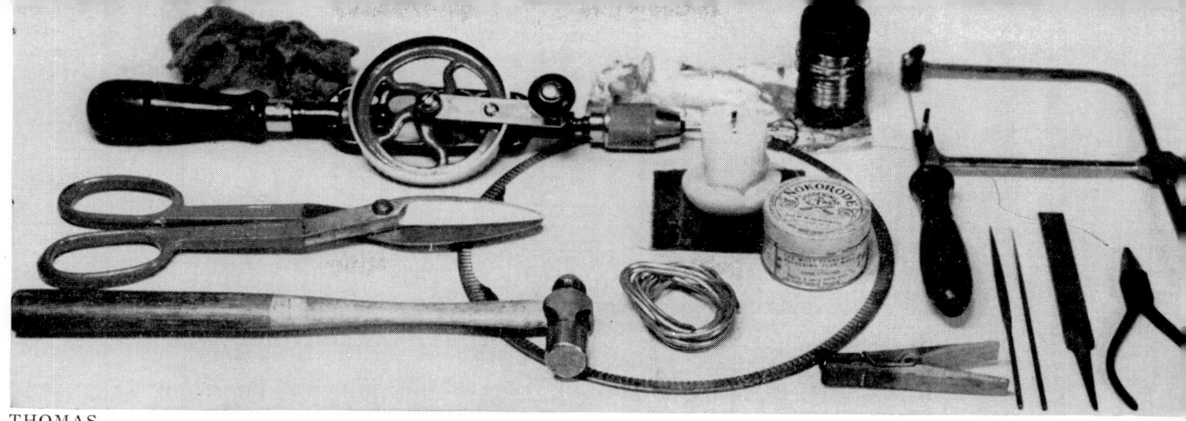

THOMAS

METAL BUTTON EQUIPMENT

A few more tools are needed but all are easily obtained. The jeweler's saw frame and saw blades might prove the least easy to acquire.

wood, and a candle, simple metal buttons may be made very inexpensively. The two metals best suited to this purpose are pewter and copper, used singly or in combination. The simple forms suggested for the wooden buttons may be adapted to this medium as well, and they may be decorated with file cuts or by hammering with the ball peen hammer.

Buttons built up in layers need to be soldered together. This is a very simple matter if using layers of pewter, or light weight copper and pewter. Cut the layers of metal to the desired size and shape, then place upon a hard smooth surface and pound with a wooden mallet until absolutely flat. Unless this is done the soldering will not be successful. The two surfaces of the metal that are to be soldered together should be cleaned with an abrasive such as whiting, fine steel wool, or emery cloth, then coated with the ordinary soldering paste. Before putting the two layers together, a piece of lead foil cigar wrapper cut the size of the smaller piece of metal should be placed between them. Grasp this metal and soldering paste "sandwich" gently with a pair of pliers that have a smooth gripping surface. A spring clothes pin may be substituted for the pliers, though the wood becomes charred during the soldering process. Wave the metal forms slowly over a candle flame. Do not allow the flame to touch the metal as it melts pewter in an instant. It is even safer to place the metal upon an asbestos pad such as one uses when cooking, then hold pad and all over the candle. As the metal becomes warm, the paste flux will bubble from between the layers and the lead foil will melt just a second later. One can tell when this happens by watching for a gleam of molten metal at the edge of the smaller layer of pewter. When this occurs, withdraw the button quickly from the flame, place on a block of wood and press firmly with a second block of wood until the metal has cooled slightly. Speed and precision are needed to produce a good piece of soldering.

Since the lead foil method is scarcely strong enough for heavy copper, it is better to use a regular soft solder paste, which comes ready mixed with flux; or glycerine, or the regular paste flux, and wire solder (without the acid core). Follow the directions printed on the tube when using the paste form of solder. The wire solder method involves quite a different technique. Hammer the solder wire into a very thin strip. Cut off small slivers of the solder. Paint with the glycerine or coat with the soldering paste all metal surfaces that are to be soldered together and place them in position. With a pair of tweezers, carefully place the tiny pieces of solder as close to the joint as possible. Heat carefully over a candle. When the metal reaches the right temperature, the strips of solder will melt and flow between the layers of metal. Remove from the flame and allow to cool. Sometimes excess solder remains on the outer surface and must be filed away.

If filing would be difficult, the following method will leave a cleaner outer surface. Paint glycerine over each of the surfaces

METAL BUTTONS

Pewter alone or pewter combined with copper was used for these buttons.

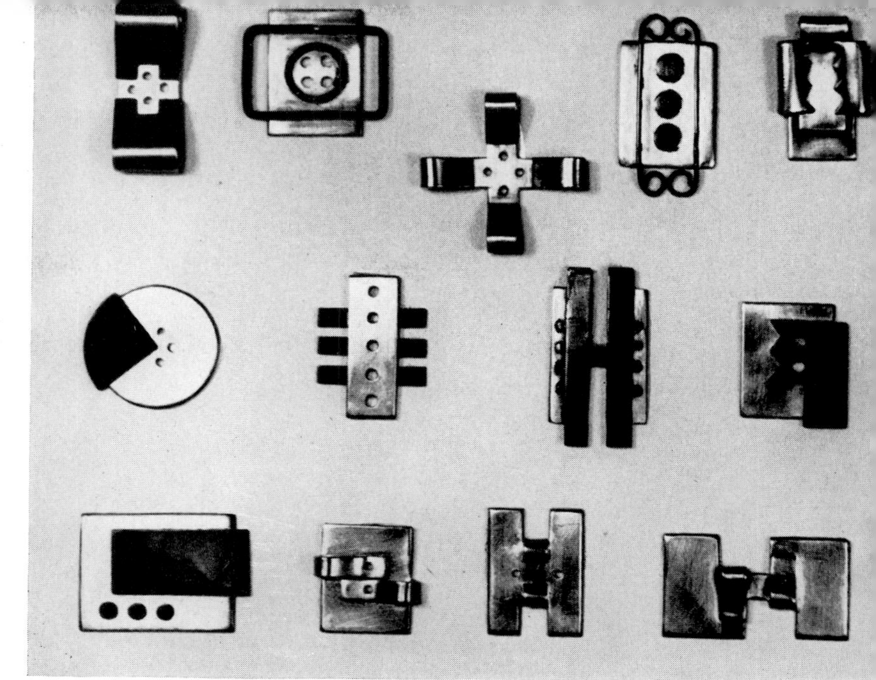

THOMAS

to be soldered. Sprinkle finely cut solder wire over each painted surface. Hold each piece separately over the flame until the solder melts and spreads. Permit the metal to cool. If any of the solder particles fail to melt, file them down to an even surface. Repaint both pieces with glycerine, place them together, and hold over the flame until the solder has melted a second time. Remove and cool.

Place the button on a wooden block, and with a metal drill bore the necessary holes for sewing. A small loop made of copper wire may also be soldered on the back. Shape the loop like a written letter "e." The bits of wire extending at the sides furnish a base for soldering.

The quality of the finishing is the determining factor in the quality of the final product. All of the rough edges and surface solder must be removed with a file, emery paper, and finally, pumice. Number 3/0 steel wool is also useful for burnishing the metal surfaces. A satinlike finish is in far better taste than a high polish. It is well to note that metal buttons are quite heavy and should be planned for use upon a fabric with considerable body. This quality of weight also limits the size of the buttons. A necessary precaution when planning the design is the elimination of any sharp corners which might tend to catch in the fabric or injure the wearer.

Chapter IX

For Frosty Fingers

THERE IS LITTLE DOUBT ABOUT THE FACT THAT A SNUG PAIR OF mittens is far better protection against wintry blasts than any pair of gloves ever will be. Most of us can remember that, as children, these were an accepted part of our winter's wardrobe. Perhaps the mittens were of a practical black Germantown yarn knit for us by a thoughtful grandmother, or perhaps they were of a less practical, but far more attractive, angora yarn. As we grew older, we discarded these childish things in the interests of sophistication and adopted gloves to protect our hands from frostbite. Of course there are many occasions to which gloves are a necessary requisite, but is there any valid reason for completely disregarding the extremely utilitarian properties of the mittens of our earlier years? There are times when an attractive and gay pair of mittens will be useful additions to any wardrobe. On such occasions they may label one with an air of the ultimate in sophistication.

The cost of making a pair of these fanciful mittens is very slight—about fifty cents a pair—if they are made of coating that sells for three dollars per yard. One third of a yard of coating will make two or three pairs of mittens, depending upon the width desired for each mitten. There is no reason, either, why scraps of material left from previous sewing shouldn't be used, providing that the material is of the proper weight and quality.

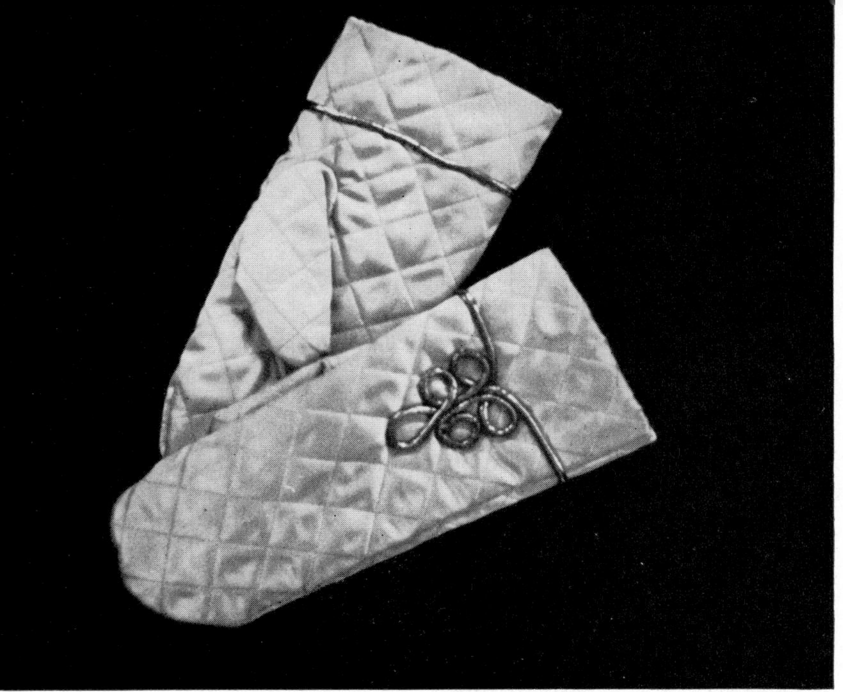

Photograph by Lloyd Matterson

QUILTED MITTENS

by Dorothy Mereness

Another version of the mitten theme.

One will be fascinated by the speed with which the mittens can be made and by the effective designs that can be applied to them with a small amount of bright yarn and the use of simple stitchery. Mittens such as these are a welcome solution to the Christmas gift worries that beset those with large families or many friends. Since the steps for designing the embroidered decorations to be applied to the mittens were thoroughly discussed in the chapter on design, the following material will deal only with the construction of the mittens.

The materials needed are very few. One third of a yard of coating will make two or three pairs of mittens. If one plans to embroider any decorative units on the backs of the mittens, a plain fabric will be the best choice. However, undecorated mittens would be very attractive in a bright plaid fabric. The material should be heavy enough for warmth and wearability. Fleece coating is an excellent choice. If yarn embroidery is to be used, Shetland floss in one or more colors is suggested. Necessary tools include a needle with a large eye and a number eight crochet hook.

The width and length of the mittens will be decided by the width and length of the hand for which they are intended. Place the hand palm down on a piece of paper and draw around it with a pencil. Make the pattern slightly wider than the rough drawing. Straighten the outside lines on the drawing with a ruler. Keep the line which corresponds to the thumb side of the hand perfectly straight for this line is to be placed on the fold of the material. Flare the outer edge slightly at the cuff to permit ease of putting on when finished. Point or round the fingertip end of the pattern. Place the inside, or thumb side, edge of the pattern along the fold of the fabric, pin the pattern securely, and cut. Reverse the pattern, pin again to a piece of fabric, and cut another piece for the other hand.

To make the thumb hole, measure from the tip of the index finger to the upper part of the thumb joint—this length will determine the position of the top of the thumb hole. Then measure down across the thumb joint itself—this length will be the length of the hole. Cut the opening on the palm side of the mitten about one-fourth inch from the fold of the material. Round the hole slightly at the bottom and cut to a point at the top. It should be only about one-half inch wide across the widest part.

When making a pattern for the thumb section, draw around the outstretched thumb, allowing a bit of extra width for freedom of movement. Straighten the outer line with a ruler and true up the curve at the tip of the thumb. Join the upper and lower lines at the base of the thumb with a slight outward curve. Cut out pattern and adjust to fit thumb hole in mitten proper. Place the straight line on a fold of the fabric and cut the thumb section.

The mitten is put together with crocheting which should be done in a color that will compliment that of the fabric itself. Crochet with Shetland floss once around the entire outer edge of the mitten fabric, working always on the right side of the material. Repeat this around the thumb opening and around the thumb section. If a design is to be embroidered onto the back of the mitten, it should be done at this point. Draw the design onto the fabric with tailor's chalk or outline it with basting threads. Embroider the decorative units with Shetland floss, using simple stitchery such as chain stitch, outline stitch, cross stitch, or satin stitch.

When the embroidery is complete, fold the mitten along the original folded edge and press it with a warm iron and damp cloth. If the embroidered side is placed face down on a piece of toweling or similar padding it will not be unattractively flattened out during ironing. Crochet the outer open sides together with the same or a contrasting color of yarn. In the same manner, crochet the folded thumb section along the top edge and then crochet into the thumb hole. Sometimes several rows of crocheting around the wrist opening will enhance the mitten because of the wide band of color or colors that this finishing touch produces. The stitches of all of the crocheting should be kept closely and evenly spaced in order that the final result will look professional.

There are almost no limitations to the number or kind of designs or colors which can be adapted to this craft for clever fingers. Peasant designs lend themselves particularly, since their very nature seems to be part of the gay informal occasions with which mittens are usually associated. Tassels of yarn may be added at the cuff for further whimsy. One with a young imagination will see in this project endless possibilities for the application of that imagination.

Chapter X

To Top It Off

SOME OF THE BEST IDEAS FOR TRICKY LITTLE CAPS AND HOODS may be garnered from drawings or photographs of peasant or period headgear. Probably the peasant costumes from rural European communities are most adaptable, for these need only slight alteration to fit becomingly into American winter sport wardrobes. However, period costumes, such as those of the moyen âge, will tempt the imaginative person into planning amusingly different creations.

There will be no attempt to present a treatise on millinery in these pages, but rather a few concrete suggestions for caps or hoods that could be worn with skating or skiing costumes. Fetching little bonnets that are quickly and simply made will give that final touch of the unusual that adds so much to a costume.

In planning a hood for an individual, it is best to build it, as much as possible, on the head of the person for whom it is intended. Whatever the source of inspiration for the general design may be, a few tucks here or an added fraction of an inch there will make the bonnet a pleasing frame for the face or not, as the case may be. The first plan or pattern may be done in muslin, and put together with pins. After a satisfactory effect has been achieved, the muslin may be used as a pattern for cutting the actual fabric.

Many kinds of fabrics may be used for these hoods. Felt,

snow suiting, quilted challis, coating, corduroy, or velveteen are appropriate for wear with snow togs. These fabrics may be left plain or they may be decorated with quilting or yarn embroidery. If the bonnet is lined with a bright contrasting color, a turned back visor will show this bright color and will add a gay note to an otherwise plain hood.

It should be remembered that these hoods are designed not only for the decorative effect they produce, but also for a practical purpose. They are to be worn in the more severe winter weather and should be warm and comfortable; and they should stay put during expert or amateur participation in strenuous winter sport.

Directions for Making a Hood

The hood pictured is becoming to many people. It was originally made for an individual by the suggested method of planning mentioned before, i.e., that of designing it of muslin upon the head of the person by whom it is to be worn. It was based upon an idea suggested by a Dutch girl's hood. The woolen hood retains characteristic earmarks of its ancestry, such as the peaked top and winged side effect. To make it more suitable for winter sports use, it was designed to tie snugly under the chin. The peak was modified to a square line which was more becoming to the wearer and less extreme than a high pointed effect.

For warmth in a rigorous climate and for a texture that would be harmonious with the usual togs, wool fleece coating of the same kind as has been suggested for mittens was used for the hood. Incidentally, matching mittens were made to be worn with it. It was embroidered with Shetland floss in a very simple design.

To make this hood, cut a paper pattern to the following directions: Cut a rectangle eight by twelve inches. From the two cor-

THOMAS

THE FINISHED HOOD

by Barbara Weismann

The two vertical seams in the crown of the hood are made by faggoting together the two edges formed by cutting away the squares mentioned in the directions.

ners of one of the narrow ends cut away a two-inch square of paper. The opposite end of the paper should be reduced from an eight-inch length to a four-inch length by a series of five evenly spaced darts which radiate from the lower edge. The longest and center dart is three and one-half inches in length, the shortest two and one-half inches. These darts form a decorative spoke arrangement at the nape of the neck. At the same time they bring in the lower edge of the hood back to make it fit the head snugly. At the upper edge the two edges formed by cutting away the square are brought together to create the squared-off peak. These edges are held together securely by faggoting. A seam allowance is unnecessary since the material does not fray easily and the stitchery is sufficient to protect the edges.

From the left-hand square corner of the lower back edge of the hood measure up along the side a distance of two inches. From the bottom of the center dart draw a slightly curved line up to the two-inch marks on the sides, thus rounding off the corners. Cut along this line. This curved edge should measure approximately five inches. Repeat this process from the center dart up the right-hand side of the hood.

Cut another rectangle from paper twenty inches long and six and one-half inches wide. Label one of the twenty-inch sides *front* and the opposite one *back*. Fold this rectangle in half, bringing the short ends together. Measure up three inches from the short ends and draw a line across from front to back. Along the short end measure in three inches from the back edge toward the front. From the last mark draw a straight line to the point where the first line drawn meets the front edge. This line should measure about five and one-half inches. Cut off the large triangle formed by these measurements.

On the folded end measure in five inches from the back edge. Along the front edge draw a slightly curved line from the lower corner to the five-inch mark. This curved line produces the winged effect on the hood.

Pin all of the darts into position and pin the back edge of

the front section to the main part of the hood, beginning at center front down along either side. If the two lengths do not exactly coincide, they may be trimmed to match. Try on this paper model and make any necessary adjustments. The paper pattern may prove to be somewhat unyielding. Cutting the hood from muslin may prove more satisfactory for fitting purposes. The front section is to be turned back to form the winged effect.

Use this paper form as a pattern from which to cut the material for the hood. It is necessary to cut two front sections since one is to be used as facing.

Put the two front pieces together, and crochet around the edges with an evenly spaced single crochet stitch. Faggot the darts together and crochet around all edges of that piece. Pin the front and back pieces together and crochet together with another row of single crochet stitch, catching through the loops of the previous crocheting on both sections. Crochet a second row around all of the outside edges of the assembled hood. This may be done in a harmonizing color of yarn. Crocheted or braided cords finished with a yarn pompon or tassel fastened at the sides of the hood may be used to hold the cap snugly in place.

Decoration of the Hood

The method of fastening together the various sections of the hood is, in itself, quite decorative and should prove sufficient if a plain hood is desired. The costumes with which hoods are most frequently worn, such as ski suits, skating skirts, and jackets, may be made of a figured or plaid material which would make it necessary that the hood be plain.

The yarn used for crocheting the seams together and finishing the edges need not match the fabric of which the hood is constructed, but could just as well pick out and repeat one or more of the colors found in the costume. The most suitable area for the application of stitchery is found either on the area surrounding the face or on the crown of the cap.

In the hood used for the illustration, a very simple border following the upper edge of the cuff was used. It was made up of two rows of crosses, each cross formed by two horizontal parallel stitches over two vertical parallel stitches. A very small cross stitch of contrasting color was placed over the center of the large cross. A row of outline stitch was embroidered along the inside of the crocheted edge. This was whipped with a contrasting color to give a cablelike effect. For the embroidery the colors used were the same as for the crocheting except that one lighter value gave emphasis to the decorative stitchery. When the costume with which the hood is to be worn permits, a much more elaborate design may be applied to the front cuff. The hood itself finds its ancestry among peasant headgear, so it would seem most suitable to adapt one of the naive, colorful designs found in peasant embroideries. These usually are of a type which cover the surface rather solidly. The nature of such designs calls for careful consideration of the colors to be chosen, because when used in so large an area, and so close to the face, they must be becoming to the wearer as well as harmonious with the complete ensemble. The more elaborate the decorative design, the greater the necessity to be guided by the shape of the section to be decorated.

The most suitable stitches for the more solid designs are the satin stitch, a chain stitch worked closely over an area, or an outline stitch done in the same way. Pompons for finishing the cord ends may match or contrast in color. The hood illustrated has one dark brown and one rust colored pompon. To make these little balls of yarn is a simple matter. For the reader who is not already familiar with the process, directions follow:

Cut a rectangle of fairly strong cardboard the width of which is the same as the desired radius of the ball. Wind a goodly amount of yarn around the width of the cardboard rectangle. The more yarn used, the fuller the ball. After this has been done, slip a length of yarn, preferably doubled for strength, along one edge of the cardboard and under the yarn. Tie this short length of yarn as tightly as possible, drawing up all the wrapped yarns into a very small bundle. Cut the wrapped yarn at the opposite edge of the cardboard. This causes the cut ends of the yarn to spring out into a neat ball. Sew the ball onto the end of the braided cord used for keeping the hood upon one's head.

It is hoped that these detailed directions will serve only as an inspiration for other ingenious designs of one's own devising.

Chapter XI

Oaks from Acorns

To some people home is where they hang their hats. A few moments of thought given to this state of affairs will uncover several easily changed contributing factors. Usually, when a home, or better a house, no longer acts as a central living unit, it is not because the physical setup is lacking. Palatable meals may still be set on the dining room table every day, inner spring mattresses may still lure one to rest at night, but the house often has an unattractive personality. It may be drab, colorless, and unimaginative. It is well to determine whether or not the rooms are arranged interestingly, or if the appointments in the house are things which have become contemptible through prolonged familiarity.

Current magazines offer many suggestions for redecorating a single room or an entire house. Modern commercial advertising constantly puts new ideas and plans before the public, most of whom spend at least part of their day in a home, whether it be a mansion, a bungalow, or a rented room. Sometimes the plans or suggestions as outlined in the articles involve costly refurnishing or remodeling. If one can afford to do so, this is unquestionably one of the most satisfying ways of injecting new life into the commonplace.

Perhaps a better understanding of the problem of making a house take on the personality of a home might be brought about by comparing the house to the wardrobe. Small things, cleverly and tastefully selected in the way of accessories may brighten a dull wardrobe or mark it as individual. In just the same way can small accessories, well selected and used in a home, add to its atmosphere. One might call these little things the grace notes of a harmonious home. We do not mean to suggest that one clutter up his home with knickknacks of heterogeneous selection, but we do wish to impress him with the fact that a few well chosen accessories will go a long way toward brightening a room.

Many small accessories may be made at home after the housework is done. And many such accessories will not only add sparkle to the house but may be used for very acceptable Christmas or birthday gifts. Some of the articles suggested later in this section are things for which one cannot even find duplicates in our larger stores. Most of them can be made at a very low cost and with a minimum of effort and will repay the individual who creates them.

After reading through the directions which follow, it may seem to the reader that we have selected a rather unrelated group of craft problems. This is true to a certain extent, but careful planning will coördinate articles made into a harmoniously related group. There are among these articles things which may be used not only decoratively but also in the utilitarian sense.

In planning anything which is to find a useful place in the house, it is first necessary to consider the relation of the article to the things with which it is to be combined. This involves consideration of all of the material on design and its principles as presented in the first section of the book. Not only should the principles apply to the object itself but also to the object as seen in relation with all of the other things it may be used with, i.e., the room decorative scheme, the furnishings, the textures, and the other accessories of the room. It should also reflect the personalities of the persons using the room, since it is to be a measuring stick of their tastes.

Amusing Rusticity

One of the very easiest items to make and one which is very attractive and useful may serve as a welcome first lesson. We give this suggestion at the beginning of this section since it concerns an article which is very quickly completed. It is a plain wooden salad bowl, painted on the outside with some bright color—blue, or red, for instance. How may it be used? Fill it with fruit and use it for a centerpiece on an informal table. Use it for salad or popcorn. A large salad bowl may be accompanied by half a dozen individual bowls to add gay spots of color to an otherwise ordinary table. The large bowl might be painted blue, and the smaller bowls various other bright harmonizing colors. Remember, the bowls are by nature informal, so your colors may be informal as well.

Bowls for this purpose may be purchased at the five-and-ten-cent store. If the outer surfaces have been waxed—they usually are—the wax must be removed completely with sandpaper before the paint is applied or the paint remains tacky indefinitely. Oil paint or enamel may be used to put the color on the bowl. The paint may be put on with an inch-wide paint brush and should be so applied as to keep the surface free from brush strokes. If one chooses to use enamel, there will be directions for its use on the can in which it comes. Two coats should be sufficient to cover the the surface well. After the first coat is thoroughly dry, sand it lightly with number 4/0 sandpaper or number 3/0 steel wool before applying the second coat of paint. When the final layer of paint is dry, wax

PAINTED BOWLS

by Kate Anderson

Decorative when empty; delightful for serving dry food.

Photograph by Helen Ludwig.

both the inside and the outside of the bowl with either a paste or liquid wax. This will protect the painted surface.

If one wishes, and if one has faith in his ability, one might paint a simple border design in contrasting colors around the upper edge of the bowl. This should be done with a small water color or oil paint brush after the surface of the bowl has been painted, but before the bowl has been waxed. Such a design may be very simple, a scalloped edge with a dot between each scallop, for instance. It will add a note of distinction to the bowl if carefully drawn and painted.

Sometimes a design placed on the inside of the wooden bowl is more effective than a border design. This is particularly true if the bowl is a shallow one where the outer edges curve under so as to obscure any outer decoration. However, if a design is to be placed in the center, the bowl must be used either as a purely decorative object or as a container for dry foods—nuts, fruits, popcorn, etc.—since one must be able to clean it by wiping with a damp cloth

THOMAS

RUSSIAN BOWLS AND BOX

Native designs from the far flung reaches of the earth are worthy of being added to one's collection.

only. When planning a design for the center of the bowl, several things must be considered. The design is to be applied to a curved surface so the measurements should be planned for the curve rather than just from side to side. And since the design is to conform to a circular form, it is essential that it be well related to the structure. Probably a design based on a circle would be most successful for this problem. After the design has been planned on paper, its various units may be cut out to be used as patterns. This makes transferring the design to the bowl much simpler, in as much as it is difficult to adjust the complete paper design to the inner curve. The separate pattern units may be placed in position in the bowl and then outlined with a pencil. Of course before this is done, it is necessary to remove any wax surface that may have been on the bowl when purchased.

In summing up the types of designs suited to the decoration of a bowl one finds that there are: a border on either the outside or the inside of a bowl, the inner circular motif, and, if desired, an

MEXICAN PLATE

Another good design to adapt to one's own needs.

THOMAS

allover design applied to either the outside or the inside of the bowl.

For finishing the inside of the bowl follow the directions as given above for the outside, namely, shellacking and waxing.

Another possibility for useful decorative objects may be found in wooden plates which make serviceable serving trays. These plates may be stood on edge to form a background in a grouping of several related objects. A decorative arrangement such as this will create an interesting note in a dining room or kitchen, according to the type of design used on the plate. The wood itself suggests an informal setting and should be combined with like objects and be used in a room of the same spirit.

These wooden plates cannot be as easily purchased ready-made as the bowls. For this reason, it may be necessary that they

Photograph by Helen Ludwig.

WOODEN PLATE

by Ardis Swanson

The repetition, with variations, of the small scallop motif unifies the design.

be made by someone having access to a lathe. Any town which has a carpenter will also have a lathe—sometimes a high school boy who can use school equipment may be found to turn out one or several plates.

Since it may be impossible to purchase these plates, it is necessary to furnish a pattern to the carpenter. The most usable designs follow two main types. The first is modeled after a standard dinner plate but may be made to almost any dimension. It has a rim proportioned to the size of the whole plate. If one takes the measurements of a dinner plate of pleasing design and increases or decreases the relative measurements of the flat inner portion and the rim according to the same ratio, it may serve as a standard for the wooden plate. The second design and one particularly useful for serving is without a rim. It is a flat plate with the outer edge

WOODEN PLATE

by Barbara Weismann

A stylized figure such as this is far more effective than one weakened by sentimentality.

Photograph by Helen Ludwig.

turned up slightly to give depth to the plate. It is somewhat easier to plan a design for this type of plate since one need not consider the rim as a limiting factor. The design may be planned in much the same way as was the design for the inner surface of the wooden bowl.

When planning the design for the plate first mentioned, it is essential that the rim and the center be thought of as related to one another. A border design following the rim with the center left plain is one successful method. Another reverses this process and puts a design in the center with the rim left plain or painted a solid color. A third treatment involves the decoration of both the center and the border. If this is done, it should be remembered that either the center or the border should receive the most emphasis and that the other should complement the dominant part of the design.

Photograph by Helen Ludwig.

WOODEN PLATE

by Marian Ogard

Simplicity is the keynote of this distinctive design.

The beauty of the wood should play a prominent part in the finished product and it is not usually advisable to cover completely the center surface of these plates with paint. Frequently the grain contributes a great deal to the character of the design, and certainly the inherent color of the wood is often so beautiful as to warrant preservation. A simple design which makes use of these qualities is in the best taste and will give the most satisfactory results. Occasionally imperfections in the wood such as knots or too dark areas occur. Sometimes they may be incorporated into the design, but often such flaws make it necessary to cover the wood completely with paint.

After the design has been painted on, these plates are finished in the same way as the wooden bowls, with shellac and wax. However, since they come from the carpenter without any protective

MEXICAN PLATE

This engaging design might some day be adapted to needlework.

THOMAS

finish having been applied, it is necessary that they be thoroughly smoothed with sandpaper and given a single coat of white shellac before the design is put on. This acts as a filler to close the pores of the wood. It also protects the raw wood from becoming soiled with handling. When the shellac has thoroughly dried, sand it lightly and just enough to remove the shine. Oil paint or enamel is suggested for the painting. If oil paint is used, one should thin it with turpentine only enough to facilitate handling. If it is thinned too much, it is apt to run along the grain of the wood and thus obscure the design.

Plates of this nature are best used with heavy linens or homespun cottons. Woven straw mats are very pleasing in texture and color with them. Remember that these plates are informal and call for informal articles when used in combination.

Tea for Two

Another wooden craft article for which materials are more easily obtained is a tile for use under hot dishes, or as a decorative note in itself. It is a small square of wood set up on fat round little legs made of wooden kindergarten beads. A simple but effective design may be applied to the colored surface, then finished with a spar varnish, which is heatproof as well as waterproof. One of the nicest features of this tile is the low cost of the materials necessary for its making, and if more than one tile is made, each one costs proportionately less, since some of the needed materials can be used over and over again. The supplies that one will need are:

One piece of *unwarped* pine, bass, or similar wood. A good size for most uses is three-quarters inch thick by six and one-half inches square. This can be obtained at the local lumber yard, cut to size for about ten cents. The cost is usually lower on quantity orders. Four round wooden kindergarten beads (purchased at five-and-ten-cent store or a store handling school supplies, usually listed in phone directories under the heading of book and stationery stores).

Sandpaper, medium and very fine, four flat-headed nails (shingle nails) long enough to fasten the beads to the tile. Water color paints of the ordinary school box variety, and a small jar of white tempera paint are used. White poster paint is a good substitute for the tempera. Oil paints may be used instead of the water colors. If oil paints are preferred, then the technique given for painting wooden bowls should be followed. Use a watercolor brush big enough to hold paint well, but be sure it points up for the small areas and lines. Spar varnish is used as a finish. Ordinary var-

TEA TILE
by Dorinda Johnson

An entertaining design of great simplicity.

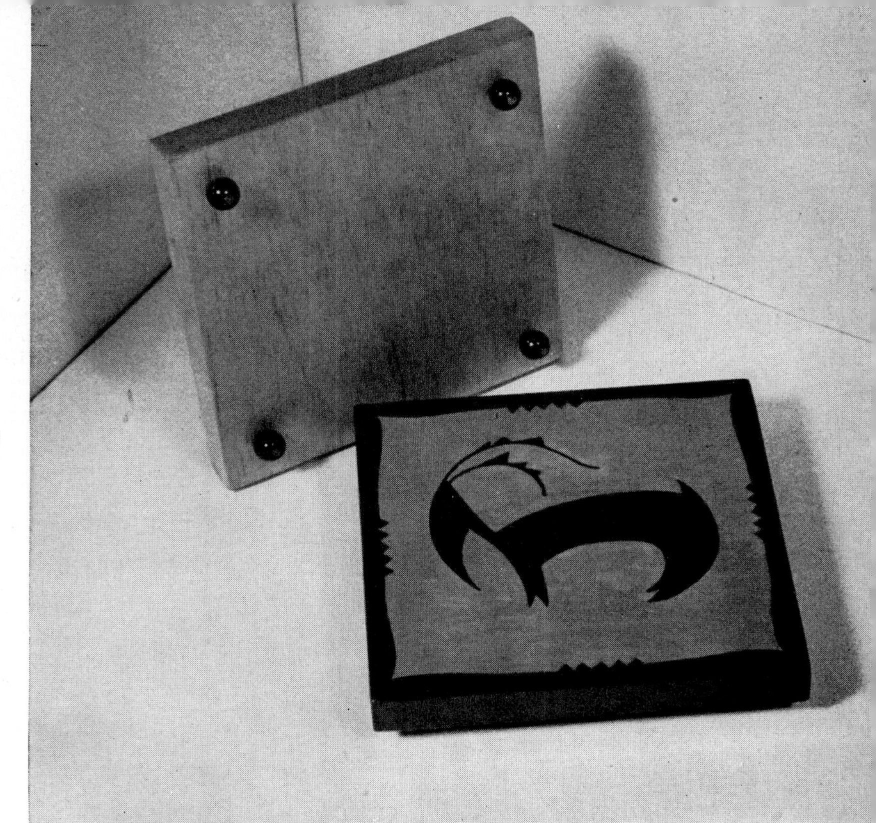

Photograph by Helen Ludwig.

nish is not practical for this purpose. The varnish is most easily applied with a brush about one inch wide.

To make the tile, the wooden block should be sandpapered to a smooth finish, rounding all edges and corners slightly. The desirable character of the wood itself is lost if the corners are rounded too much. A certain severity of line is preferable to a soft, curved edge. When sanding the flat surfaces of the wood, be careful to work with, rather than against, the grain.

If desired, the wood may next be colored. This coloring process is done by mixing clear water color paint and water to the desired value and intensity. Be sure to mix an ample amount so as not to run short of paint while working. Paint all surfaces of the block as quickly as possible with a fairly large brush. If the color does not appear dark enough, apply a second or even a third coat after the first coat is almost dry. Another method of coloring the wood is by the use of leather or batik dyes. A dye bath of the desired color and in a quantity sufficient to permit completely submerging the wood is necessary. In order to prevent warping the wooden block, the dye must be strong enough to dye the wood to the right value and intensity instantly. The strength of the dye may be easily tested with small scraps of the same wood as that being used for the tile. After the tile has been dipped into the dye bath, it should be stood up on end to drain and dry. Do not force the drying process by placing in a warm place, for that often causes the wood to warp and crack.

When the paint or dye has dried into the wood, trace the design, planned carefully, onto the top surface. If an error is made at this point, the entire surface may have to be resanded, since the traced lines cannot be erased.

Prepare the colors one desires to use for painting the design by mixing transparent water color with some of the white tempera or poster paint. The tempera will give body to the paint and will prevent its running out of the boundaries of the design and along the grain of the wood. It also gives the paint an opaque quality which enables one to apply one color directly on top of another with satisfactory results. Varnish will change the appearance of the colors slightly. In order to prevent disappointment, it is wise to varnish over trial patches of color. These need not be painted on wood; the trial colors mixed and tried on paper will serve the purpose well. Varnish has a yellow cast, even when the most transparent kind is used, so that either the hue or intensity of the colors is changed in almost every case.

Paint the design. If the design calls for black in some of its areas, use the plain black water color without the addition of white. Use water sparingly. The paint should be just liquid enough to cover the surface of the wood easily without becoming caked. It may be necessary to apply more than one coat of paint to some parts of the design.

After the design has been painted onto the tile surface and around the edges if desired, the tile is ready to have the legs attached. Nail one round wooden bead onto each of the corners of the underside of the tile. Measuring one-half inch in from each corner on the diagonal has proved satisfactory. Sometimes the wooden beads come in a variety of shapes. The cylindrical and square beads can also be used for legs if the design is in character with that form.

The final step in the process is that of varnishing the tile to preserve the design and to make it heat resistant. Apply the spar varnish in two or three successive thin coats, allowing the varnish to dry between applications.

The design itself should be carefully considered. If it is kept very simple and conventionalized, or geometric, it will be more attractive and in far better taste than if a realistic basket of flowers or a Scotty dog is used for the decorative motif. Many Swedish designs are particularly appropriate for this practical, decorative article.

Pandora Never Had These

Boxes, too, may be decorated. Many common commodities come packed in wooden boxes that lend themselves to this treatment. To mention just a few: cigar boxes that have mitered corners; cheese boxes, the round as well as the square; dried fruit boxes, stationery, chalk, and many others. Besides these packing boxes, it

THOMAS

RECLAIMED CIGAR BOX

A spirited design, five wooden beads (four were used for legs), and a little time.

is possible to purchase very attractive wooden boxes for only a few cents at ten-cent stores and book and stationery stores.

The uses for these decorative boxes are unlimited. The small ones are fine for cigarettes, pins, costume jewelry, sewing supplies, and a dozen other things. The larger boxes, the round cheese box for instance, afford convenient storage space for hats, knitting or sewing, or toys. Give a box to any member of the household and he will find a use for it. Either the oil paint or water color processes may be used to finish the boxes. The surfaces should be prepared carefully, of course, before any process is employed. Boxes have so many possibilities for decorative treatment that every box designed offers at least two more ideas for other boxes. There is the top cover, perhaps the most obvious choice for decoration. Except that it may be rectilinear rather than round, it lends itself to exactly the same variety of treatments suggested for plates. The sides of the box might be the center of attention, or the outside of the box may be painted a beautiful, rich color that harmonizes well with the sur-

WOODEN BOX FROM POLAND

Just border designs were used. Similar ones might be adapted to wall hangings, draperies, or place mats.

THOMAS

roundings, and then an interesting design placed inside the top cover, to be enjoyed every time the box is opened.

After one has experimented on simple objects as have been mentioned, it is hardly safe to look at the panels of a cupboard door or breakfast nook windows without being stimulated to action. Utmost care must be taken when undertaking the enrichment of anything so permanent as furniture or architectural details of a room. Every part of the room must be considered in relation to the planned design. Are the draperies of such nature that another design can be added without competing with them? Is the furniture simple enough? Is the spirit of the room itself of informal nature? Other suggestions are beside the point, since anyone who has become interested in this craft will find many opportunities to make use of it. Great is the satisfaction to any one who has become proficient in this process when comparing it with the results obtained by the frequent misuse of commercial transfers or decalcomanias of poor design.

THOMAS

MEXICAN BOX

Boxes such as this are a valuable aid when learning space division and shape harmony.

The beautiful texture of wood has a great appeal to many people, and if one belongs to this group he may hesitate to superimpose any design motif upon the natural grain of the wood. Such a person might investigate the possibilities of several products manufactured by General Finishes, Inc., 111 South Second St., Minneapolis 1, Minnesota.

Chapter XII

Fanciful Fabrics

IT IS INTERESTING TO ENUMERATE THE VARIOUS USES OF TEXTILES in the room in which one ordinarily spends the evening. The upholstery upon the chairs, the rug, the draperies. and the glass curtains, wall hangings, table scarves, pillows—to mention the most obvious. These will demonstrate to one how important fabrics are in the home, and the close relationship they bear to the other furnishings of the room. Because of this widespread use of textiles in the average home, a wider scope for the application of design presents itself. The use of fabrics is one of the most important items in the decoration of one's home, owing to the fact that they are used in such large areas, and play such an important role in determining the complete color scheme and the spirit or personality of any room.

Not all the fabrics in a room lend themselves to home crafts. For instance, it would hardly be practicable to attempt to design a large piece of upholstery or room-size rugs. On the other hand, hooked rugs of a small scatter size, or a needle-point chair seat or footstool cover, or a wall hanging, among other things, are very feasible. The article which is least familiar to the average person and which one seldom finds used in homes, is the wall hanging. This may be used not only as a substitute for the ordinary framed picture, but as a decoration is often far more suited to the other

BLOCK-PRINTED DRAPERIES
(Courtesy of the Milwaukee WPA Handicraft Project.)

The well proportioned stripes furnish a splendid complement for the bold motif.

BLOCK-PRINTED SCREEN
(Courtesy of the Milwaukee WPA Handicraft Project.)

Stenciled material would be equally satisfactory for this purpose.

BLOCK-PRINTED MATERIAL
(Courtesy of the Milwaukee WPA Handicraft Project.)

Only two small blocks are necessary for this feminine pattern—a single flower and a length of stem bearing eight leaves.

textures used in the room. Wall hangings frequently complement the spirit of the room more adequately than does a picture, since the wall hanging is usually designed for a particular area in a given room. There are a number of techniques adaptable to wall hangings which range from the very simple to the intricate.

Old Art into New

Block printing is one of the more simple techniques and has innumerable uses. It can be used expediently for making greeting cards, book plates, table covers, and draperies as well as attractive wall hangings. Block-printed material, either paper or cloth and designed to suit one's fancy, can be used for making book covers, pages of books, wrapping paper, covering for boxes, and for unusual bags or purses. The possibilities are limited only by one's ingenuity.

As a rule materials for block printing are not too difficult to assemble. The linoleum may be obtained in two forms: mounted blocks, or battleship linoleum which is used for floor coverings. The blocks are carried by art supply shops; the battleship linoleum in floor-covering departments of most furnishing stores. It is often possible to buy remnants or scrap pieces.

There are tools especially manufactured for this craft consisting of V- or U-shaped gouges; or razor blades and pen knives may be used. The best printing medium is regular printer's ink, though oil paint may be used. For cleaning up and protecting the work table, one needs plenty of old newspaper, rags, and turpentine. Kerosene is effective for cleaning off the printing blocks, rollers, and glass if turpentine is not handy. Never use the kerosene as a thinner for the ink or paint. A piece of glass or a smooth stone slab is necessary for rolling out the ink or paint. A rubber or composition roller, called a brayer, is used to apply the ink to the cut linoleum block. A photographer's squeegee roller works well on small blocks. This is a small rubber-covered roller which can be purchased for about twenty-five cents, though for long usage, gelatine rollers of a six-inch length are preferable. The latter must be hung up when not in use as they have a tendency to flatten, especially in warm weather.

If cloth is used to print upon, it should not be of too coarse a texture, because ink will remain only on the upper threads, destroying the effect of the design. Percale, pongee, linen, or fabrics having similar textures are suitable.

Careful, even painstaking, attention should be given to the

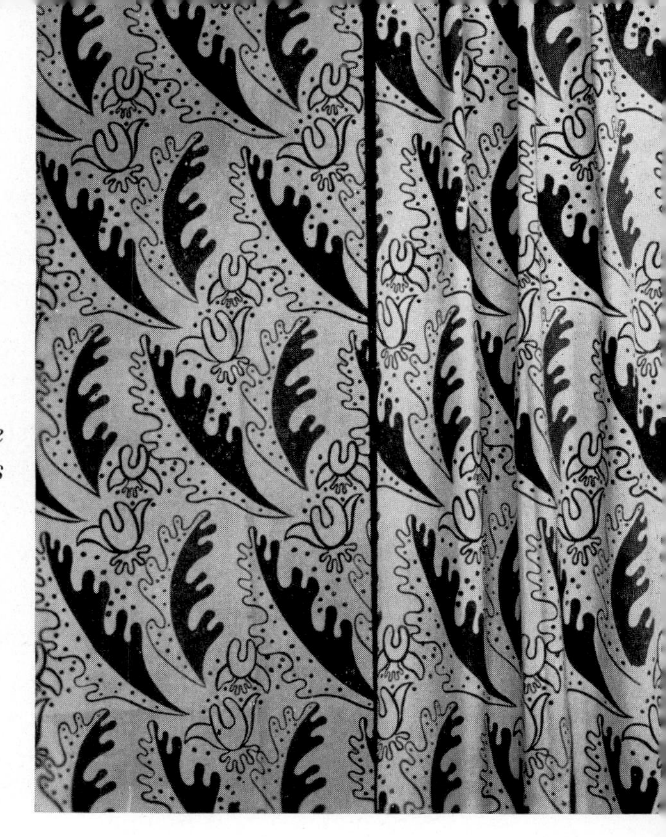

BLOCK-PRINTED MATERIAL

(Courtesy of the Milwaukee WPA Handicraft Project.)

Strong rhythmic movement and value contrast are responsible for the spirit this design displays.

preparation of the block for printing. If the linoleum has a hard, waxy surface, sandpaper this off carefully with fine sandpaper. If desired, the sanded surface may be painted with white poster paint or flat white oil paint to facilitate tracing the design. Commercially mounted blocks frequently come with a white surface.

Trace the design very accurately upon the block. Graphite paper underneath the design is an expedient method; or the back of the design may be blackened with a soft pencil. *Precaution:* If the design depends upon a certain direction of line, either to the right or to the left, it will have to be traced in reverse upon the block. This applies to lettering especially. It is provoking, to say the least, to find words on greeting cards turned backwards.

Using a simple motif over and over in simple repeat patterns gives attractive results. If this is desired, measure the parts of the

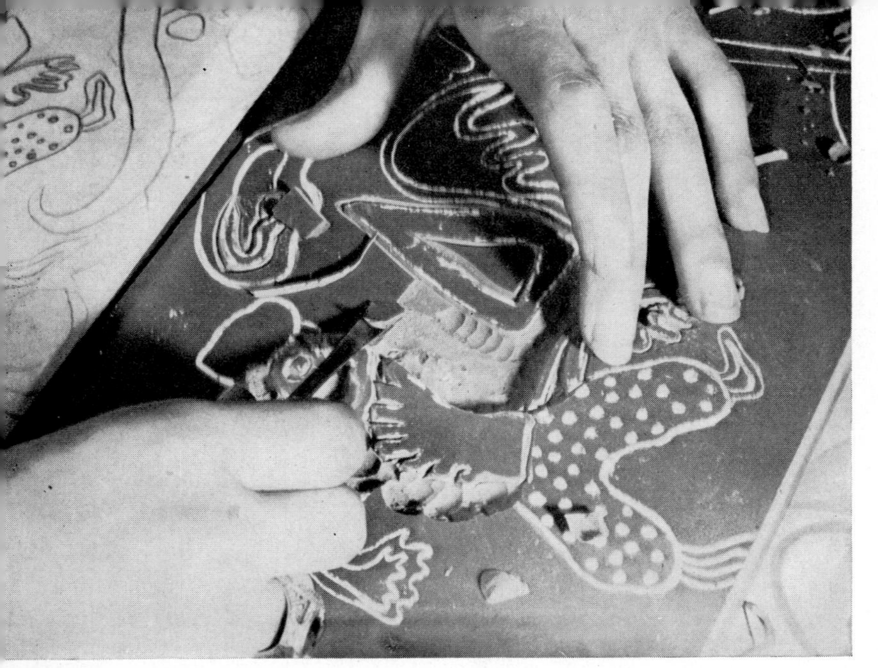

CUTTING A LINOLEUM BLOCK

(Courtesy of the Milwaukee WPA Handicraft Project.)

An area is outlined with a V-shaped groove before being gouged out.

motif that serve as connecting units very carefully in order that they may match when used in this manner.

Slow, exact cutting of the block pays dividends later. Before making a single nick in the surface of the linoleum learn the principle that all parts to be printed are left the original height of the linoleum, unprinted areas are dug out or cut away.

In general there are three main techniques used in cutting:

1. Outlining the entire design with a V-shaped gouge or a razor blade. When using the razor blade cut around the design, holding the blade at an angle slanting away from the part of the design to be printed. This is to prevent undercutting. Then cut a line all around the design, holding the razor blade slanting toward the printing surface of the design. This cuts a V-shaped groove all around the design. A block cut in this manner is called a white-line block; when printed, the design appears in lines only.

A COMPLETELY CUT BLOCK

(*Courtesy of the Milwaukee WPA Handicraft Project.*)

Each unit is broader at its base than at its printing surface.

2. ROUTING. Proceed as for outlining; then, with a U-shaped gouge or pen knife, dig out all areas not to be printed.
3. DETAILING. This is a combination of methods 1 and 2. By using the tools in various ways to show the direction of the stroke of the cuts and varying the width of the cuts, very interesting results may be obtained. Analysis of blocks cut by others, close observation of prints made from blocks, and actual experimentation will develop skill in cutting blocks this more elaborate way.

There are a few pitfalls one may avoid if the following rules are kept firmly in mind:

1. Wide spaces are cut deep. This prevents paper or cloth from picking up excess ink that may have gotten on the background areas.

2. Narrow spaces are cut shallow.
3. Deep vertical cuts are bad, undercuts are worse. Fragments of the linoleum break off, leaving ragged printing edges.
4. Square off the outside edges of the block with a vertical cut, not slanting either in or out. The block is more easily keyed into its proper position for printing if this rule is observed.

About the time enough cutting has been done on the block to let one recognize the design there is a great urge to rush the task in order that a print can be made. It is wiser to take the time to test results frequently while cutting in order that one may forestall accidents. There are two popular methods: Put the block, cut surface up, under a piece of paper. Hold the paper securely, then rub the lead of a soft pencil back and forth over the block; the cut surfaces will appear white or very light gray in contrast to the raised parts. Or if brown or gray linoleum is used, the cut parts may be filled with starch or talcum powder, then the raised parts wiped off clean. A white-surfaced block may be blackened with ink if this method is to be used.

It is wise to have both the original design and the one traced on the block worked out in dark and light to be used as a cutting guide. Darken all parts to be left the original height of the linoleum.

The actual process of printing with a linoleum block is simple. All the attention given to careful preparation of the materials used will be well repaid later. The cloth or paper must be free of folds or wrinkles. Prepare the cloth or paper for printing by indicating guide lines with pencil dots (not lines) pointed off where the corners of the block are to be placed. Spread the material out

ALL READY FOR PRINTING

(*Courtesy of the Milwaukee WPA Handicraft Project.*)

More than one brayer is a convenience for multicolor work. Neatness and order are a necessity for all crafts.

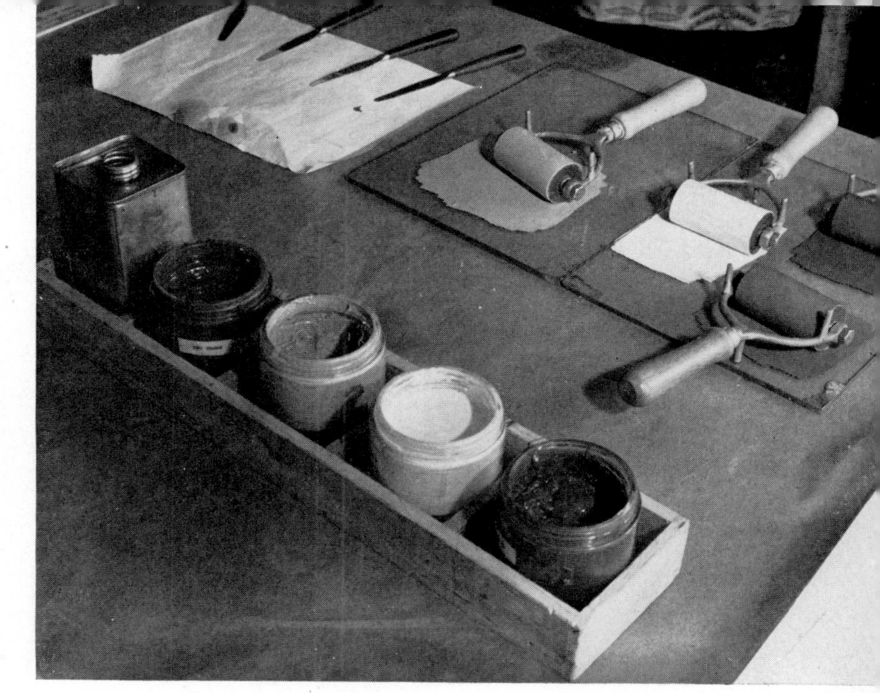

INKING THE BLOCK

(*Courtesy of the Milwaukee WPA Handicraft Project.*)

A squeegee roller would prove a good substitute for the professional brayer.

PRINTING
(Courtesy of the Milwaukee WPA Handicraft Project.)

Pounding the block with a mallet is one of the best ways of applying pressure.

over an even pad of newspapers; then tack it down to a flat surface if necessary.

Printer's ink or oil paint may be used, the ink preferred. If it is necessary to thin the ink, use a reducer produced by the ink manufacturer; for the oil paint, use linseed oil or turpentine, but this should be done very cautiously. Oil also slows down the drying process. Either the ink or the oil paint should be of a tacky consistency.

Place a little of the ink (or oil paint) on the center of the piece of glass. Roll the brayer over it until the ink is nicely distributed upon the roller and the surface of the ink is velvety rather than shiny. Roll the brayer back and forth over the cut surface of the linoleum until the block is covered completely with a thin coat of the ink.

With the inked side down, place the block in position on the cloth (or paper) as indicated by the pencil dots. There are several ways of producing the pressure necessary to make a perfect im-

THE PRINTED RESULT
(Courtesy of the Milwaukee WPA Handicraft Project.)

Finger smudges or marks made by a block that slipped would mar the work beyond repair.

pression of the design upon the material to be printed. The size and nature of the problem at hand will dictate the best method. Some favorite procedures are listed.

1. Pound the block with a wooden mallet over its entire surface to transfer the ink to the cloth, or
2. If the block is small, pressing everywhere with one's thumbs is often sufficient, or
3. Have the material and pad on the floor, step on the block a number of times, facing in different directions in order to distribute the pressure evenly. The preceding methods are especially suited to printing allover patterns on large pieces of material.
4. Book plates and greeting cards may be printed by putting the padding, the paper to be printed, and an unmounted piece of linoleum on a very thin board, then on top of all of this a piece of tin, or heavy cardboard. Put all this through an old clothes wringer.

PRINTING WITH AN IRREGULAR BLOCK

(Courtesy of the Milwaukee WPA Handicraft Project.)

Both convenience and economy are often served by cutting the block the shape of the motif.

5. Ink the block as usual and place upon the paper. Press into place firmly. Turn the block cut side up so that the paper is uppermost. Rub over the entire surface gently with the bowl of a tablespoon. Be very careful the block does not slip at any time. Remove the block, re-ink, and print as before.

Always clean the glass, roller, and blocks thoroughly with turpentine or kerosene when through printing at any time, even though the entire process is not finished.

Block printing need not be confined to printing with one color. A separate block is needed for each color used. Until one has practiced this craft enough to gain considerable confidence, limiting oneself to a few colors or values is a wise decision. The more complicated procedure for multicolor block printing follows. Take time to think through each step before going ahead. It is worth the extra effort.

HAND PRINTED MATERIAL

(Courtesy of the Milwaukee WPA Handicraft Project.)

It is not the subject matter but the manner in which it is used that determines the success of a design.

1. Cut a master block first. The entire design outlined with a V-gouge is used for this.
2. Ink the block very thoroughly.
3. Make a print on hard-surfaced paper.
4. Place a second linoleum block, cut to match the master block, carefully upon this fresh print. Register the corner accurately. Press gently to make the paper adhere to the new block. Turn the block, paper adhering to it, upside down and rub the paper with a tablespoon to transfer the design to the linoleum.
5. Allow this block with the printed design upon it to dry before attempting to do any cutting. The ink will smudge if not dry and will cause inaccuracies.
6. Indicate upon this block all the areas to be printed in any one of the colors needed in the original design.

7. Cut the color block carefully, following the guide lines of the master block, or the cutting may be done with a fractional allowance for overlapping.
8. Prepare a new block from a fresh print of the master block for each color desired. After all have been printed, cut away all the areas of the master block not to be printed in the darkest color. Each color block should have raised areas for a single color only. Cut all other parts away.
9. In printing, start with the lightest color first, the darkest last. This last should be the master block. On the reverse side of each block, mark corresponding corners plainly to avoid turning the block accidentally and hence printing upside down.

Borders on wall hangings present their own problems. Suggestions for designing corners were made previously. A few hints for avoiding difficulties during printing follow:

A special corner block may be cut. This facilitates printing but adds to the cost of the finished product. When planning for a special corner block, care must be taken to measure the border blocks accurately to insure a perfect fit around the center unit. The border may be printed either before or after the center of the hanging has been printed.

The center area should be measured off with a row of pencil dots against which the border blocks are placed. Mark the base on the back of the block in order to avoid reversing it when laying it on the cloth. Every fraction of an inch of the border must be accounted for before printing a single unit of the border. It is probably safest to follow this procedure. Have a piece of material large enough to allow for very ample margins. Using the border blocks

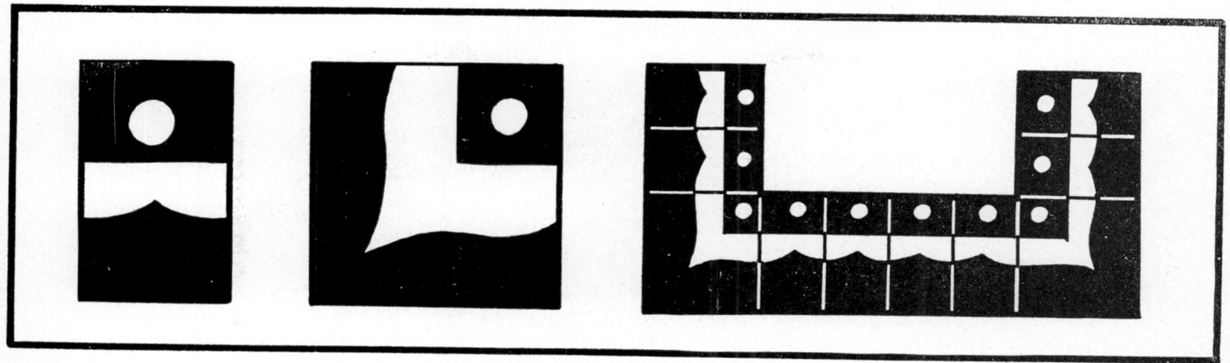

WEISMANN

BORDER DESIGN WITH SEPARATE CORNER BLOCKS

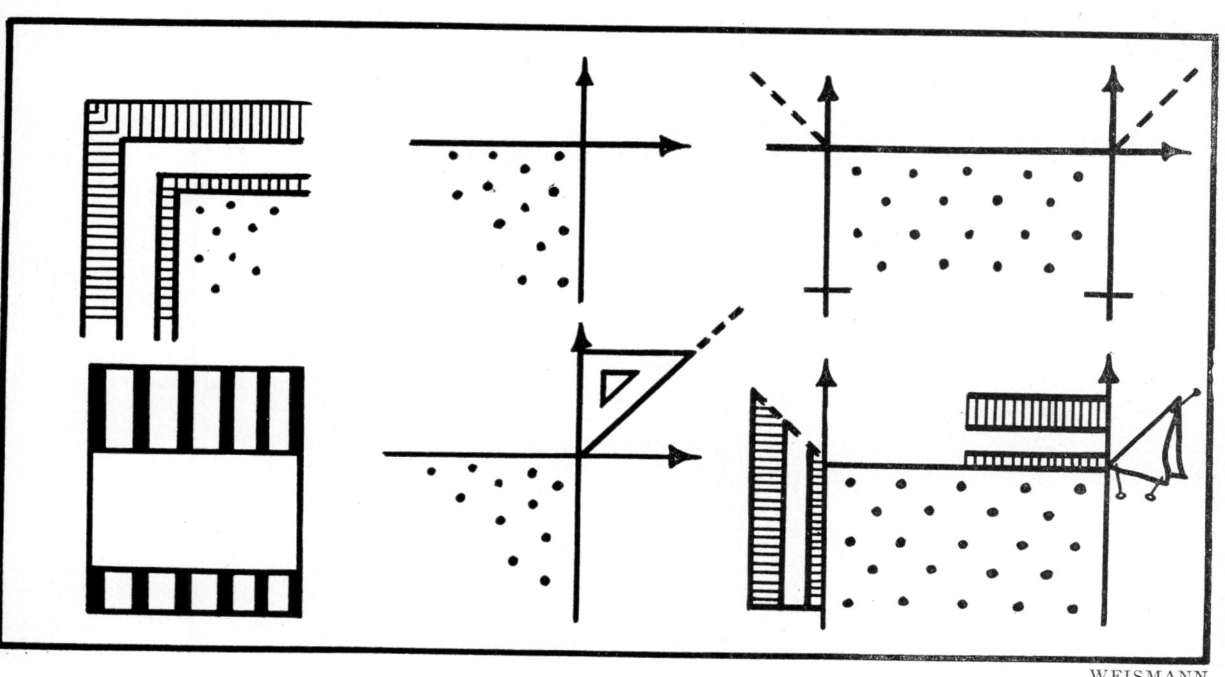

WEISMANN

PLANNING AND PRINTING A MITERED BORDER

HAND PRINTED MATERIAL

(Courtesy of the Milwaukee WPA Handicraft Project.)

Good proportions and a variety of shapes and sizes are essential to good design.

as units of measure, plan the placing of the blocks as accurately as possible. Use faint pencil dots to indicate the position of each during the printing. After all has been carefully planned, start printing in the middle of the top border. Work out from this unit to both the right and the left until the desired amount of border has been printed. Next, print the two top corners and continue with first one side, then the other; finally the bottom corners and the bottom border. The center of the wall hanging may now be printed, adjusting the inner margins for pleasing proportions. This seemingly backward procedure prevents gaps or unfortunate overlapping, because the linoleum block simply won't stretch or shrink if the last space to be printed and the size of the block are not the same.

When printing borders without special corner blocks, the corners are mitered. Before printing, indicate with light pencil marks the center square or rectangle; draw in the diagonals. Extend these lines an equal distance beyond the corners, the distance depending upon the width necessary to accommodate the border. Connect the

BLOCK-PRINTED MATERIAL

(Courtesy of the Milwaukee WPA Handicraft Project.)

Two blocks identical in size were printed alternately.

ends of these lines with a faint dotted pencil line. Measure the sides of the central square or rectangle thus formed and point off the exact center of each side. Lay the border block with one corner at this mark and print. Follow this procedure, printing until the corner is reached.

Fold a piece of paper of a size large enough to serve as a mask and lay the folded edge along the line extending from the center unit, pinning or tacking down the paper so that the corner about to be printed is neatly bisected, the paper protecting the part of the corner to be formed by the border not yet printed. Print the uncovered area in the same manner as before, right over the masking paper, the result being, after removal of the block and the paper, one-half of a mitered corner. Repeat this process in the other direction from the center mark. The printing is continued in this manner on the remaining three sides of the center motif. The resulting border will have an unbroken movement around the corners of the hanging.

BLOCK-PRINTED MATERIAL

(Courtesy of the Milwaukee WPA Handicraft Project.)

This design requires that the two blocks be perfectly keyed.

CHAIR BACK AND DRAPERY

(Courtesy of the Milwaukee WPA Handicraft Project.)

It would be more economical to stencil than to block print the drapery design.

Paper, Paint, and Brush

Stenciling is equally as effective for wall hangings as block printing. It offers some advantages not found in a block-printed textile, since it permits the use of a wider range of colors and the covering of larger areas with color. Another distinct advantage is that of enabling the craftsman to see just what his results are going to be during the process itself. It is usually found that the materials required for the making of a stenciled wall hanging are less expensive than those used for block printing.

There are numerous other projects for which stenciling may be used. It may be wise for the beginner to experiment with this new technique on some small item before attempting so large an article as a wall hanging. In general, stenciling may be used as a means of applying surface decoration wherever block printing would be suitable; and in addition upon wooden and metal objects such as furniture, boxes, woodwork, and plastered walls. The materials are quite easy to assemble. The sten-

Photograph by Helen Ludwig.

STENCILED DRAPERY

by Helen Ward

Inexpensive Osnaburg was used for these draperies.

cils themselves are best when cut from a flexible, hard-finished card-board. It is possible to buy stencil board, but the results obtained when using Manila tag board or very heavy wrapping paper are satisfactory. The cutting is done with a razor blade, small pointed scissors, or a special stencil knife.

The designs for stenciling may be very elaborate, using many colors, or as simple as a polka dot stenciled in only one color. Somewhere along the gamut of possibilities is a degree of complication suitable to anyone. When designing the unit to be used keep in mind that each color calls for a separate stencil, with each "hole" in this particular stencil surrounded completely by at least a small pathway of the stencil board. To some this pathway between all units of a stenciled design is the distinguishing characteristic, for it is the type of stenciling used by many interior painters for years. Not many of these old stenciled borders would pass as good designs, for they are weak and spotty in appearance. A carefully executed stenciled design need not have a single trace of the background material separating the various colors used unless it is desired for part of the design itself. However, this pathway serves as a protective mask during the stenciling process, so it does appear on the separate tag board stencils.

Tubes of oil paint, turpentine, a piece of glass or an old plate, and a palette knife or other device for mixing the paint, along with thumbtacks and clean rags, are about all one needs besides the tag board or heavy paper. As is true with block printing, the material upon which the design is to be stenciled should not be too coarse or flimsy in nature. Osnaburg, sugar or flour sacking, linen, crash, sailcloth, and dull-surfaced oilcloth are all suitable. The purpose of the finished product will have to govern one's choice.

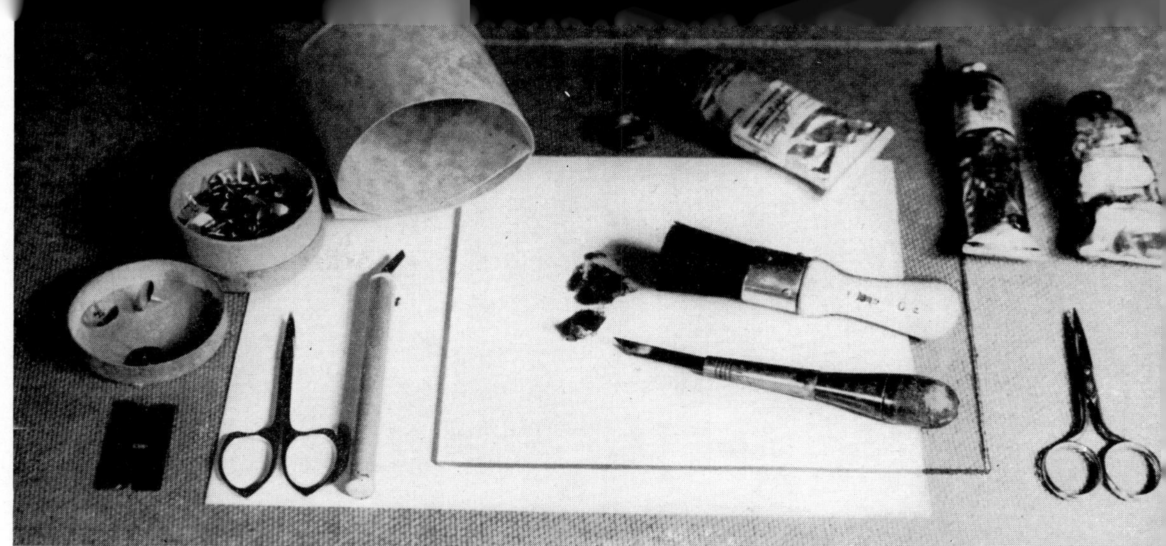

THOMAS

EQUIPMENT FOR STENCILING

One or more sharp cutting instruments, a stencil brush, stencil board, oil paint, and a piece of glass to mix it on are the tools of stencil craft.

As mentioned before, a stencil will be needed for each color. Trace all the sections of the design which are to be in one color onto one piece of the stencil board. Allow at least one inch of margin around the outside of the entire group of spots to be cut out. This provides a thumb-hold quite necessary when doing the actual stenciling. Follow the same procedure for each color, taking care to trace each unit accurately or the finished piece will not key.

With a razor blade or scissors cut away the outlined sections. It is advisable not to use more than four colors, at least on one's first project. If one uses four colors there will be four stencils.

If the stencils have been cut from square or rectangular cardboards of a uniform size, the following method may be used for keying: Make a frame from a large piece of cardboard by cutting in the center of it a hole the size of the small cards upon which the design has been cut. Hinge the stencil sections with gummed tape to the sides of the hole in the frame unit. This will look very much like a doorway with four doors, each one hinged to a different side of the opening so that any one of them may be used separately. It will be necessary to determine which edge of the small card should be hinged to the frame in order that the stencil may take its proper position when turned down over the opening in the frame. Test the accuracy of the position by turning down any two at a time and holding the frame up to a strong light. The cut out areas should just meet or overlap evenly just the smallest fraction of an inch. If gaps or large overlaps appear, shift the small cards at the hinged side, or trim the cut edges judiciously until a satisfactory matching is effected. This is termed "keying." When in use, these flaps are turned down one at a time over the portion of material to be stenciled, starting with the one through which the lightest color is to be stenciled. When done carefully, and if too much paint has not been used, the various colors will not smudge. Clean, clear-cut edges are characteristic of a good stenciled design.

A second method of keying and one which sometimes is more easily used, especially for allover patterns, is as follows: Trace the entire unit on as many cards as there are colors in the design, but cut each card so that it accommodates only one color as before. Now on the second stencil, or the one to be used for the next to the lightest color, cut peepholes that fit accurately over two, better three, parts of the areas stenciled through the holes in the first card. It is not necessary or even advisable to cut out the entire areas. They may be just small holes that register a sharp corner or a distinguishing curve in the design. Let these holes be well separated and far enough away from the areas to be stenciled through this card to prevent the bristles of the stencil brush accidentally carrying an unwanted color onto the material exposed by them. If the design permits, the same peepholes may be cut into the remaining cards.

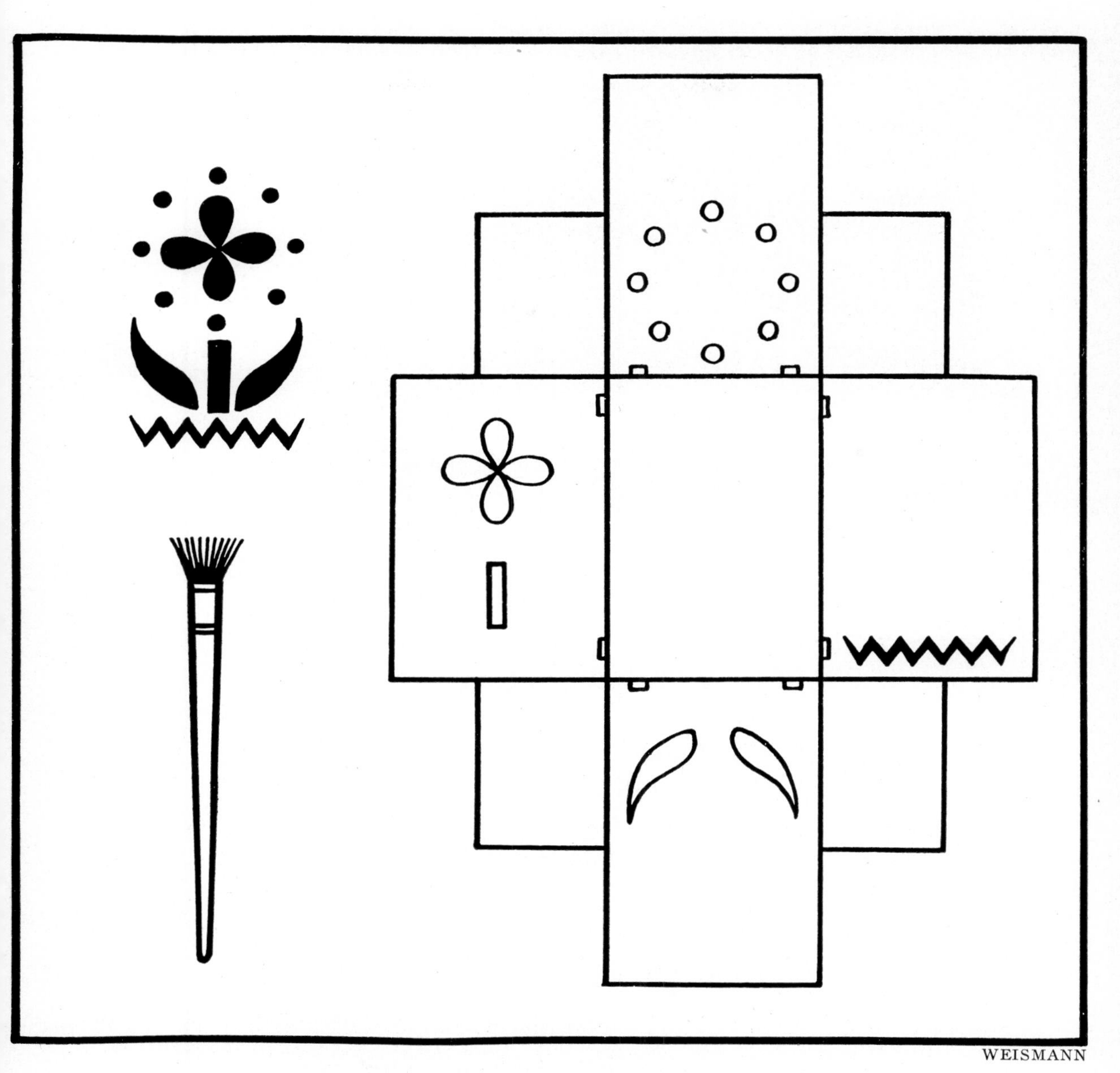

KEYING A FOUR-SECTION STENCIL

Photograph by Helen Ludwig.

STENCILED WALL HANGING

by Ruth Justine

The vigor of this design lies the fact that only th stencils were used.

If not, cut them elsewhere; it is care that counts here. Test the keying of the stencils by holding any two of the cards up to a strong light to see if the outlines of the design on one card coincide with the peepholes and cut out areas on the other one. A stenciled area is always a bit smaller than the hole through which the paint has been applied. This may be compensated for by a slight overlapping of areas when keying the design. Be sure to correct all errors even though one or more of the cards has to be cut over more accurately.

When the stencils are keyed satisfactorily, mix a sufficient quantity of oil paint of the desired color to permit stenciling all the areas of that particular color. Do not thin the paint with turpentine without testing the consistency first on a piece of the fabric to be used. If thinning appears to be necessary, do so with great care. Paint which is too thin will run under the stencil edges and cause a blurred design. Spread a thin layer of the mixed color upon

STENCILED WALL HANGING

by Jean Montgomery

A small design such as this lends itself to block printing as well.

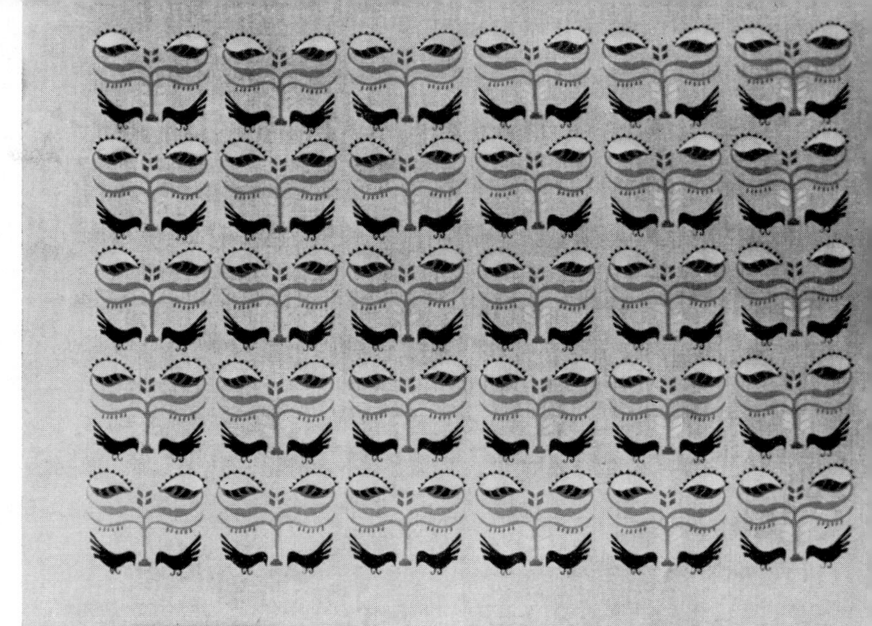

Photograph by Helen Ludwig.

the surface of a piece of glass or a plate. Keep the remainder of the pigment in a compact mass covered with waxed paper to prevent it from drying before it is needed.

The material should be firmly tacked to a smooth surface. Place the keyed stencil in the desired position upon the material. Fasten the stencil down with thumbtacks and, if using the hinged type, fold the first stencil over into position. Apply the paint gingerly. First tap the flat surface of the stencil brush into a thin layer of the prepared paint, using care not to get too much paint on the bristle ends. Hold the brush perpendicular to the material and tap the bristles briskly with short, swift strokes over the exposed area of material until the desired color has been obtained. Shading may be accomplished by varying the amount of pigment used within an area. Interesting surface textures may be obtained by experimenting with various brush strokes and through the application of more than one color within a single area. Keep the underside of the stencil free of paint. Always clean the brush thoroughly in turpentine and wipe it well on a rag before using it for another color.

The time required for the paint to dry depends upon the amount of paint applied and the weight of the fabric used. In most cases the paint should dry out overnight, but this is not always true. Try to prevent the paint from forming a thick coating on the surface of the material. When stenciling a piece of fabric, the fibers of the material should absorb the paint. This is accomplished by tapping the brush more frequently over any area rather than using more paint to obtain darker values. The texture of the fabric is an integral part of the design and should not be obscured by too much paint.

The color may be set by covering the material with a cloth dampened in a fairly strong solution of vinegar and water and pressing it with a hot iron. Usually fabrics treated in this way can be washed if care is taken. This is not always so, however, because the quality of paint varies. It is well to test a small piece of stenciled fabric for color fastness.

Experience will develop ways and means suitable to each individual and to the task at hand, but a few variations of procedure may be of assistance. Scotch tape or masking tape will hold stencils firmly in place when thumbtacks are impractical. Just the steady pressure of one's fingers is sufficient to keep small, simple stencils in place.

A large wall hanging or a decoration to be stenciled directly on a wall may be attacked quite differently if the design calls for good sized motifs that are not repeated over and over. If this is the case, draw the design very lightly directly upon the surface to be decorated. Any small units that are used for allover or border pattern within any of the large areas may be omitted from the drawing and taken care of by the usual procedure, but all the large areas do not necessarily require a true stencil. Instead cut a variety

WALL HANGING

(*Courtesy of the Milwaukee WPA Handicraft Project.*)

The main lines of a design of this type might be drawn directly upon the fabric. The characteristic clean-cut line of stenciling could be obtained by using a variety of curved and straight line shields; only the clover leaf requires a regulation stencil.

of curved and straight-edged pieces from sheets of tag board. Have the pieces wide enough to permit one to handle them easily. Twelve inches or more is a good length. Firmly hold or tack the piece of tag board which happens to be cut with the right curve along the corresponding line drawn upon the design. Stencil the area thus protected; then shift that curved mask along to another part of the line or substitute a piece that fits better. Not many pieces will be required. Start out with a few straight strips, a large and smaller circle, a piece shaped like an S, a shallow concave piece, and a shallow convex piece. A roll of waxed paper or a bread wrapper or two that may be snipped for small pieces now and then is a handy addition to one's equipment.

Sometimes one wishes to stencil a spot within a spot, and there is no way of holding the parts of the stencil together without destroying the unity of the design. A piece of stencil board cut to the right shape and size, and held in place with pins or thumb-tacks, solves that problem. It may be used to protect the material while color is being applied, or to protect the color while another color is being stenciled in an adjacent area. These protective pieces used independently of the stencil proper are called positive stencils. The cards into which holes are cut are called negative stencils.

A very satisfactory textile color is distributed by the American Crayon Company of Sandusky, Ohio. It is easy to use, and when the very simple directions for setting the colors are followed accurately, the colors are resistant to fading and are washproof.

Oil paints are not satisfactory for stenciling upon paper. After a few hours an unsightly ring of oil begins to appear around the colored areas. Poster, tempera, and water color paints are far better for this purpose. The procedure is the same. Never use too much paint.

For quick effects colored chalk may be used on fairly rough paper. The chalk is powdered and pounced through the stencil. Decorations made with this medium are not practical unless kept under glass as a framed picture or set by blowing a fixative upon them. A dilute mixture of denatured alcohol and shellac, sold for fixing charcoal drawings, may be applied with an atomizer. Just as good, and easier to prepare, is a mixture of one tablespoon of mucilage in one-half cup of water. Have the design thumbtacked to a flat horizontal surface and blow this fixative over it so that the mist falls down upon it. Do not disturb until quite dry.

Oriental Magic

Up to this point we have discussed types of wall hangings which have the design applied to their surface with a medium for-

BATIK WALL HANGING

This batik design is based on a schematic diagram of a vacuum tube.

THOMAS

eign to the fabric itself. Another method which dyes the design directly into the fiber of the fabric and which leaves the material with its original softness and flexibility is that of batik. This technique is used chiefly on the islands of Java and Bali, but is also found in the other Oriental countries. Fabrics dyed in this fashion are used for wearing apparel and household accouterments.

Cotton is generally conceded to be the fabric most charac-

THOMAS

EQUIPMENT FOR BATIK

Strips of lath and clamps, or a frame with mortised corners, wax, brushes, tjantings, and dye are essentials for this method of resist dyeing.

teristic of the batik technique. For this purpose a finely woven cotton is most suitable. Nainsook is a very good choice.

Silk may be used; it definitely produces a more brilliant color—a quality which might be desirable for certain purposes. Crepe de Chine, silk crepe, or pongee are usable if one wishes the brilliance of color and softness of texture that may be achieved with these fabrics. Whatever fabric is used, it must be thoroughly washed to remove all traces of sizing, as this may interfere with the application of the dyes used to produce the design.

Carefully draw the design onto the fabric with pencil. It is not necessary to make the lines very dark but they should be strong enough to remain visible after the fabric has been dyed the first light colors. Sometimes if the material is light weight enough the original design planned on paper may be placed under it and the lines redrawn onto the fabric.

The batik process is a dye-resist method with wax used as the resist or as a protective coating over the fabric. Any area which is covered with a thin coat of wax will not take the dye. Thus the design is brought out by dyed and undyed areas. In order that the wax may be applied to the areas which are to remain undyed, the fabric must be stretched smoothly over a wooden frame. This may be made very simply of four laths fastened together at the corners with small metal clamps. The fabric should be tacked securely to the wooden sections with thumbtacks and the laths adjusted with the aid of the clamps until the tension is absolutely even on all parts of the material.

Another method is that of tacking twilled cotton tape to the laths, allowing a portion of it to extend over the edges. The fabric may then be pinned to this tape. When the laths are assembled the tape should be to the inside of the square formed by the four pieces of wood.

Beeswax is the best for the purpose of batik since it is pliable and the least liable to crack when the material is placed in the dye bath. However, if the cost of beeswax is prohibitive, a substitution may be made with a mixture of one-half beeswax and one-half paraffin. Some art supply stores carry specially prepared batik wax.

The wax is heated slowly to the melting point over hot water and applied to the areas which are to be covered with a small watercolor brush or, if fine lines and dots are desired, with a tjanting. This last-mentioned object is made from a piece of thin copper in a cuplike form with a tiny piece of copper or brass tubing at one corner to act as a spout. The cup is fastened to a wooden handle. These tjantings may be purchased at some art stores or may be secured through dealers in art supplies. A substitute for the tjanting may be made if one has the use of a wire drawplate. A strip of very thin copper about three-sixteenths of an inch wide and three inches long should be cut on the diagonal to form a point at one end. This point is then inserted into a small round opening on the drawplate and the entire strip pulled through. It will emerge in tube form and may then be cut to lengths of about one and one-fourth inches. The cutting process will close the openings in the tube, but these may be reopened with a pin or similar pointed instrument. The lengths of tubing should be bound at right angles to the end of a wooden stick about the size of a small paintbrush handle. The tube or cup of the tjanting is filled by dipping into the heated wax. The tube is then drawn or dotted over the material. It should be held at right angles to the material when this is done. A piece of waste cloth kept handy in the other hand to catch superfluous wax will prevent any accidental dripping into an undesired area. If the wax has a tendency to solidify in the tube too quickly pass the tjanting through the flame of a candle. The wax should be put onto the material in a thin layer of a thickness sufficient only to cover the fiber. After the waxing of the top surface, the fabric should be turned over and waxed on the back in such places as the wax failed to penetrate. When the waxing has been finished, the fabric should be removed from the frame and dipped into lukewarm water so that all the exposed areas are wet through. This will help to insure an even dyeing.

For dyeing the batik, a special batik dye may be purchased at art supply houses or an ordinary dye especially prepared for the kind of textile being used will be quite satisfactory. Following the directions upon the package, mix a dye bath of sufficient quantity and strength to cover and dye the material the color desired. The dye bath should be lukewarm so as to prevent the wax from cracking but not so warm as to melt the wax. Remove the fabric from the frame and submerge it in the bath and allow it to remain there

BATIK

The boldness in the design of this batik is not unlike many Javanese designs.

THOMAS

until the dye has penetrated thoroughly. Remember that the color will lighten as it dries, so that it is necessary that it appear darker than desired while the material is wet. It is a good idea to test the dye with a scrap of the same material as used for the wall hanging before attempting to dye the wall hanging itself.

After this dye bath, the fabric should be rinsed in clear water to remove any excess dye, and then hung up to dry away from heat.

When thoroughly dried, the wax must be removed. This is done by placing the material between newspapers and ironing, thus melting the wax which is absorbed into the paper. Repeat this until all of the wax that can be removed with heat is out of the material. There will still be a stiff quality to the fabric owing to a residue of wax in the fibers. The fabric may be sent to a dry cleaners where the last traces of wax will be cleaned from it, or it may be rinsed out in naphtha at home. If this is done, the usual precautions in using naphtha should be carefully observed. Nonexplosive cleaning fluids may be used in preference to naphtha.

From the directions given up to this point, the reader will probably have assumed that a batik is a piece of fabric decorated with a dyed design produced with one color plus the basic color of the fabric itself. This is not necessarily true. It may be a design embodying several related colors, one dyed over the other. Before each successive coat of dye is applied, the areas of the design which are to remain the color of the previous dye bath should be covered with the protective wax. It is to be remembered that the dye color should be successively darker since it is impossible to dye a light color over a dark one. The effect of one color over another should also be considered since the two colors will often combine to produce a third. This follows the same principle as that of mixing transparent water colors.

Where small areas of color are desired, it is not always necessary to dye the entire fabric. A wax outline may be put around the area to be colored, and the dye may be painted onto the cloth with a brush. This is a time- and wax-saving device which is quite successful.

Small geometric designs or designs using very decorative and conventionalized animals, birds, flowers, and fish are usually most successful for this technique.

Attractive wrapping paper is delightful to use, but doesn't it always seem that the design and color one selects is always the most costly of the lot? Try batiking some paper. After the dyeing process remove as much of the wax as possible by pressing with a hot iron between old papers. Omit the naphtha bath. The finished paper has a feeling similar to parchment. The paper one has collected from parcels can be used. The process requires the paper to be rumpled a bit during the dye bath anyway so a few wrinkles to begin with will be quite all right. It isn't easy to work over creases and bumps so it is wise to press the paper with a moderately hot iron before beginning to work. Keep the designs simple and fairly bold, and one color is quite capable of producing a rich effect. The fine crackle lines that appear are characteristic of the medium. Beeswax and lukewarm water accompanied by gentle handling will keep the number of these lines at a minimum. Or one might wish to capitalize on this natural crackle. Coat the paper with wax—use up the old paraffin from jelly glasses—rumple the paper until the line pattern is as fine as one wishes, then dip the paper into the dye. The process can be repeated if more than one color is to be used. Press out the wax between old newspapers as suggested before.

Chapter XIII

Scintillating Stitchery

WALL HANGINGS HAVE BEEN DISCUSSED AT LENGTH UNDER other techniques; but for the woman who enjoys plying an embroidery needle, decorative stitchery lends itself admirably to the making of decorations for walls, and of course, to many other objects that might add an individual note to one's home. To anyone the least bit sensitive, the so-called art needlework shops or departments are really chambers of horror. It is amazing to find that so many sweetly sentimental boys and girls, "cute" little puppy dogs (or kittens, to say nothing of squirrels and ducks) can be maligned to such an extent. If one looks carefully, one might find a fine adaptation of a Swedish tapestry, or directions for simple decorative edges on linens for various purposes; but there is an overwhelming display of "real" roses, daisies, and forget-me-nots, stamped hither and yon upon otherwise beautiful material. The same may be said about most of the stamped articles offered for sale in needlework sections of magazines, or of the transfers so profusely filling pattern books.

The designs found on stamped goods, or offered to the public on transfer patterns, are generally poor in that they lack suitability to the use to which they are put. Many are realistic to the extreme; others add to this mistaken conception of design a great deal of sentimentality. The actual organization of many of these

DETAIL FROM MEXICAN AYATE

A rich collection of source material is a good antidote for that helpless feeling.

Photograph by Lloyd Matterson.

designs is very loose, lacking almost entirely the desired quality of unity. When the design is stamped upon the material, all too frequently the same design is used for aprons, bedspreads, dish towels, and rompers for the baby without regard for the structural design of the object to be decorated.

Designs should be suitable to their use. We have rather universally accepted the humor of walking over a bed of cabbage roses every time we cross the floor to the other side of the room, and few people would buy scatter rugs nowadays that have a lifelike portrait of Rover taking his nap. Unfortunately, we have not let this understanding of the harmony of idea to be expressed in a design carry over to all household objects. Little kittens are often scorched on the handles of hot skillets, luscious purple grapes twine themselves up over the shoulders of dresses, and glasses are often wiped and polished upon images of themselves. This statement deals with a number of ill-conceived ideas concerning design. The little kitten should have been conventionalized to the point that it had become an interesting motif, based upon the animal form, but not a realistic representation of the animal. The grapes, besides being too realistic, do not strengthen the structural design of the dress. They, too, would have to be conventionalized to give character to the garment. The pictures of utensils upon towels is too obvious a label, the texture of the linen ordinarily dictates the use. A simple border in suitable colors would be ever so much more attractive hanging over a towel rack.

While dealing with the matter of suitability of design, it might be well to mention the use of monograms. That form of decoration has been misused to such an extent that monograms have fallen into disrepute. A monogram should always be considered a design, not merely a label. If it is good, it will serve both purposes. When making a monogram, the source of inspiration is one's initials. These should be treated no differently than a flower or an animal used for this purpose. It should be simple, of beautiful proportions, consistent in size and shape with the object to be so decorated, and finally, placed upon that object in such a way that the structural design is given added strength. If these suggestions were followed, there would be few script or old English letters trailing off a pillowcase on the diagonal, or on blouse fronts telling the passerby that one's name is Jane.

It is hoped that the preceding paragraphs do not discourage anyone. It is merely hoped that they will create the desire to find truly excellent source material. A few suggestions for sources are: English crewel embroidery, Scandinavian tapestries, peasant embroideries on wearing apparel, Mexican decorative stitchery, and Oriental needlework. It is not necessary that one find actual examples of stitchery for inspiration. If one knows a few simple stitches,

MEXICAN
EMBROIDERY

This type of handicraft furnishes abundant source material for today's needlework.

THOMAS

and has an active imagination, a painted box, a bit of beautiful leather tooling, or perhaps some simple wood carving is all the idea one needs. Just by way of caution: some designs are not suitable to development in stitchery, but are better expressed in some other medium, for instance, stencil, or perhaps batik.

MOTIF IN CHAIN STITCH

(Courtesy of the Milwaukee WPA Handicraft Project.)

Pretty as Pictures

After one has tentatively considered a suitable design for a wall hanging in a specific room, one's attention should be turned to a fabric that answers one's needs. It should be harmonious in texture to the other textiles used in the room. It should be consistent with the idea of the design, and above all, have a texture of its own that permits the stitches applied to it to become almost an integral part of the fabric, rather than remaining conspicuously upon the surface. There are a number of fabrics that fulfill these specifications, for instance, the finer monk's cloth, linen and linen crash, and Osnaburg, which can be dyed a desirable color or used in the natural state. Other drapery fabrics, woolen materials, and cotton crashes add many possibilities. For a very social home, some silks and satins are suitable.

For the stitchery, yarns are very good. The most suitable are the Shetland flosses, Germantown, and tapestry and peasant yarns. Among the cottons are six-strand embroidery flosses and moss yarn. For wall hangings there are really no suitable linen threads; the soft textures are too fine, and those heavy enough to give character to the design are apt to be stiff and wiry.

The character of the design itself will suggest stitches most suitable for its portrayal. Some of the most adaptable stitches are: the chain in all its variation, the cross stitch, outline, darning, and satin stitches.

Assuming that a design has been planned that satisfies the requirements, it is necessary to transfer it to the material. Some designs, especially those worked in cross stitch or darning stitch, are easily executed by merely counting the threads of the fabric. This is not too difficult, since a fairly coarse material is ordinarily used for wall hangings of this type. For other designs, the motifs may be traced upon thin paper, then basted to the fabric. The stitches to be employed are then carefully worked over the paper. After the embroidery has been completed the paper is torn away from the stitches. If this method is used, be careful to place the long lines of the motifs with the thread of the fabric. It is possible, of course, to trace the design upon the fabric, but very often the pencil or carbon marks discolor the embroidery floss or smudge the plain background areas.

The actual stitchery should be executed with the utmost care. Long floats of thread should be avoided because they easily catch and snag. The stitches should be firm enough to have character, but not pulled so tightly that the fabric becomes warped.

To finish the hanging, it should first be pressed carefully, face down on a well padded board. A damp cloth helps to steam

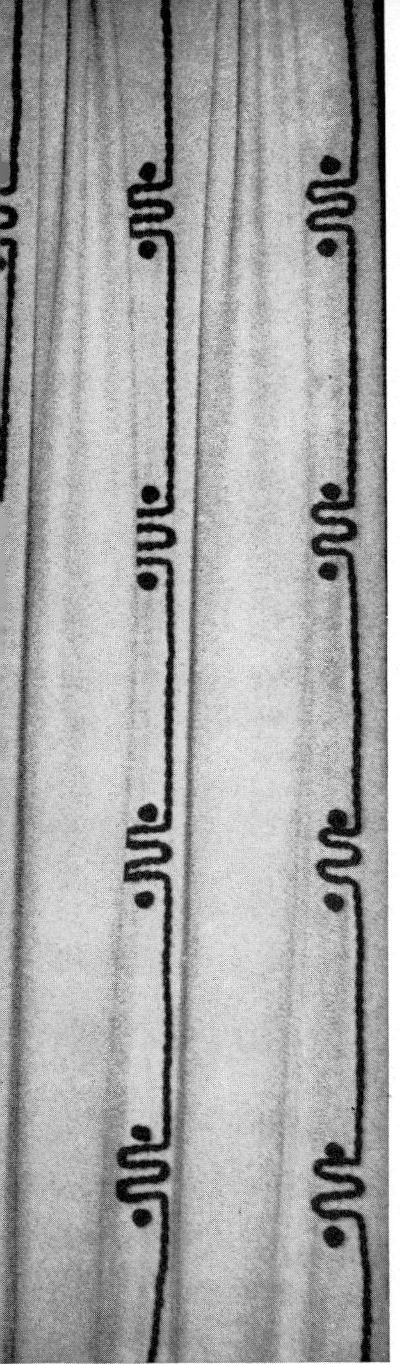

THOMAS

EMBROIDERED DRAPERY

by Helen S. Petersen

A simple, bold design carried out with roving couched into position and accented with balls cut from ball fringe.

the fabric back into shape and renew its original finish. After that fold back the raw edges enough to form the margins necessary to set off the embroidered design. If the turned back edges are wider than one-half inch, the excess material is best cut away. A lining should then be slip stitched to the top and sides. If the bottom edges of both the lining and hanging materials are hemmed, but not stitched together, the wall hanging will lie more flatly against the wall. The principle there is the same one often applied when lining a coat or jacket; for a space directly in the back, the lining is not fastened to the hem. The hanging may also be lined by cutting a piece of suitable material the same size as the embroidered fabric, the two placed face to face, then stitched on the machine around the sides and top. The bottoms should be hemmed separately when this method is used also. Suitable lining materials would be sateen or percale, depending upon the choice of the material of the hanging itself.

The lining may also be considered as part of the design. In this case it is cut large enough to permit suitable margins to be brought over the hanging to form a colored border. The corners should be neatly mitered. If this is done, the lining material should be carefully selected for texture and color.

To hang a wall decoration of this type, whether embroidered, stenciled, or produced by

JUVENILE WALL HANGING

(*Courtesy of the Milwaukee WPA Handicraft Project.*)

This hanging shows an engaging freedom.

some other medium, rings or tabs should be provided at the top through which a rod may be placed. For the rings, wire or bone are suitable. The wire rings are best sewn to the back, concealed from view. The texture of the bone rings is harmonious with many of the fabrics suggested for use as wall hangings and therefore may well be fastened to the very top edge of the hanging if desired. In

THOMAS

EMBROIDERED DRAPERY

by Helen S. Petersen

The strength and simplicity of the design make drapery of this type suitable for many rooms.

case the natural color of the rings is not harmonious, they may be dyed by soaking in a cup of dye solution. There are also on the market rings made of plastic material in a number of pleasing colors. If rings are not available, tabs of material may be made and applied to the back, or again to the top edge.

Rods may be either of wood or metal and should be appropriate in color. Usually the less conspicuous the better, since an over-elaborate rod will detract from the character of the hanging.

The rod should be suspended from the picture molding by means of two wires or cords that hang vertically and parallel to each other. A single wire or cord forming a triangle above the hanging (or a picture for that matter) leads the observer's eye away from the hanging to the picture hook up in the vicinity of the ceiling. This is hardly complimentary to the hanging itself.

More Stitches and Time

While a wall hanging offers a fine opportunity for the use of needlework, many homes do not have the right wall space for such decoration. This does not mean that embroidery for household accessories need be relegated to the guest towels hanging in the bathroom. Among the articles which might be enhanced with stitchery are many that will take their place in the living or dining room to add to the character and individuality of that room.

Pillow tops may be decorated with simple conventionalized or geometric designs. These may be based on border designs or well scaled allover designs of simple units. If one chooses to make a pillow top, there are several points to be remembered. The embroidery should be simple in character, should harmonize in line and spirit with the furniture in the room, and should be done with

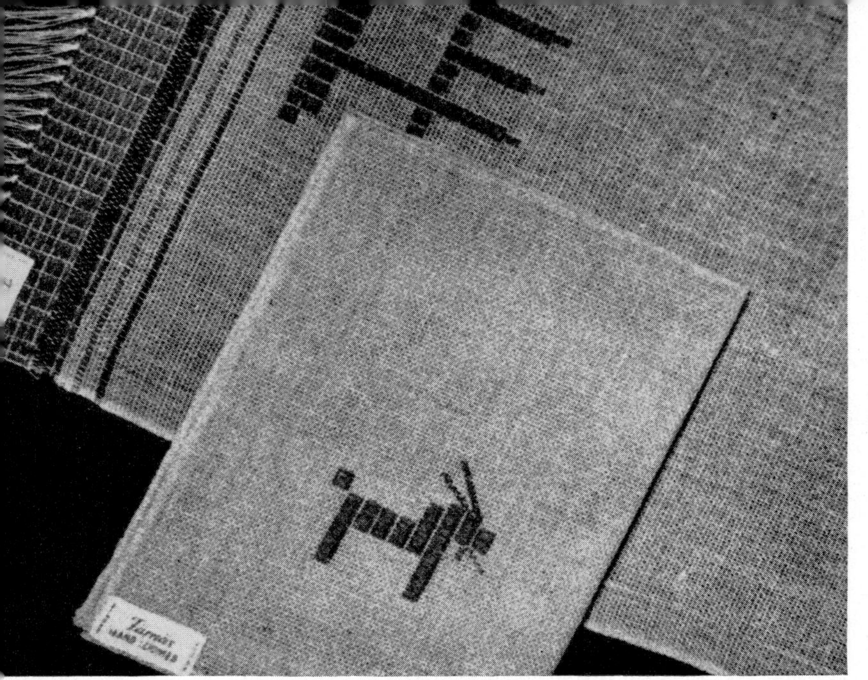

THOMAS

WOVEN MAT AND NAPKIN

The motifs employed for the design of this Swedish place mat and napkin are adaptable to embroidery.

stitches which will withstand the often rough handling that a well used pillow receives. Many stitches lend themselves to this purpose; namely, cross stitch, chain stitch, outline stitch, needle point, and a closely worked satin stitch. Long floats of yarn, which are apt to catch and pull, should be avoided. The texture of the fabric and the yarn are also important considerations and should be selected with thought for the rest of the room. The pillow may be planned to repeat the color of the upholstery fabric used on the furniture, or it may repeat some accented color found in the decorative accessories in the room. It is wise, however, to avoid colors so bright that they tend to focus the attention on the pillow itself.

Frequently one wishes to protect the top surface of an end table or some other piece of furniture in the room. Or perhaps in the dining room, a few attractive changes in place mats would be appreciated. Table scarfs and place mats may be made quickly and inexpensively and may be very attractive if done with simple and effective designs. Well planned proportions and well selected colors

EMBROIDERED MAT AND NAPKIN

by Helen S. Petersen

The embroidered motifs are well placed and in scale with the linen upon which they are used.

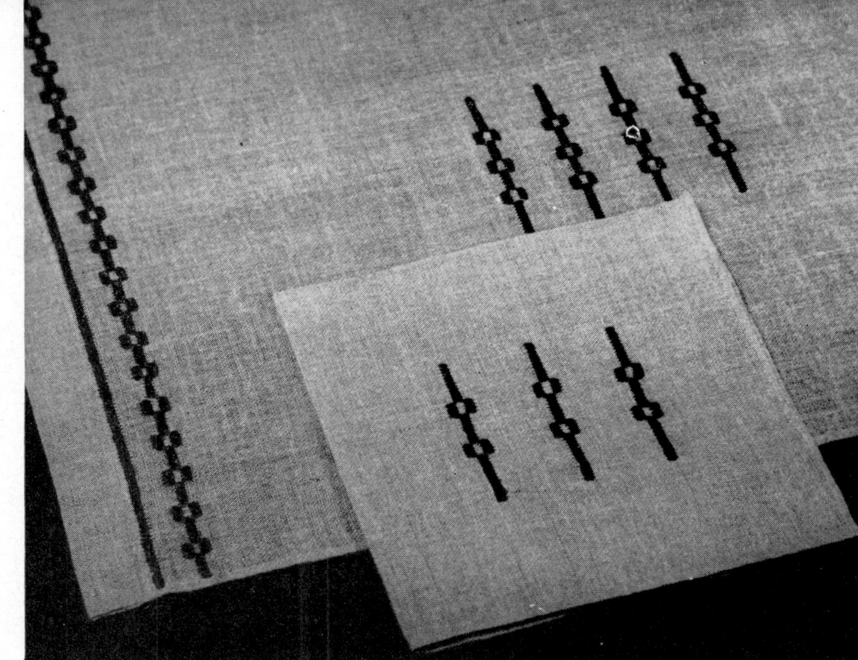

THOMAS

used in a border design of simple stripes or units will provide adequate and distinctive decoration. For table scarfs, the fabric may be as informal as heavy monk's cloth or of finer textures such as linen. On the heavier textures, yarn may be used, and on the finer textures, a floss of appropriate weight, such as six-strand embroidery floss. Place mats should be planned to be of the correct size for the china, silver, and glass as well as for the particular meal of the day for which they are intended. A good luncheon size is eleven by eighteen inches. They may be made of the finest linen, delicately embroidered or hemmed with single hemstitch, ladder stitch, antique hemstitch, or Italian hemstitch for more formal occasions when fine china and glass are used; or of heavy linen, cotton crash, or like textures for more informal occasions. Color selection is important since the mats should harmonize with the dishes to be used with them, as well as with the general color scheme of the room. For the more informal occasions, bright colors may be used. Very attractive informal mats may be made quickly by stitching rows

THOMAS

ONION SACKING TABLE MAT

Coarse nets, jute cloth, or various sack materials are all quickly decorated with cotton rug filler.

of bright but harmonious colors of rickrack trimming in a striped border on either end of the mat. Plain, solid-colored napkins repeating one of the colors in the braid would be attractive with them.

Mats and scarfs need not necessarily be trimmed with borders. Small motifs made up of geometric forms in two or three colors may be arranged over the surface of the fabric in an allover design. Remember always that a simple, unified design well related to the structural lines of the fabric itself will be in far better taste than elaborate or realistic motifs of the sort seen all too frequently.

Guest towels and finger towels may be thought of in much the same way as place mats and table scarfs since they are of about the same proportions. The fabric may differ in as much as it should be selected for its absorbent qualities. Simple border designs, allover designs, or a single well planned unit placed so as to be attractively displayed while the towel is hanging on its rack are wise

DETAIL FROM NEEDLE-POINT CHAIR SEAT

by Helen S. Petersen

Variety in texture has been attained by changing the direction of the stitch in alternate stripes.

THOMAS

selections. Monograms may be used, but should be considered in the light of the paragraph dealing with them at the beginning of this section.

Needle point has been mentioned as a possibility for pillow tops. This particular technique has many other uses in the home as well. Chair seats or footstool covers done in needle point may be beautiful in texture and design. Most department stores sell partially completed needle-point canvases, but these are usually of inferior design, consisting of realistic wreaths of roses or the like. One may plan designs from well selected source material belonging to the period represented by the furniture in the room, or from related periods. Here, too, simple geometric or conventionalized motifs will be the most successful. It is not essential that the design be executed in a wide range of colors. A few well chosen colors will probably be more pleasing than a great variety.

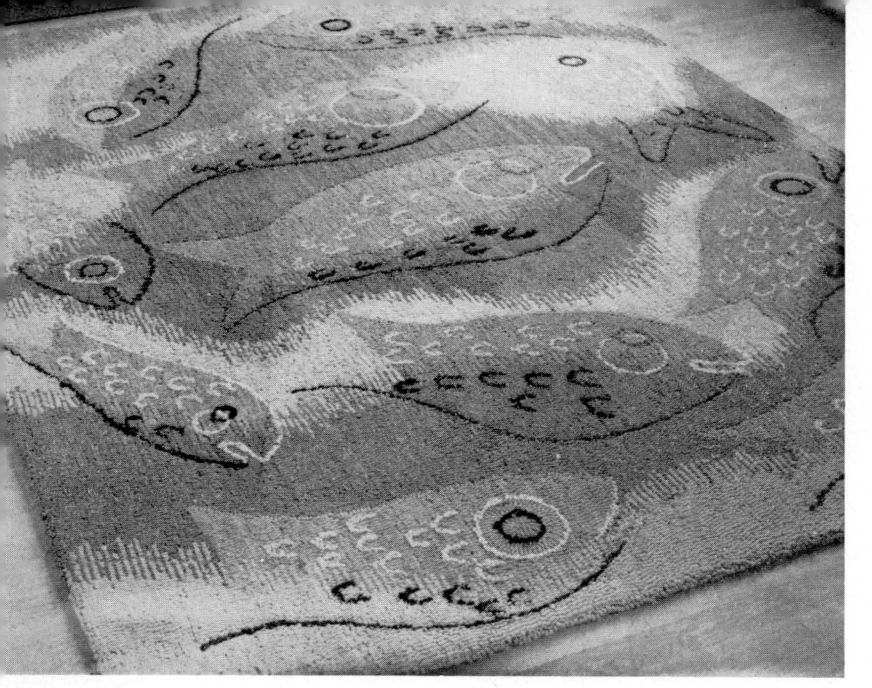

HOOKED RUG
(Courtesy of the Milwaukee WPA Handicraft Project.)

The strong movement of the design is counteracted by closely related color values.

HOOKED RUG
(Courtesy of the Milwaukee WPA Handicraft Project.)

A simple repeat is one of the most adaptable of designs for a rug.

HOOKED RUG
by Barbara Weismann

Solid or broken stripes are a welcome relief from the floral patterns so frequently employed for hooked rugs.

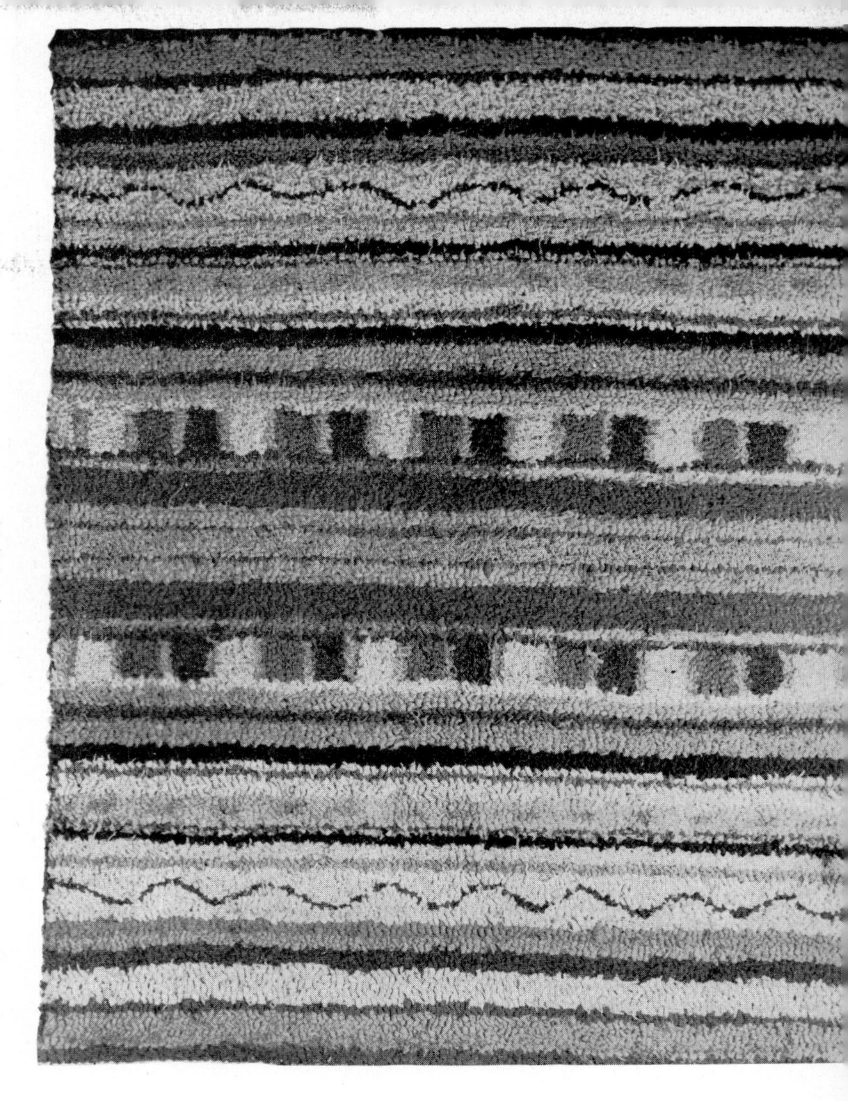

Always Under Foot

Any library reference shelf will provide well detailed books on the art of making hooked rugs. For this reason, we are omitting a lengthy discussion of them here. However, we do feel that a brief mention of the possibilities of this technique and of the materials which may be used for it will encourage some to do further research along this line.

A HOOKED RUG

(Courtesy of the Milwaukee WPA Handicraft Project.)

A welcome departure from the usual hooked rug design. This rug would be most appropriately used in a distinctly modern setting.

HOOKING A RUG

(Courtesy of the Milwaukee WPA Handicraft Project.)

The appliance shown in the photograph is one of the best for the craft. It may be purchased in the needlework departments of most large stores.

DETAIL FROM AN OLD QUILT

Heirlooms such as this furnish good source material.

THOMAS

THOMAS

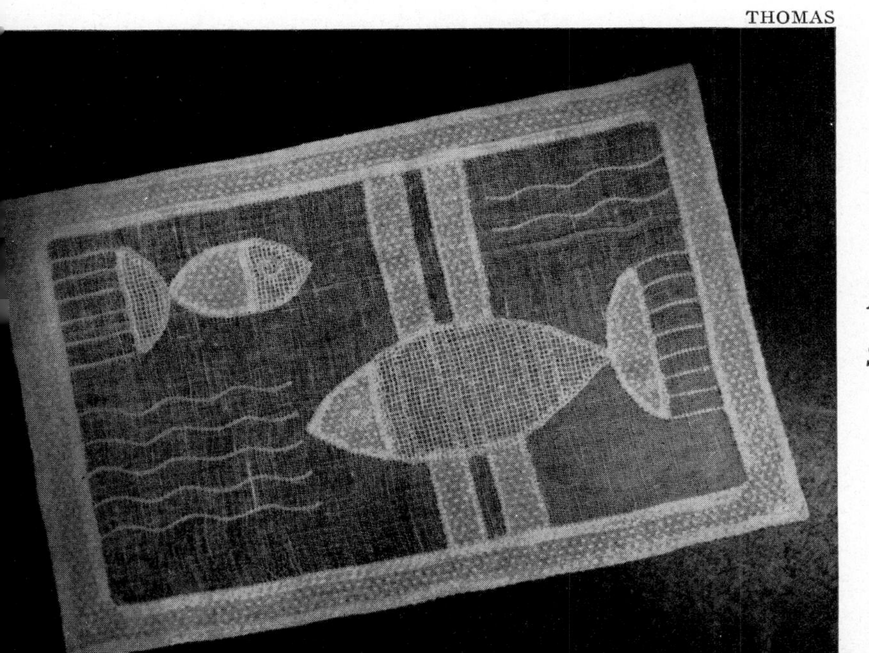

APPLIQUÉ PLACE MAT

Sheer materials may be used for unusual effects.

THOMAS

PATCHWORK PILLOW TOP

Abstract designs lend themselves admirably to modern patchwork. This pillow top combines appliqué and regular patchwork techniques.

Scrap materials which might otherwise be discarded may be saved and cut into lengths for such rugs. Woolen fabrics from old garments may be dyed to the colors desired or may be used in their original color if it is suited to the design. Silk stockings and underwear may also be dyed beautiful, subtle colors and worked into rugs. Yarns may be used, but as it is usually necessary to purchase these, the original cost of the rug is a great deal more than if waste materials are used.

Striking abstract designs for modern rooms are well adapted to this old technique. One will find that most of the designs shown in references dealing with hooked rugs are of the realistic flower garden sort. Research, however, will uncover reproductions of lovely old colonial designs which may be used as they are or may be modified to fit into many interiors.

APPLIQUÉ COMBINED WITH QUILTING

(*Courtesy of the Milwaukee WPA Handicraft Project.*)

This technique is adaptable to wall hangings and table covers as well as to coverlets.

Needles for hooking rugs may be purchased in the needlework departments of the larger stores. Burlap or monk's cloth is usually used for backing for these long wearing rugs.

THOMAS

APPLIQUÉ WALL HANGING

(*Milwaukee WPA Handicraft Project.*)

Simple forms, sensitively combined, are often more effective than elaborate motifs.

Priority on Patches

It would be fun to list all the ideas for the uses of patchwork and appliqué one might conceive while turning the pages of any one of the fine books available on old patchwork quilts. Per-

APPLIQUÉ WALL HANGING

(*Courtesy of the Milwaukee WPA Handicraft Project.*)

The introduction of embroidery unifies the entire design. The freedom of the design is the noteworthy element of this work.

THOMAS

EGYPTIAN APPLIQUÉ

The large simple forms and fine distribution of values provide a good object lesson.

THOMAS

APPLIQUÉ DRAPERY

(Milwaukee WPA Handicraft Project.)

haps one has to be in an analytical mood, but once he has begun thinking about the possibilities of this technique, he is likely to wail because time passes too quickly! Just the borders found on beautiful old quilts could be used as the decorative design for tablecloths, place mats, draperies, smocks, beach coats or robes. The units making up the body of the design lend themselves to mats, pillows, chair seats, holders, and unusual bags or purses. Or one might make a miniature version of a complete quilt, quilting and all, and use it as a most distinctive table cover. After all these ideas are taken care of, adaptations based on the designs would permit one to continue on and on.

Once the craftsman is familiar with the technique, he may wish to employ contemporary designs. The illustrations in this section will provide some good suggestions, and the drawings in the chapter on design might have been made to order. There are a few technicalities to keep in mind. If the finished product is to be laundered, be sure that all the material used has been shrunk before any of the pieces have been cut. It is also necessary to keep the correct position of the warp and weft threads throughout the work. This care prevents unsightly puckers later. All edges must be carefully prepared. In true patchwork each edge becomes part of a seam and is thus protected, but frayed edges might appear on appliqué unless the edge of each applied piece were turned under evenly before stitching into place.

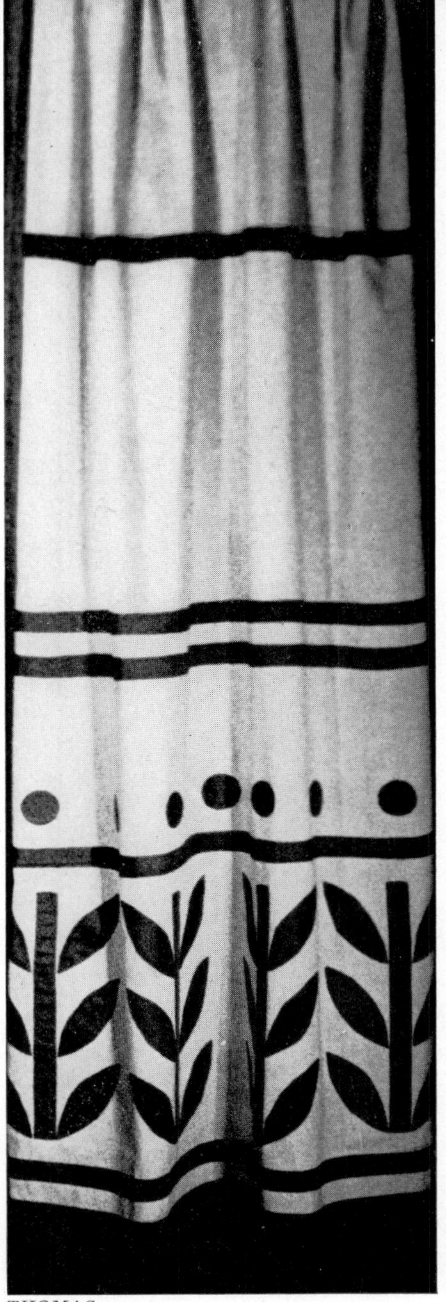

THOMAS

APPLIQUÉ DRAPERY

(Milwaukee WPA Handicraft Project.)

THOMAS

APPLIQUÉ DRAPERY

(Milwaukee WPA Handicraft Project.)

Firmly woven materials may be sewed to the foundation material with a diagonal overcast stitch; these small stitches can later be covered with decorative stitches. Simple couching as well as couching combined with other stitches such as the buttonhole stitch are the types most often used. Chain stitch is likewise effective.

A very effective wall decoration can be made from an appliquéd panel mounted in a picture frame. When the work is to be protected by glass in a manner such as this, less attention need be paid to the edges. Textures which would be most unhappy partners if sewed together for a place mat that would be laundered can be combined in appliquéd pictures to give interest and variety. Embroidery is a nice addition to give accent to some of the areas.

Our great-grandmothers produced some very beautiful appliqué and patchwork, but there is another source well worth investigating. The Egyptians make many interesting pictures of cloth in appliqué technique. The colors are bright and the design is highly stylized. The most effective of these panels are almost room high, but small squares about the size of a pillow top have much of the same spirit.

Chapter XIV

Practical Portfolios

THERE IS A CERTAIN FASCINATION TO THE CONSTRUCTION OF portfolios that might well be strong enough to make this craft one's major hobby. Drawing ability is not a prerequisite, for one may choose material distinctive in design and color in the shops with which to make the book covers or similar projects. At the same time this craft provides a splendid way of using stenciled or block-printed fabric or paper.

Only slight variations of procedure need be considered in order to successfully carry through any number of projects based on the fundamental principles of construction. Everyone's problem is quite apt to be specialized. The following directions for a telephone book cover are typical and should prove helpful as a starting point from which departures may be made.

Decide upon the Material To Be Used for the Cover

Heavy cardboard used for book binding comes in fifty-pound bundles. The weight or thickness of cardboard is designated by a number. This number actually represents the number of sheets in the bundle, so that the smaller the number, the thicker or heavier the cardboard. Number 30 therefore would be thicker than number 40, etc. Number 30 is recommended for portfolios in general. Smaller notebooks could be made of lighter weight material, usu-

ADJUSTABLE PORTFOLIO

(Courtesy of the Milwaukee WPA Handicraft Project.)

The wide strips of binder's linen used to fasten the flaps to the cover make this portfolio adjustable to either a few or many plates.

ally large ones of heavier material. Keep the covers in scale with the size of the book.

If one is using cardboard that happens to be on hand, examine some of the books one has. Most covers are almost an eighth of an inch in thickness. It is quite possible to employ suit boxes, tablet backs, or the cardboards the laundry uses to fold men's shirts around; paste as many layers together as required to make cardboard of the desired thickness. Be sure to place under a heavy weight, and allow several days for drying. Warped covers are most unpleasant. Discarded posters or display material from the local stores are very useful. Just remember to paste the brightly colored sides together when fabricating the cover board; the bright inks might discolor the material used to cover the book.

Cut and trim all edges with a razor blade. Use a metal-edged ruler and be sure the corners are square. When binder's board is purchased for a particular project the dealer will cut it for one, but he charges so much per cut. It's rather costly unless large quantities

PHOTOGRAPH ALBUMS

The leather that enriches the bindings of these albums was salvaged from an old purse.

THOMAS

are being used; then one's own time may be worth a great deal more than the ten cents or so it costs each time the knife falls.

Some sort of cloth is needed for the back binding. Paper is not strong enough to withstand any wear on this part of the book. There is upon the market regular bookbinder's linen, which comes in a variety of colors and textures. The price of the linen varies, depending upon the quality desired. Dress linen, crash, hand toweling, drapery and slip-cover material, as well as sailcloth, cotton suitings, percale, ginghams, and denims are all suitable and are sometimes more attractive for particular problems than are the commercial bookbinder's linens. The book linen has been impregnated with a substance which makes it very durable. For most uses in the home, material from one's piece bag will be quite suitable.

Fabric or paper may be used for covering the front and back covers. If fabric is selected it should be of a firm weave—any in the foregoing list would be suitable. The design (if a patterned material is used) and color should be carefully selected to harmonize with the surroundings. This may be the place to add pattern interest if plain colors predominate, or to come smashing through with a color note that makes the color scheme of the room distinctive.

If paper is used it should be fairly tough. Kraft paper is ideal, but is not always suitable in color. Construction paper—the heavier

THOMAS

TELEPHONE DIRECTORY COVER

The soft toned chintz is far more pleasant on the desk than the taxicab advertisement it conceals.

of the usual colored papers—is good if not too old. Old paper cracks at the corners because it has become brittle with age. Commercial cover papers give one a wide selection and are not very costly. Wallpapers open up still another possibility, and after one once learns to visualize the finished product before any work has been done on it at all, ideas for the uses of materials, alone or in combination, will be so numerous that the average person just couldn't get all the books visualized made. One does have to sleep, even though a beautifully bound leather portfolio for the desk is ever upon one's mind.

The portfolio will need a lining. Choose any of the aforementioned materials, but remember the little matter of suitability. It's fun to introduce drama in the lining of a book. If the book cover from necessity had to be plain, here is an opportunity for striking pattern, or for some color to be brought to full intensity. It has something of the same effect one experiences when a brilliant bird is seen for just an instant as it flies across the field of vision.

PORTFOLIOS AND SCRAPBOOKS

(Milwaukee WPA Handicraft Project)

Types vary with the use of each folio.

THOMAS

The choice of an adhesive is important. Use Higgins Vegetable Glue, really of a semi-opaque pastelike consistency, or any other library paste that is permanent. Some adhesives fail to hold after several months. Pastes have different effects upon colors also. Avoid one that stains the fabric or cloth easily. Rubber cement deteriorates and a strain may make the cemented parts give way after a short time. Glue is useful to have on hand and is used in one step. It is too difficult to use for ordinary pasting. Mucilage is messy too, and does not hold well enough.

The recipe given in the Boy Scouts' Handbook for bookbinding paste is satisfactory; or if the paste is to be used immediately just flour and water boiled together until transparent and of rather pastelike consistency will do. Rye flour is superior to wheat flour for this purpose.

A few more materials will be needed. A thin coat of white shellac or clear lacquer may be put on the finished cover. This helps to keep it clean and to harden the surface. A little wax or Venetian Shoe Cream is all that one needs on leather. Too high a polish is out of keeping with the idea of a book. In many cases it is not necessary to coat the surface of the book at all. The use to which the book is to be put will decide this.

Use cord, carpet warp, leather thong, or wire to fasten the book into the cover. A telephone book is revised several times a year, so it is best to have a means of readily replacing the body of the book.

MEASURE THE BOOK FOR WHICH THE COVER IS TO BE MADE

Telephone directory 8¾″ x 11⅛″ x 1¾″.

Be accurate. When measuring the thickness of the book do not compress the pages, but measure it as it normally closes. Skimping on this measurement might cause the covers to spring open at the front of the book.

PREPARE ALL THE MATERIALS NECESSARY FOR THE CONSTRUCTION OF THE COVER

The foundation cardboards should measure 9¼″ x 11⅝″. Cut two pieces. Notice that ¼″ has been allowed for extensions of the cardboard cover over the edges of the original paper cover of the directory. For a smaller book this extension is about ⅛″ on each edge. In a straight box binding, such as this portfolio, ¼″ is also allowed at the back edge. In a regulation book of the nature of a textbook or novel the back of the book proper extends slightly beyond the cover boards.

Of thinner cardboard cut one piece measuring 2″ x 11⅝″ and another measuring 1⅝″ x 11⅛″. The length of the larger piece of cardboard matches the length of the cover boards, the width is

¼″ wider than the thickness of the book to compensate for the thickness of the cover boards and the thickness of the cloth (or paper) used to cover the cardboards, as well as for the thickness of the lining papers. The smaller piece is shorter to permit the cords or thong to function without extending beyond the top and bottom of the book. It is narrower to prevent crowding the cover boards when the book is closed.

A strip of the cloth or bookbinder's linen measuring 6¾″ x 13⅝″ is needed for the back binding. The width of the piece of bookbinder's linen or cloth used for the back binding is optional. As it is placed across the back and over the back edge of the cover boards a pleasing relationship of areas should be sought. If striped or patterned material is used the design will also govern the width. A stripe or motif should be cut to the best advantage of the design. Bookbinder's linen or leather is sometimes so heavy that a lapped seam would be too thick. In that case the edges of the binding material and the cover cloth or paper are just brought together neatly rather than overlapped. If overlapping is desired a ⅛″ or ¼″ lap is adequate. This amount then must be allowed on both sides of the binding material. The length of the cloth or binder's linen should be 2″ greater than the length of the cover boards.

Cloth, paper, and leather are all suitable for covering the cardboard. Two pieces measuring 8″ x 13⅝″ are needed. The width of this material is somewhat governed by one's decision when determining the width of the back binding. One should allow for the following: If the seam is an overlapped one or if the material, such as the chintz used for the telephone book cover, might ravel easily, and is thinner than the binding material, allow ¼″. Add 6¾″ to take care of the part of the cardboard not covered by the back binding (this measurement varies with the project). For turning over the edges, add another inch of material.

Paper is most frequently used for lining the covers of a book. Cut two pieces that measure 9″ x 11⅜″ and one piece 3⅝″ x 13⅛″. The lining papers are cut just enough smaller to permit about ⅛″ of the edge of the material used to cover the outside of the book to show inside. A larger area of the cloth or bookbinder's linen will show on the inside at the center of the book.

To increase the strength of the back binding, cloth is used to line the inside of the back of the book. The strip 3¾″ x 11⅜″ is cut to extend one inch beyond the front and back hinges, but should be the same length as the lining paper.

Construct the Cover

Provide plenty of old newspapers and clean rags before the actual construction is begun.

Paste the two cover boards and the back board to the strip of bookbinder's linen or cloth. A one-inch shellac or varnish brush is a great convenience for quick pasting.

Be sure the strip of cloth or bookbinder's linen is cut on the thread or has followed the pattern of a stripe or other design. Press out any wrinkles present. Put a coating of paste on one side of the largest back board. Place it in the exact center of the reverse side of the bookbinder's linen or cloth. The ends extending at the top and bottom should each be about one inch long, the side pieces equal, the size depending upon the project at hand.

Lay the two cover boards in position, one on either side of the back board. Leave a space that equals the thickness of the cardboard one is using between each of the covers and the back board; this is necessary to allow the book to close. Sometimes the cloth

Repeat the process for the other side of the book. At this time the extra material just extends beyond the cover board on the outside edges.

When paper is used to cover the book, lap the paper over the back binding ¼″ instead of folding any of the paper toward the wrong side. A very light pencil mark placed on the binding material is a helpful guide when covering the surface of the cardboard with paste. It is essential to get plenty of paste along the edges. Any spot that has been neglected during pasting will cause an unpleasant bump on the cover later.

The pasting process is a much happier one if the work rests on a dozen or so loose sheets of an old magazine or newspaper. Then after every step the top paper can be pulled out from underneath the book quickly. Most paste leaves a stain that is not readily removed, and a paste-stained product is unsightly.

Miter the Corners

Open the book cover and place it inside uppermost on the table.

Cut off each of the four corners of the cloth extending over the corners of the cardboard so that about ⅝″ or ¾″ of the cloth remains. This is cut at a 45° angle. Fold this narrower piece of material down over the corner of the cardboard. It will form a diagonal line across the inside of the cardboard. Paste into position. Always keep the material as close to the edge of the cover boards as possible. Now paste the material that as yet extends beyond the edges of the cover to the inside of the cover boards. If carefully done all the edges of the cardboard have been concealed.

Mitering paper corners is slightly different. Fold the top and bottom of the extending pieces of paper over the cardboard as tightly as possible. Crease. Be gentle; paper is sometimes so brittle that it cracks or punctures easily. Open these folds out again, and repeat the process for the side edge. Open it out again after the crease has been made. Now fold the top edge and the side edge over the cardboard at the *same time*. The corner of the paper sticks up in a shape not unlike a dog's-ear. Pinch the "ear," adjusting the two edges until the top and side pieces meet at a perfect right angle on top of the cardboard. With one hand hold these edges firmly in place; with the other fold the "dog's-ear" down first to the left, then to the right. When the edges are opened again, a diagonal crease has been made far enough away from the corner of the cardboard to insure full coverage. To be doubly sure, cut 1/16" beyond this crease as one cuts off the corner triangles thus formed. Repeat for all four corners. Paste the top and bottom flaps onto the inside of the cover first. Put paste on the side flap, but before folding it down into place, tuck in the little projections at the top and bottom that were formed when the top and bottom flaps were pasted down, then when the side flap is in place all raw edges and cardboard have been concealed.

Line the Book

Paste in the center lining. This should always be cloth. Center it accurately. It should come to within 1/8" of the top and bottom edges of the book. Hold a ruler firmly along one crack and close that cover. Repeat for the other cover. This is to prevent the lining from bulging or slipping out of place.

Line the front and back covers. Coat the wrong side of the lining papers with an even layer of paste. This piece, if measured accurately, should permit a 1/8" margin of the cover paper to show beyond its edge at the top, bottom, and side when placed in position on the inside of the book. Usually the edge toward the center of the book then takes care of itself. It should come to ⅛″ of the nearest center fold. The book will not close well, or the lining will wrinkle badly, if this piece of material overlaps the center fold at all. Repeat.

Fasten the Telephone Book into the Cover

Paste the 1⅝″ x 11⅛″ piece of cardboard exactly in the center of the 3⅝″ x 13⅛″ piece of lining material, miter the corners, and paste the extending pieces to the wrong side. Cut three to five 36″ lengths of cord, carpet warp, or leather thong. The length, of course, is determined by the size of the telephone book. They should be twice the length plus enough to make the tying of knots easy. Coat the wrong side of the cardboard just covered with a heavy coat of glue. Paste is not strong enough. Place the cords lengthwise upon this bed of glue at equal intervals, the long ends of the cords extending equally beyond the ends of the cardboard. Put another coating of glue over the center section of the book cover. Do not carry it to the edges; the cardboard to be placed there is smaller than the outside piece. Carefully place the cardboard in the book cover, sandwiching the cords between the two pieces of cardboard. Before going any farther place the completed cover, open, upon a smooth clean surface. Cover with a clean paper and weight down with a big pile of magazines, books, or other heavy material. Allow the book to remain under the weight until the glue has hardened.

To fasten the book into the cover, open the cover out flat, laying the cords out beyond the top and bottom. Place the telephone book, back binding down, upon the back binding of the cover, then open the book at the place indicated by the center cord

JAPANESE BINDING

This method of binding is particularly suited to thin paper and is used where heavy cover boards are not needed. The booklet should not be too thick if it is to be flexible enough to open easily. Fold the paper as indicated in the first diagram. Each folded section should be as large as the page size desired and may contain as many folded pages as the paper size will permit. Gather the folded sections together with folded edges to the outside. Punch, drill, or pierce an uneven number of holes at the back edge of the gathered sections, spacing the holes evenly. For cover material, a folded piece of heavier paper should be used at the front and back. Sew together as indicated.

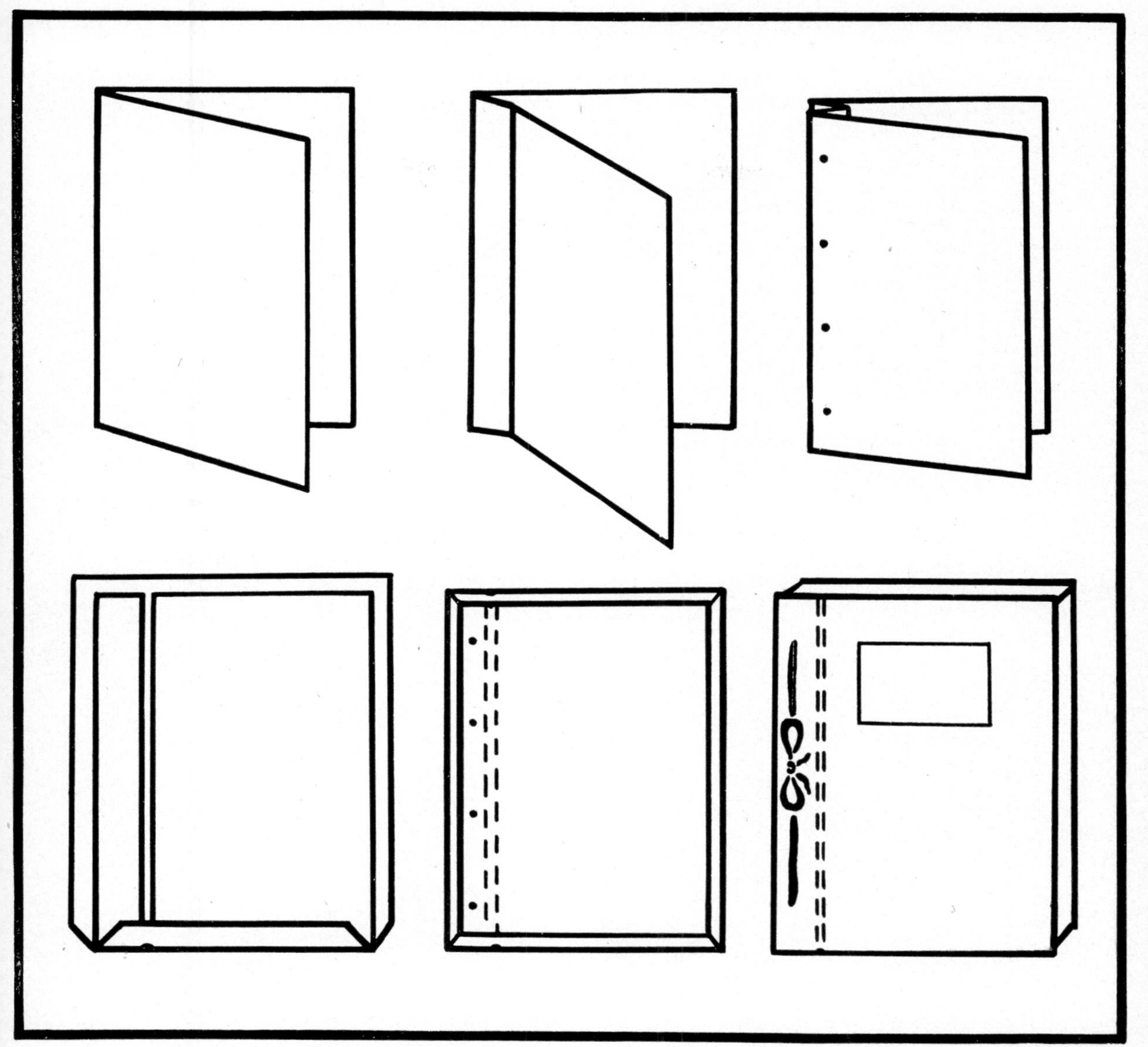

STUB BOOKLET FOR PHOTOGRAPHS OR SCRAPBOOK

When a folio for mounting is desired, it is necessary that some form of stub be used in order to prevent it from springing open when the thickness of the mounted material is added to the original book. The above diagrams show how this may be achieved in simple fashion. At the same time the loose-leaf characteristic of this portfolio allows for the addition of more pages at will. The pages may be made of a fairly heavy paper—folded in the manner indicated to make the stub. Separate covers are made of cardboard sections covered and lined with fabric or bookbinder's linen. The booklet is fastened with cord strung through punched holes.

fastened to the cover. Tie the two ends up over the open book. Remember there will be a new directory some day, so use knots that will come open when one wishes them to, and leave ends long enough to use again. Tie the remaining cords inside the book in like manner, always opening the book above the cord first. If the cover feels the least bit damp slip wax paper between the cover one has made and the original cover of the book, then place under the weights until thoroughly dry. This is necessary to prevent the book from warping.

Chapter XV

Alchemy

If one has tired of the quieter crafts that we have mentioned so far and would like to try a more exuberant technique, metalwork will let one give vent to any excess of energy he may have. It is not the kind of work that one can do in an apartment building without losing all of his friendly neighbors, but if one happens to live in his own home with an understanding and patient family, he may surprise them with a number of beautiful and useful household accessories. (Perhaps surprise is the wrong word, since this technique does not lend itself to secrets.)

The soft silver gray of pewter carries with it all of the qualities of gracious hospitality and blends beautifully with the subtle colors of a well planned room.

Copper reflects a warm orange light and may be used to brighten or accent a color scheme. Brass and the several new alloys now on the market may be used to equal advantage alone or in combination. The textures and colors of these metals combine well, and decorative effects may be obtained by a simple well planned use of two of any of these metals.

Perhaps to the novice the very contemplation of metalwork is overwhelming. Actually simple things may be made with few tools, a little time, and no previous training. We do not mean to suggest that this is not a complicated technique; it is, but very

THOMAS

PEWTER HOUSEHOLD ACCESSORIES

by Dorothy Tillotson

It is important to choose pewter in a gauge consistent with the function of the object.

beautiful objects can be made by the beginner who may then graduate to the more difficult articles. There are many texts dealing with metalwork which give directions for objects requiring more skill and knowledge than those suggested in this chapter. Since this book is dedicated to the untrained beginner, we have selected the easier and more fundamental things that may be made. After skill has been acquired with the following of our suggestions, the interested person may obtain further directions for advanced metalwork in any library.

Among those things within the comprehension and skill of the beginner in this technique are plates, bowls, serving spoons, salad sets, candle holders of simple line, salt and pepper shakers, and napkin rings. Of these things listed, the plates and bowls which require pounding but not soldering are the most simple to make. Pewter may be obtained through dealers in art supplies or through companies dealing in artists' equipment and tools for craft work. These companies also handle the newer alloys that are becoming

THOMAS

PEWTER CANDLESTICKS
by Helen S. Petersen

Domes, discs, and cylinders of pewter were the simple units which were combined to produce so effective a result.

popular in metal craft work. Copper and brass may usually be purchased locally in shops using these metals or through one's hardware merchant. Of the metals mentioned, pewter is the softest, and therefore the easiest to manipulate. A simple first problem in this metal would be advisable in order that the technique be learned with as little difficulty as possible. The metal may be purchased in discs suitable for plates or bowls and cut to the diameter desired. The diameter of the disc determines the diameter of the finished bowl or plate. Pewter, as well as the other metals, comes in a number of thicknesses or gauges. A satisfactory gauge for ordinary use in bowls and plates is number 16. Lighter weights are numbered higher and heavier weights lower.

As already mentioned, the equipment needed for the first problems is relatively little. To form the hollow of the plate or bowl, the metal is pounded with a suitable hammer. Mallets for metal pounding are usually made of wood, leather, or rubber, since these materials do not tend to nick the metal during the process. Rubber or wooden mallets may be obtained at auto supply stores. If a wooden mallet is used, care must be taken to prevent the wooden surface from becoming roughened during pounding, as it is apt to do. Sometimes this may be prevented by tacking a soft piece of leather over the head of the mallet. If this is done, the tacks must be placed at the sides of the wooden head so that they will not come in contact with the metal surface. If one does not have other leather suitable for this purpose, old glove leather will do. Careful observation as to the condition of the surface of the wood during the pounding process will lead one to discover any roughing of the wood before it becomes serious. The surface should be sanded with a very fine sandpaper immediately if such a condition becomes apparent. After sanding, the wood must be wiped carefully to remove any grains that may have become loosened from the sandpaper.

Vessels, Deep or Shallow

There are a number of ways of forming the depressed area in bowls or plates. The carved or turned wooden mold, shaped to the desired curve and depth, is perhaps the most satisfactory for the beginner. The first step is to secure a block of wood that is at least three-quarters of an inch thicker than the envisioned design of the plate or bowl, and one inch greater in diameter than the diameter of the plate, including both the rim and center area. If one is planning on making the mold himself, pine is the wood to choose. A carpenter, or someone having access to a lathe, can turn out a more perfect mold in a very short time, if those arrangements can be made. A hard wood, turned on the lathe, produces a well wearing mold.

Assuming that one is making the mold himself and has found a suitable piece of wood, the following directions should suffice:

1. Find and mark the center of the top surface of the block of wood.
2. Using the above mark as a guide, draw the circumference of the plate on the wood. Use a compass.
3. Using the same center mark, draw a line indicating the inside of the rim and the beginning of the sunken area of the plate.
4. With a wood chisel gently hollow out the center of the mold until it conforms to the desired depth and shape planned for the finished plate. While doing this keep in mind that the metal is to be pounded into this wooden form until the back of the plate fits perfectly into the lowest part of the mold. Any uneven portion or groove will be apparent on the finished product. Hence, chip out the excess wood carefully, just a small bit at a time, always working with the grain of the wood.
5. Sandpaper the carved portion to satinlike smoothness.

Any person who turns out the mold on a lathe will need a paper pattern to guide him in reproducing the design. Make a template of heavy paper or tag board that represents a cross section of the plate as it would be seen at the eye level. The back of the plate is the important part. The top may be left perfectly straight, since the pattern would be inserted into the area being hollowed out on the lathe or measured with calipers. That is why a fairly stiff paper should be used for the pattern. This method of checking the mold is likewise valuable to anyone hollowing out the mold with a chisel. It is so very easy to deviate from the original plan if some plan for control is not used.

It is not necessary to have any contrivance to guide the formation of the rim, since the disc of metal may be cut just to fit inside the first pencil line drawn on the wood to indicate the outside edge of the plate, then held there with the left hand while pounding the plate into shape. However, there are two ways of helping oneself make this easier. The entire area representing the rim may be lowered to the depth of one-eighth inch, then smoothed with sandpaper as before. The metal should then be of a size to just fit into this depressed circle easily.

More simply, the metal may be kept in place by pounding about six small nails part way into the wood, just beyond the pencil line indicating the outside of the plate, and deep enough to stay in place so that they will not be jarred out of position during the pounding process. The nails should be placed at equal distances from each other around the circumference of the plate.

Another way of guiding the formation of the lowered part of a plate—it is not satisfactory for bowls—is by the use of two pieces of smooth, hard wood. They should exceed in length the diameter of the entire plate by a number of inches, be at least an inch wider than the rim, and be thick enough to permit a desired depth to be attained to form the center of the plate. To use this method the two sticks are clamped, or nailed, to an old table; they should be parallel to one another and the space between the two inside edges of the boards should be the same as the diameter of the lowered part of the plate to be made. To keep the metal disc in place, nails

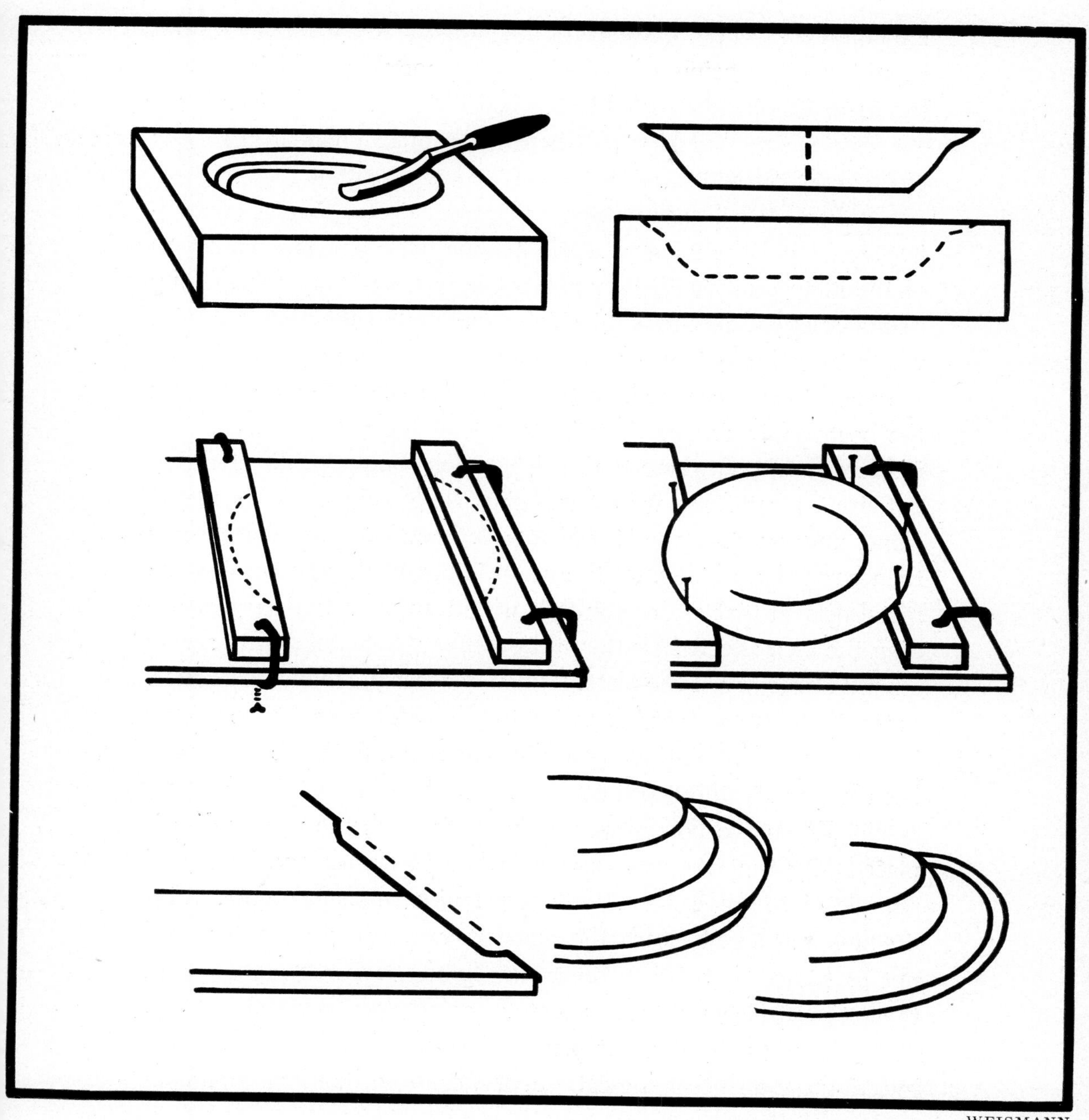

WEISMANN

PLATE AND BOWL MOLDS—TURNING PLATE EDGE

are pounded into the wood to form an arc that keeps the plate from slipping as it is being worked upon. If a portable mold is desired, the two sticks can be nailed to a board of the necessary size.

The actual making of the plate is simple. The first directions given apply to the "two-stick" mold.

Place the disc of pewter inside the nails forming the confining arcs. Hold the metal steady with one hand and tap the center of the plate firmly with the mallet. Direct the blows of the mallet so that they fall just to the inside of one of the sticks at the point where the stick is tangent to the circle indicating that portion of the plate to be depressed. In order that this be a fixed spot, mark the board plainly where it extends beyond the rim of the plate to indicate the place where the mallet strokes should be directed. Do not exert great force when pounding. The weight of the mallet alone, under a steady series of beats, lowers the metal more evenly than hard, sharp blows. As the metal is pounded, keep turning the metal disc so that each blow falls within an area partially overlapping the area affected by the previous blow, but progressing slowly around the center of the plate. Remember that the mallet is directed at exactly the same spot in relation to the wood, but that the pewter is turned slowly. Continue pounding the metal until the center has been lowered to the depth planned.

When the hollow wooden mold is used, the pewter disc is placed over the scooped-out area, held firmly with one hand and pounded into shape with steady overlapping blows as before. With a complete mold beneath the metal to shape it, the pewter need not be turned, but the mallet blows should be worked evenly over the entire surface, until it has been lowered to conform to the mold.

When pounding out plates or bowls, there is the danger of lowering the dish to too great a depth, causing the metal to stretch to such a degree that it is paper thin or gives away entirely. Do not attempt to use 16 gauge pewter for a bowl that exceeds two inches in depth. Thicker metal, of course, would permit greater stretching without breaking.

To strengthen and finish the edge of the plate, the extreme outer edge of the plate may be rolled under. This is most easily accomplished in the following manner:

Hold the plate at an angle, top side up, against the sharp edge of a table or piece of hard wood that is stationary. The metal edge should not extend more than one-eighth inch over the edge of the wood. With a mallet, pound this extending edge over the wood, turning the plate during the process until the edge has been pounded back slightly all the way around. Care must be taken to maintain the same width for the rolled edge all around the plate or the circle is destroyed. After this edge has been pounded to almost an upright position around the plate, place the plate upside down on a flat surface and pound the edge back upon itself. Be sure that the top of the plate is protected from anything that might mar or dent its surface.

The size of the plate governs the finish required for the edge. A nine- or ten-inch plate needs a rolled edge; a larger plate frequently needs reinforcing by the addition of a wire placed inside the rolled edge, before it is pounded back on itself. Smaller plates are quite satisfactory if just filed smooth.

The surface of the plate requires some attention before it is ready for use. If there are any rough edges, these should be smoothed with a fine metal file and strips of very fine emery paper. The large surfaces of the plate are polished by first going over the entire plate with very fine emery paper, or number 3/0 steel wool. A rotary motion around the plate gives the best results. A further degree of satin smoothness is achieved by rubbing the plate with a soft cloth that has been dipped into oil and then powdered pumice. Maintain the rotary motion. The plate will look very smudged and black by this time, but a bath in warm, soapy water will remove the grime and expose the dull satiny surface. Pewter is at its best with a finish of this sort. It should not look like chromium.

Witches' Brew

Sometimes it is desirable to etch a simple design upon the surface of a metal object. A border, a surface pattern, or a single centered motif are all suitable choices for the enrichment of a bowl or plate. The design should be worked out on paper very carefully, following the previously prescribed methods. Pewter does not lend itself to too fine or intricate a design, nor does the process of etching when done by the beginner. As one's skill develops, more intricate patterns may be attempted safely.

The design is traced on the metal by using carbon paper, strengthening the lines with pencil afterwards; or by pricking through the paper pattern with a sharp, pointed instrument such as a darning needle or a victrola needle set into a handle. After the paper pattern has been removed, the pricked dots may be connected with scratched lines. For a simple pattern made up of large areas the design may be cut out of paper and drawn around with a pencil, or more clearly with a needle.

The etching process involves the use of a resist and an acid capable of eating away the exposed parts. For the resist, asphaltum is used. This may be purchased at any hardware store or ten-cent store. It is a thick, viscous substance that hardens within twenty-four hours. It should be painted over any part of the metal that is to be protected from the action of the acid. This part of the design will stand out in relief on the finished plate. Besides protecting parts of the design, all undecorated parts of the plate should also be covered carefully with a coating of the asphaltum. This includes the back and edges. Try to avoid air bubbles forming in the asphaltum while painting with it. These permit the acid to reach the metal and give a pock marked effect over the surface. Allow the asphaltum to dry for at least twenty-four hours before the etching process is attempted.

For the etching process a container large enough to permit the complete immersion of the article to be etched is necessary. A glass dish, usually a glass pie pan or casserole, is adequate; but for very large articles, a piece of roofing paper folded up at the corners to produce a tray of sufficient size and depth is usable. Metal containers cannot be used, since they are susceptible to the action of the acid.

The acid most frequently used for etching pewter is nitric acid. A solution made of ten parts of water to one part of full strength nitric acid is usually strong enough. Put the water in the container first and then pour in the acid. Keep the face away from the fumes, and avoid splashing. Nitric acid burns one's skin. Immerse the prepared metal object in the acid bath. Very soon small bubbles will form on the surface of the metal exposed to the acid. If these are gently brushed away with a feather, the etching process will be hastened somewhat. When the metal appears to have been eaten away to the desired depth, remove from the acid bath and rinse in clear water. A spring clothes pin makes a good device for removing most pieces, or a piece of string may be placed under the plate so that the two ends hang out over the edge of the large acid container. These may be used to lift one side of the plate out of the

THOMAS

ETCHED NAPKIN CLIP
by Doris Cox

Pewter, pottery, and the coarser linens are harmonious.

acid. If the acid bath seems to be working too slowly, carefully add a small amount of acid and agitate the solution to mix thoroughly.

After the etched object has been removed, rinse very thoroughly in water to wash away any trace of acid. All of the asphaltum now has to be removed. This may prove to be tedious, but if it has been carefully applied in the beginning to form clean-cut edges, and a coating entirely devoid of air holes, there is great satisfaction in the emergence of a design free from the dark, unpleasant-looking puddle of asphaltum and kerosene. Kerosene or turpentine, generously applied to the asphaltum and rubbed with a soft cloth to speed up the process, is the most satisfactory for removing the acid resist.

The film of kerosene or turpentine should be washed off with warm water and soap. The surface of the metal will take on a more pleasant sheen if rubbed briskly with powdered pumice stone and oil. Water may be substituted for the oil. It works quite as well for this purpose. In case the edges of the plate are pock marked where the metal was not fully protected from the acid, a bit of filing or rubbing with fine emery paper will do much to restore the softly beveled or rolled edge that was originally produced. Another bath with warm water and soap and a final buffing with a soft cloth will complete the plate, making it ready for use.

There are many articles that lend themselves to decoration produced by etching. To mention only a few, one might consider: paper knives, napkin rings or markers, bracelets, clips for paper money, or clips to be worn with a suitable dress. Decorative pins for costume wear are easily made from any variety of shapes, and a quite satisfactory method of fastening can be provided by soldering a safety pin to the underside of the pin itself, after all decoration has been applied to the metal. Before soldering the safety pin, be sure to figure out the best way for the head of the pin to face. If it is put on in reverse, it would have to be opened and closed with the left hand. That is a little difficult for most people to manage. Buttons, either all pewter or made of a combination of pewter and copper, could also be etched. Copper etches very well. However, if the two metals are together, do not try to etch a design into both metals at one time. The speed of the action of the acid is not the same for each. One part of the object would be either underetched or overetched if this were attempted.

Better Than Fingers

Sometimes a special serving spoon, useful for dressing, jellies or jams, salads, or nuts adds to the unusualness of the dish. These spoons should, of course, be designed to go well with the other silverware used during a meal, yet they may differ enough to supply a decorative effect to the table. The use to which they will be put will determine the general size and shape of the spoon—a wide, short-handled shape for nuts; long-handled and rather shallow but large shapes for salads.

The making of a spoon calls for some knowledge as to the properties of the metal which is being worked and involves somewhat more work and skill than that needed for pounding a simple bowl. It is not, however, a difficult problem and may be done by one with patience and some familiarity with the techniques.

A sketch should be made of the spoon showing the size and shape of the bowl and its relation to the length of the handle. This proportion should be planned so that the handle will balance the bowl of the spoon and at the same time allow for easy manipulation.

The handle of the spoon should be made of one or several lengths of pewter wire. This wire may be obtained through companies dealing in pewter and comes in various sizes and shapes. Square, round, and half-round are among the most common. Since the strength of the handle is determined by the size of the wire (pewter is a very soft metal) it is well to order a rather substantial size. It has been found that three-sixteenths to one-quarter inch square or round wire is very satisfactory. If the handle is not to be too long, one length of wire is sufficient. If a long-handled spoon or fork is being made, two lengths soldered together are more advisable.

The bowl of the spoon or fork is made from a small disc of pewter which may be of 16 gauge if the spoon is a small one or of 12 gauge if a large spoon such as a salad spoon is being made.

To make a pewter spoon, a few more supplies than those listed for the bowl or plate will be needed. This is a project which involves soldering, and an electric soldering iron is adequate and easy to use. One may purchase such an iron at any hardware store or at a five-and-ten-cent store. A metal file should also be bought at the same time to be used for keeping the point of the iron clean at all times. A small bottle of glycerin will serve as flux for the soldering process, and one or two small screw clamps will aid in holding the pewter in place during the soldering. Soft pewter solder may be obtained from the company that handles the pewter. This comes in lengths of wire and may be cut into small pieces for use.

To make a suitable mold for pounding the bowl of the spoon, follow the directions given for making a bowl mold in the preceding chapter. Sometimes the lower part of a larger bowl mold will have enough of a curved surface to make it a satisfactory spoon mold. In general, a serving spoon or ladle does not need to have a deeply curved surface. Follow the directions given for pounding a pewter bowl when shaping the spoon. Actually the problem is the same except for size.

The next step in the making of the spoon is forming the handle. The wire should be cut to the length planned, with an added amount of about three-fourths of an inch to permit soldering to the bowl of the spoon. If any decoration is to be applied to the handle, this should be done before the two main pieces are soldered together since it is easier to work on them separately. The handle may be treated in many ways. Small pewter balls may be soldered to the sides of the wire; small file marks nicely spaced may be in-

PEWTER SOLDERING EQUIPMENT

Clamps, files, tweezers, pewter solder, a small bottle of glycerine, and the soldering iron.

THOMAS

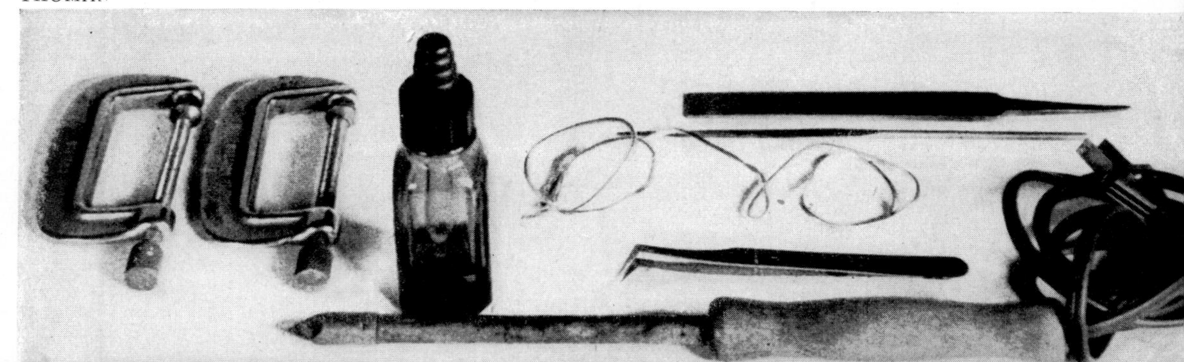

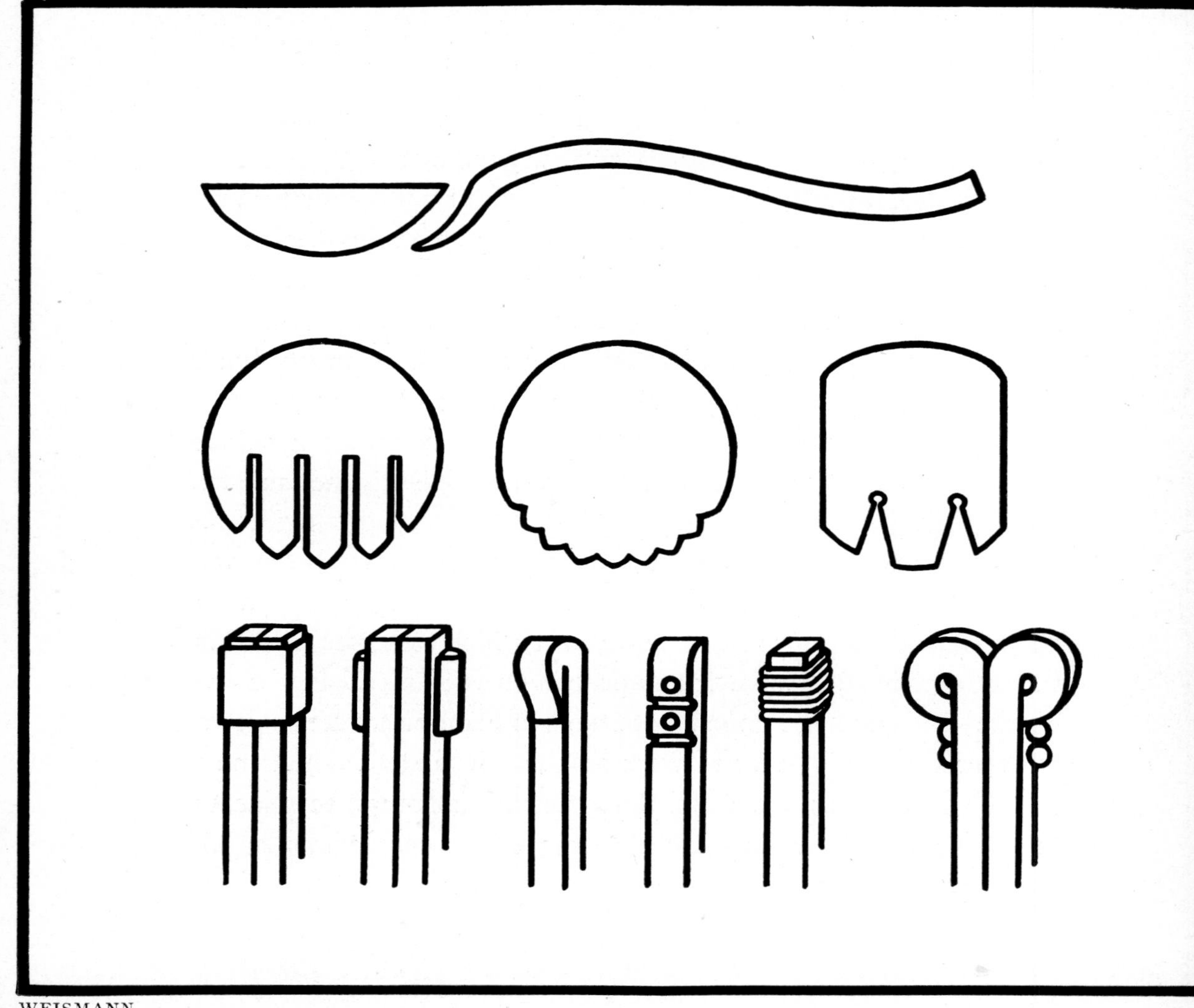

WEISMANN

PEWTER FORK AND SPOONS, BOWL AND HANDLE DESIGNS

cised along the length or at the end; the wire may be bent with pliers into a graceful scroll form at the end; or wire of smaller gauges may be wound or wrapped around the handle at points in keeping with the general proportions of the spoon.

When two lengths of wire are to be soldered together to form a handle, they should be absolutely straight so that the sides are flush, one with the other. Clasp the two pieces together firmly with the screw clamps. It is a good idea to put folded bits of paper between the clamps and the metal to prevent marring the pewter surface. Brush the surface to be soldered with glycerin. A medicine dropper may be used instead of a brush. Some bottles come equipped with stopper of this type. Along the line between the two wires place small pieces of pewter solder. Apply the heated soldering iron to the solder. It will be necessary to hold the iron against the solder until the metal beneath it becomes well heated, since the solder will not melt and flow between the pewter pieces until they are heated to the melting point of the solder. Solder flows over a heated surface but not over a cool surface. When the solder reaches the melting point, it will turn shiny and liquid and will flow down between the pewter. It is well to remember that the pewter melts at a temperature only slightly above that of the solder so care must be taken not to keep the soldering iron on the metal any longer than is necessary. Perhaps it would be wise to practice with a few extra lengths of wire before attempting the finished product. Decoration that must be soldered onto the spoon is handled in the same way, clamping the various pieces to the handle and soldering them. This method of soldering is bound to leave some excess solder on the surface of the metal itself. Any extra solder may be filed off easily; but in planning the original design, one should remember to keep it simple enough so that its parts may be reached with a file. Such a design is most satisfactory from every standpoint. Flat pieces of decoration may be sweated onto the wire in the same method as suggested for pewter buttons as described under dress accessories.

The part of the handle which is to be soldered to the bowl of the spoon should be filed into a tapered wedge-shaped point. All filing should be on the back of the wire handle and should be done on about the last three-quarters of the handle. This tapered length should be bent with pliers to match the outer curve of the spoon bowl. Again, with the protected clamps, fasten the handle to the bowl of the spoon. Brush or apply glycerin along the edges of the parts to be soldered and place the solder along these same crevices. Solder as before, taking care not to overheat the metal. File off any excess solder and smooth down all the rough edges of the pewter. Bend the handle of the spoon to the desired curve. This can usually be done by hand; but if pliers are needed, pad the jaws to prevent marring the metal. Polish the metal in the same way as suggested for finishing the bowl or plate.

If a salad fork is being made to pair with the spoon, the tines of the fork may be sawed into the disc with a jeweler's saw, or if very simple in design, cut with metal shears. This should not be done until after the shaped pewter disc has been soldered to the handle.

Pretty and Practical

Further projects involving the use of soldering equipment will suggest themselves once this new technique has been mastered. Aside from the many possibilities of costume jewelry, which any ingenious person can work out for himself, household accessories may be easily made. Simple salt and pepper shakers may be made in a

PEWTER HOLDER FOR A LARGE CANDLE
by Doris Cox

The candle was made from an accumulation of short ends of candles.

THOMAS

variety of forms which will fit into the accouterments of the table. The soldering may be done with an iron as suggested for the pewter spoons. These utensils should be made from flat lengths of pewter bent and soldered into the desired forms. A cylindrical form may be made by bending a strip of pewter around a piece of doweling of the desired diameter, a broomstick, or around a cylindrical iron stake such as used for more advanced pewter work (see catalogues of companies handling craft equipment). To the top of this rounded piece of pewter, a dome-shaped disc with holes of a suitable size drilled into it may be soldered; and to the bottom, a disc rounded upward slightly. The bottom disc should have a hole drilled into it which would be large enough to permit pouring in salt or pepper. A cork may be used as a stopper or a small piece of adhesive tape may be placed over the opening. The fact that the bottom disc has been rounded upward slightly will permit the shaker to stand even though a cork is used to fill the opening. The dome-shaped pieces are made in the same way as the bowls of spoons. There are other variations of shapes which might be experimented with. A flat disc might be soldered to the bottom of the cylinder and a foot, made from a narrow strip of pewter bent into a slightly smaller cylinder, soldered to the disc. The top disc might also be flat instead of domed. The salt or pepper shakers need not be round; a square or even somewhat rectangular shape could be equally attractive.

After the beginner has become familiar with the qualities and some of the possibilities of the metal, new problems will suggest themselves in rapid succession. We have mentioned jewelry only briefly. Some of the articles which are easily made are: bracelets, etched, or decorated with pierced designs done with a saw and drills, or soldered decoration; buckles and buttons; brooches and bar-pins; necklaces or decorative pendants; and clips.

Among the more easily made household accessories other than those described in greater detail are: bookends, pierced, etched or decorated with solder-work; candle holders of simple design; decorative boxes, such as trinket, cigarette, or match boxes; plant stands, etched or pierced and fastened to a piece of wood; napkin rings or clips; coasters; and many other articles.

It is hoped that the illustrations in this chapter will be used as a source of stimulation rather than as something to copy. Pewter provides a wonderful outlet for the craftsman. As with any new material, it is first necessary to learn what pewter will do. It should never be forced beyond its potentiality. The soft glow of the surface of pewter is most consistent with an easy flow of line in the structural design, decorated simply and sparingly.

After one has decided upon a design suitable for pewter work, consider which soldering method is the most adaptable. When one *layer* of metal is placed upon another, sweating the two pieces together is expedient. There is less likelihood of any excess solder

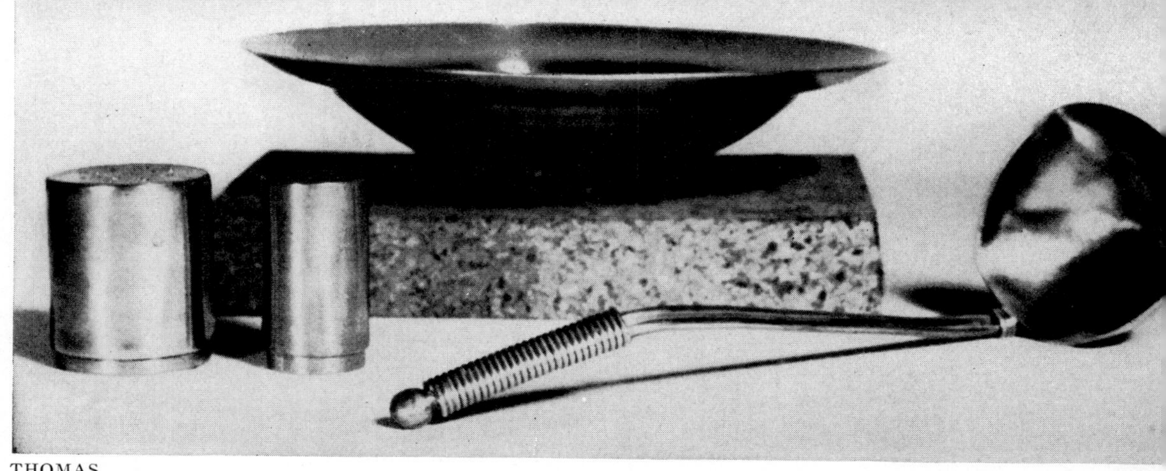

THOMAS

PEWTER BOWL, LADLE, AND SALT AND PEPPER SHAKERS

by Dorothy and Alexander Tillotson

THOMAS

PEWTER AND COPPER NAPKIN RINGS

Designed by Helen S. Petersen and executed by the Minneapolis WPA Handicraft Project

THOMAS

NAPKIN RING IN USE

An appropriate table setting for the use of pewter.

remaining upon the surface. This method is described in detail in the discussion of pewter buttons. It would be recommended for the napkin rings and clips. All the soldering is done before the metal is bent into its final form. The use of the soldering iron is the better method whenever two *edges* are to be joined, such as two wires for a spoon handle, or a dome to the top of a cylinder as might be needed for a salt shaker or a candlestick.

No matter what the craft, neglect of finishing details is quite apt to result in an unsatisfactory product. Time spent thus is never wasted.

Chapter XVI

Festive Ways

PERHAPS THE FOLLOWING THINGS THAT WE ARE SUGGESTING DO not properly come under the heading of crafts since they are of a temporary and, in some cases, perishable nature. We do feel, however, that they offer fields for the application of design which involve techniques that may be experimented with inexpensively. At the same time, these articles will do a great deal toward making some holiday or special occasion a more gala affair and are projects in which the whole family enjoys taking an active part. The danger of loss is not great, and the products resulting from such round-table effort may be startlingly attractive.

These simple techniques are also suitable for the solution of the rainy-day entertainment problem when children are most apt to become annoyances rather than pleasures. And too, some of these articles may be demonstrated to the convalescent child or even to the adult who is yearning for something with which to pass the time.

To Anyone's Heart

Many, many times during the year, fancy or unusual cookies are in demand. This is especially true when a children's party is being given, or at Christmas time. We have experimented with the old-fashioned gingerbread cooky with favorable results. These cook-

THOMAS

GLORIFIED GINGERBREAD

Confectioners' sugar sprinkled through the cut out parts of a paper "snowflake" gives a plain cake a festive air.

ies have been well received by every child who has seen or eaten them and have been equally enjoyed by the parents as well. May we pass on our two best experiments? Remember, these are not just cookies—they are works of art!

If Johnny or sister Sue have ever delighted in a handful of modeling clay, especially of the plasticine variety, the following gingerbread cookies will meet with great enthusiasm. The recipe given for the more traditional cooky is also used for the modeled cooky. Any ginger cooky recipe that is short enough to retain its shape and not puff up in baking would be suitable, but a small piece of the dough, pricked or shaped in some fashion, should be tested by baking to determine whether it really will hold its original form.

The process of forming the cooky is most elementary. First, a piece of dough is patted or rolled flat to form a sheet slightly larger than the visualized finished cooky will be. This is best when about one-eighth inch thick. The very smallest amount of flour should be used on the top surface of the dough for that would pre-

MODELED GINGER-BREAD COOKIES

(Photograph from the Photographic Laboratory, University of Minnesota.)

vent the next layer from adhering to this foundation. Then by rolling up small cylinders of dough, or small pellets, that in some cases might be flattened out to form discs, a design is made on the first piece of dough.

An active imagination is about all one needs, for the more naïve the approach, the more entertaining the result. Imagine a girl-cooky made by putting long strings of the dough side by side to form wavy tresses, or little pellets placed side by side to form curls; raisin eyes; dough pellets, small cylinders, or a raisin for a mouth; pieces of blanched almonds for a necklace; buttons of raisins, almonds, or dough; red cinnamon candies are useful for decorative notes too. The bottom of her skirt could have dough braid, ruffles or pleats; eyelet embroidery of raisins or any other decoration one's fancy might dictate. Interesting textures or designs can be made with the tines of a fork, toothpick or any other gadget found in the kitchen that would leave an interesting impression when pressed into the dough.

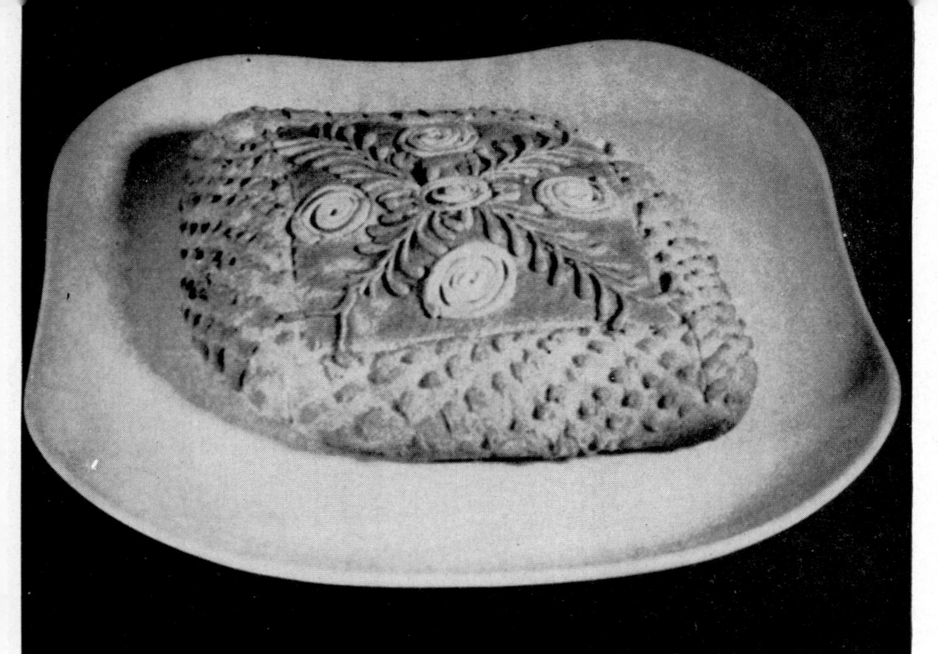

THOMAS

MEXICAN BREAD

Little rolls of the dough an
nodules made by pricking th
surface of the loaf furnishe
a most satisfactory outlet f
a Mexican baker's strong fee
ing for design.

Gingerbread men or women aren't the only things to make. All sorts of animals, birds, and fish can be concocted, and decorative flowers bloom in great profusion once the knack of using dough, almonds, raisins, and cinnamon candies for the various parts of a flower is developed. It takes about one trial to start one off. After the decorations have been applied or pricked or pressed into the basic dough, the excess is cut away, leaving just the planned shape ready to be baked. In order to facilitate moving these "masterpieces" on to a pan, the work may be done on a sheet of wax paper which is removed after the cooky has been baked. Ideas for the designs will probably be largely governed by the season of the year during which they are made.

The counterparts of these modeled cookies can be found in almost any well illustrated book on European peasant crafts. The cookies, or cakes, as they are called, are frequently very elaborate, and at a casual glance might be mistaken for wood carvings. Reproductions of them are usually found on the same pages upon which one finds carved butter molds.

A SWEET COUPLE

cardboard pattern, cookie ugh, frosting, and imagination.

THOMAS

Everyone is quite familiar with the gingerbread men that depend upon frosting for decoration. These, too, are of European origin. What joy it must have been to receive one as a gift. The bakers let imagination have full sway.

This recipe has been tested for these cookies:

Molasses Cookies

7/8 c. shortening	2/3 t. allspice
2/3 c. sugar	2/3 t. ginger
4 c. flour	2/3 t. cinnamon
1 1/3 t. soda	2/3 c. dark molasses
2/3 t. salt	2/3 c. cold coffee

Cream the shortening and sugar together well. Sift the dry ingredients together, and add to the creamed ingredients alternately with the coffee and molasses, which have been mixed together. Chill the dough thoroughly. Roll out one-quarter inch thick and cut. Bake in a hot oven (400° F.) for fifteen minutes. This recipe makes about five dozen cookies of ordinary size.

Plain Frosting

1 egg white	½ t. vanilla or
2 t. cold water	½ t. lemon juice

¾ c. confectioners' sugar

Beat egg white until stiff. Add the water and sugar. Beat thoroughly and add the flavoring. When this frosting is used for decorating, more sugar will need to be added, as the frosting should be quite firm for this purpose.

The special tool needed for this craft is a pastry bag. Many households have canvas ones on hand, but a paper one will serve the purpose admirably.

Use thin, tough paper (writing paper or fresh, clean wrapping paper) in sheets eight and one-half by eleven inches. Cut the sheets diagonally in two. Hold one long point of paper in each hand. Wrap around to make a cornucopia with a very sharp point. This point should come in the middle of the longest side.

The three corners of the triangular piece of paper should come together at the open end, where they can be turned in several times so that the cornucopia will hold together firmly. The points may be cut in one of the three ways shown in the diagram. The plain tube opening is the one most used for gingerbread men.

For elaborate work small brass tubes with different-shaped openings are for sale at kitchen furnishing stores. These metal tubes may be used in the paper cornets or in the cloth pastry bag. When using the paper cornet, cut off three-quarters of an inch at the pointed end and drop the metal tube into it, letting it project through the opening at the end. Then put the frosting inside the paper cornucopia. These paper bags are most convenient when using frosting of several different colors. When only one color is being used, as in decorating a wedding cake, a cloth bag with a metal end

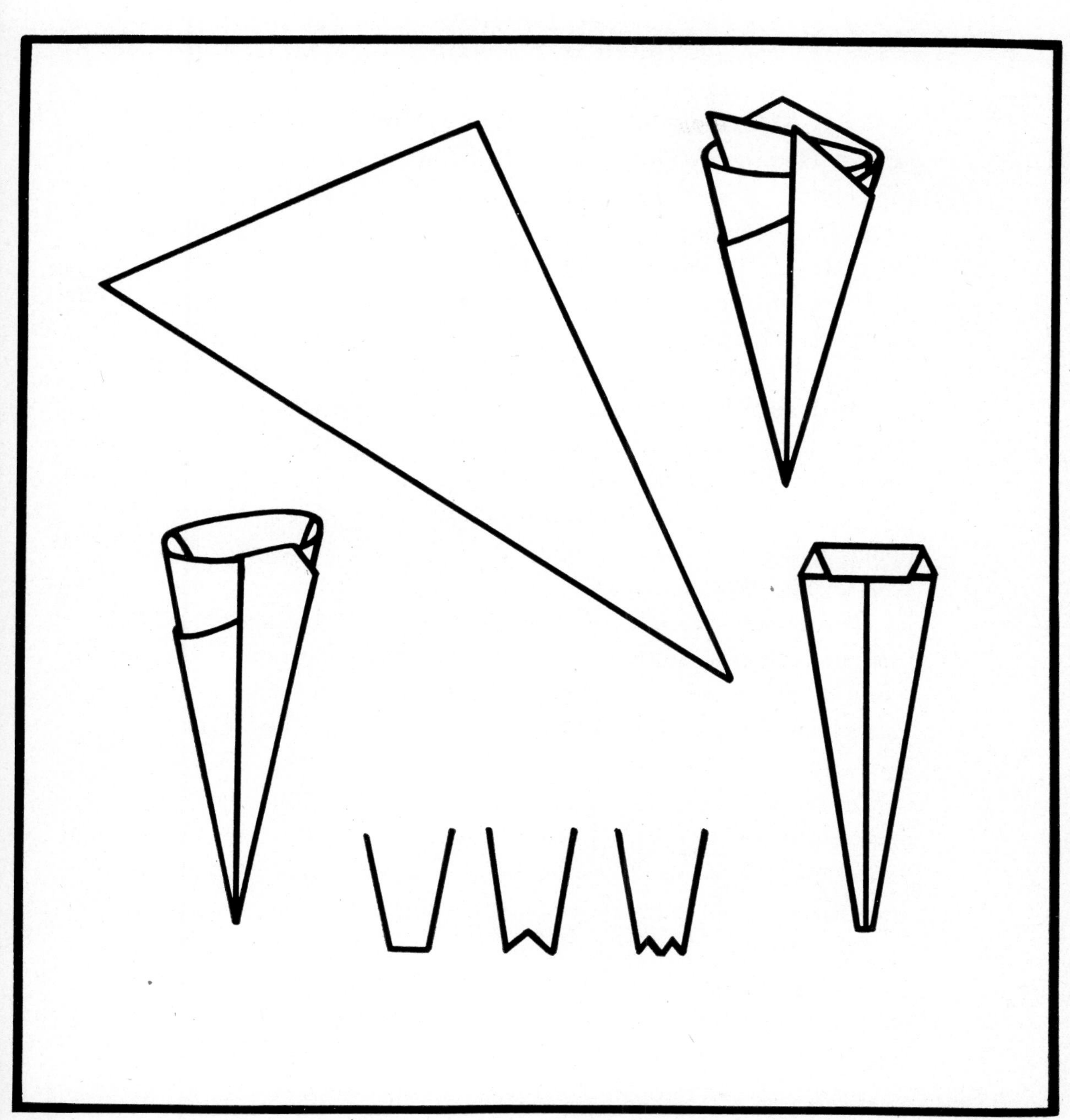

WEISMANN

HOW TO MAKE A PASTRY BAG OF PAPER

to which the tubes may be screwed will be found more convenient, as the paper bags soften and break with much usage.

Put the frosting into the bag, filling it not more than one-third full. Bring the edges of the open top together, turn down the right hand corner, then the left hand corner; then fold over twice and continue to fold the paper tube down to the frosting. If using a cloth bag, twist the bag just above the frosting. This is done in order that all the frosting may be forced out through the tube at the lower end of the bag and also to prevent any of the frosting coming out at the top.

The consistency of the frosting will be a matter of experimentation for any person mixing it. It should be soft enough to go through the tube easily, and firm enough to hold its shape at the same time. If the frosting is too stiff, it will harden rapidly and crack off the cooky very soon. A plain frosting of water and confectioners' sugar or a fudge frosting cannot be forced through a tube as it becomes hard and dry.

The principles of correct use of color values stressed in earlier parts of the book apply here. The dough becomes a rich golden brown while baking, the frosting is light; bitter chocolate melted over hot water and painted onto the cookies with a small, clean brush adds the dark value needed. The chocolate effects rare and costly velvet for skirts, boleros, or breeches. Try a villain with a chocolate moustache!

Eggs in One Basket

The mention of holidays brings to mind the fun that a session of decorating Easter eggs can provide. The batik process is a good one to use. The simplest method is to gather up all the onion

UKRAINIAN EASTER EGG

THOMAS

skins one can find and put a layer of them in the bottom of a kettle large enough to hold all the eggs one wishes to boil.

A design, simple or elaborate, is then painted with hot wax on the shell of the raw eggs. The eggs should be at room temperature. Use an old brush because it won't be usable for paints after this. Place the eggs in the kettle, adding onion skins at the same time; add water and boil the required length of time. The eggs emerge a beautiful brown with the designs showing up in the creamy eggshell color. Do not stir the contents of the kettle with a spoon while the eggs are boiling. The edges of the spoon mar the design.

Another simple method is to put the design on boiled eggs with white or colored wax crayons. It is more simple to control the crayon than a brushful of hot wax. The batik process previously described is used. Wax all portions to remain the lightest color, dip into a dye bath, wax everything that is to appear this color, dip into the next dye bath and so on until all the desired colors have been

THOMAS

CZECHOSLOVAKIAN EASTER EGG

used. So thin a coating of wax is used by this crayon method that it is not necessary to remove it. If hot wax is applied, *warm* the eggs in a very *slow* oven until the wax has melted and run off. Wipe with a warm soft cloth.

The beautiful peasant designed Easter eggs so often brought to this country are done on raw eggs which are never cooked, but are put away in a dry place for months until the contents of the shell dry up. They are given as tokens of friendship, not as food.

If the eggs are to be eaten, only vegetable dyes should be used. Eggs to be used for decorative purposes only may be dyed with wool, silk, or leather dyes. Some of the gayest colors are obtainable by soaking the color out of crepe paper. Some of the Ukrainian people who design many exquisite gift eggs each spring use this source for their dye supply. The resulting dye is not to be used on eggs to be eaten.

The batik process need not be used at all. Colored crayons may be used entirely, omitting the dye baths. Or, the designs may be painted on with water colors. If oil paint is used on eggs, they cannot be eaten, for the turpentine and oil flavor the eggs unpleasantly. It little matters what medium one uses, but to make it worthwhile, there seems little reason to paint an egg to resemble a watermelon or like object. The natural oval of the egg lends itself readily to designs that enhance the proportions of a beautiful ovoid.

Each season will suggest new uses of any talent or skill developed by previous craft experiences. The person who doubts his ability might start his hobby during this time since fewer materials and less time would be needed. At whatever end of the game one begins, a fascinating time awaits the person willing to make the effort.

THOMAS

CHRISTMAS TREE ORNAMENT

by Doris Cox

The artist-craftsman will determine whether an egg shell is to be discarded or is to become a naïve angel to hang upon the Christmas tree.

Now You Know

IF YOU HAVE NOT READ THIS BOOK FROM COVER TO COVER AT ONE sitting, but instead have read small portions of it at a time and have digested these bits thoroughly, you should be well equipped for more technical exploration in the crafts field. Perhaps you have made most of the articles described herein; perhaps you have made only a few. In any case, no doubt you have found that certain things have been more interesting to you. If this is true, then follow that branch of craft work to its very end; become an accomplished technician in that phase of art production. Much is being said today about the value of a hobby as a leisure time occupation or to mitigate emotional strain. If this book has led you to discover some interesting hobby, your life will be the richer for it. Do not allow your new interests to lag, but let them grow and develop into something of which you can be justly proud.

Of the many suggestions included in this book, some will be especially suited for use in the home, others to the enhancement of the wardrobe, many to camp or school. None of them call for an outlay of equipment beyond the means of most readers, and a large number of the articles can be made with little or almost no equipment. The directions for the construction and decoration of the various objects have been kept simple, keyed in as far as was possible to the novice. This was done by intent, since the book was planned to encourage, rather than to discourage, the beginner. Naturally, successful results are stimulating to anyone, but we would like to emphasize the fact that one or two failures do not indicate lack of ability. Patience rather than talent is of prime importance to the completion of a good craft product.

It is of utmost importance that the first few chapters dealing with taste, design, and color be understood thoroughly before even the simplest project is undertaken. This cannot be stressed too much, because the ultimate effect of the finished piece of work depends on a sound knowledge of the principles involved in its making. Constant reference to these chapters during the craft process itself will be insurance against possible failure. These first chapters are condensed and simplified, but if more information is desired, the library shelves may be referred to. We do feel that our information is complete, however, in so far as is necessary to the projects outlined in the rest of the text.

Bibliography

IT IS HOPED THAT A LIST OF BOOKS SUCH AS THIS WILL PROVE helpful in several ways to the reader. This is not an exhaustive list nor do all libraries have upon their shelves the very books mentioned, but these titles may give clues to appropriate substitutes. Often, too, one tends to narrow down source material to only those references dealing with the actual article about to be made. This practice handicaps one at the outset. There is always the possibility that new interests may be aroused by related material. If a personal clipping file is subdivided in the main as is suggested by the headings used for this bibliography, and then used thoughtfully, it will provide a rich source of stimulating ideas for years to come.

GOOD TASTE

ART IN EVERYDAY LIFE, by Harriet and Vetta Goldstein, New York, The Macmillan Company, 1940.

This book provides a sound standard upon which to build an ever-growing appreciation of both the aesthetic and the practical forms of art encountered in daily living.

DESIGN METHODS

THE ART OF COLOR AND DESIGN, by Maitland Graves, New York and London, McGraw-Hill Book Company, Inc., 1941.

A logical and simple presentation of all the basic principles of two-dimensional design.

THE BASES OF DESIGN, by Walter Crane, London, George Bell and Sons, 1898.

A good book on fundamentals in spite of the early date of publication.

COLOR AND DESIGN IN THE DECORATIVE ARTS, by Elizabeth Burris-Meyers, New York, Prentice-Hall, Inc., 1937.

The basic principles of color and design presented from the retailing angle, but interesting to the layman.

THE ELEMENTS OF DESIGN, by T. Elder Dickson, London, Sir Isaac Pitman and Sons, Ltd., 1933.

Most useful for chapters on allover patterns and counterchange.

A METHOD FOR CREATIVE DESIGN, by Adolpho Best-Maugard, New York and London, A. A. Knopf, 1927.

The creative approach presented makes designing simple, easy to understand, and fun to do.

ORNAMENTAL DESIGN FOR WOVEN FABRICS, by Stephenson and Suddards, London, Methuen and Company, Ltd., 1924.

This book was first published in 1897, but is a valuable help in designing.

PLANE GEOMETRY TEXT

The application of the theorems of plane geometry to the problem of dividing areas of all shapes into a number of equal parts saves considerable time and helps to insure accuracy.

TEXTILE DESIGN, by Anthony Hunt, New York, The Studio Publications, Inc., 1937.

There are many fine photographs in the book, which presents the material from a professional angle.

CRAFT METHODS

BATIK

BATIKS AND HOW TO MAKE THEM, by Pieter Mijer, New York, Dodd, Mead and Company, 1919.

FIRST LESSONS IN BATIK, by Gertrude Clayton Lewis, Chicago and New York, The Prang Company, 1921.

These books both contain historical accounts of the craft and of the technique employed.

BLOCK PRINTING

BLOCK-CUTTING AND PRINT-MAKING BY HAND, by Margaret Dobson, London, Sir Isaac Pitman and Sons, Ltd., 1930.

Emphasis is placed upon pictorial rather than decorative design. Good suggestions for keying color blocks are given.

FABRIC PRINTING, by W. B. Adeney, New York, The Studio Publications, Inc., 1934.

HANDBLOCK PRINTING ON FABRICS, by Thomas J. Corbin, London, Sir Isaac Pitman and Sons, Ltd., 1934.

A very complete treatise. Advanced processes are explained.

THE GRAPHIC ARTS, by W. H. Johnson and L. V. Newkirk, New York, The Macmillan Company, 1942.

This book relates the history of the graphic arts and explains their use commercially. There are good illustrations and text for linoleum engravings, silk screen process, bookbinding, and booklets. These are prepared with clear instructions for amateurs.

LINO-CUTS, by Claude Flight, R.B.A., New York, Dodd, Mead and Company, 1928.

LINO CUTTING AND PRINTING, by Claude Flight, R.B.A., London, B. T. Batsford, Ltd., 1934.

These are both good books on the subject. The contemporary approach of the latter is especially pleasing.

CARD WEAVING

CARD WEAVING, by Mary M. Atwater, New York, The Universal School of Handicrafts, 1931.

Not only are directions and patterns for weaving this braid given, but uses for the finished product are suggested as well.

References to be found in the periodical THE WEAVER:

NEW IDEAS FOR TABLET WOVEN RUGS, by Beatrice A. Shephard, Vol. 1, No. 3, July 1936.

"STUNTING" ON THE CARDS, by Mary M. Atwater, Vol. 2, No. 1, Jan. 1937.

CARD WEAVING TECHNIQUE, by Clara M. Youse, Vol. 6, No. 1, Jan.-Feb. 1941.

DRAWING DOWN CARD WEAVING DRAFTS, by Mrs. W. F. McNulty, Vol. 6, No. 1, Jan.-Feb. 1941.

WEAVING WITH SMALL APPLIANCES, BOOK II, TABLET WEAVING, by Luther Hooper, London, Sir Isaac Pitman and Sons, Ltd., 1923.

FINGER WEAVING, BRAIDING, ETC.

BRAIDING AND KNOTTING FOR AMATEURS, by Constantine A. Belash, Boston, The Beacon Press, Inc., 1936.

Good for techniques—valuable if interested in making novelty belts or unusual cords for accessories.

References to be found in the periodical THE WEAVER:

THE "OSAGE" BRAID, by Mary M. Atwater, Vol. 4, No. 2, April 1939.

A FEW SIMPLE BRAIDS, by Mary M. Atwater, Vol. 7, No. 1, Jan.-Feb. 1942.

THE FINISH OF EDGES, by Mary M. Atwater, Vol. 7, No. 2, July 1942.

METALWORK

ART METALWORK, A Manual for Amateurs, by Emil F. Kronquist, New York, London, McGraw-Hill Book Company, Inc., 1942.

METAL WORK, by R. D. and M. E. Snively, Brattleboro, Stephen Daye Press, 1940.

This book confines itself to simple problems; well illustrated with photographs.

PEWTER, Spun, Wrought, and Cast, by B. N. Osburn and G. O. Wilber, Scranton, International Textbook Company, 1938.

This treatise leads to very advanced problems, but fundamental processes are well presented.

SIMPLE METALWORK, by E. Kronquist and A. G. Pelikan, New York, The Studio Publications, Inc., 1940.

Both the Kronquist books are prepared very much as manuals. All the steps of the processes are very well illustrated with drawings and photographs. The more recent book is much more complete than the first one listed.

NEEDLEWORK

ADVENTURES IN EMBROIDERY, by Ernest Thesiger, New York, The Studio Publications, Inc., 1941.

Accessories for the home are described. The author realizes that all embroidery is not art—but may be merely patience and the ability to handle a needle. Elaborate historic and contemporary examples of the art of needlework are shown, but Mr. Thesiger understands that most needleworkers have at most only an hour or two each day at their disposal, and makes his suggestions accordingly. He insists that the work be done for a specific purpose.

APPLIQUÉ DESIGN AND METHOD, by Kathleen Mann, London, A. and C. Black, Ltd., 1937.

The author recommends a very playful, free approach to the problem of design.

DICTIONARY OF EMBROIDERY STITCHES, by Mary Thomas, New York, William Morrow and Company, 1936.

Just what the title implies. Excellent.

EMBROIDERY DESIGN, by Molly Booker, New York, The Studio Publications, Inc., 1935.

Stresses an original approach to the problem of design.

ENCYCLOPEDIA OF NEEDLEWORK, by Therese de Dillmont, Alsace, Dornach, 1890.

This book is from the D. M. C. Library. It is very old but very useful.

HOOKED RUGS, and How To Make Them, by Anna M. L. Phillips, New York, The Macmillan Company, 1925.

THE HOOKED RUG, by William Winthrop Kent, New York, Dodd, Mead and Company, 1930.

A record of the origin and development of the hooked rug. Methods of making and suitable sources for design are included.

MODERN DESIGN IN EMBROIDERY, by Rebecca Crompton, London, B. T. Batsford, Ltd., 1936.

A very imaginative approach. Some of the less-known stitches are used effectively. Well illustrated.

MODERN EMBROIDERY, by Mary Hogarth, Garden City, Garden City Publishing Company, Inc., 1933.

Presents examples of the work of many well known embroiderers. This is a good source for motifs, use of materials, and for ideas for household and costume accessories.

NEEDLEPOINT AS A HOBBY, by Geneva D. Lent, New York and London, Harper and Bros., 1942.

This book contains a historical development of needle point with an extensive and diagrammatic set of instructions for carrying on every step in the creation of needlework tapestries.

OLD PATCHWORK QUILTS, by Ruth E. Finley, Philadelphia and London, Lippincott, 1929.

This is a presentation of the history and directions for making patchwork quilts.

THE SAMPLER BOOK OF DECORATIVE NEEDLEWORK, by Louisa E. E. Judd-Morris, Leicester, The Dryad Press, 1942.

There are many useful diagrams in this book.

RARE HOOKED RUGS, by William Winthrop Kent, Springfield, The Pond-Ekberg Company, 1941.

A very interesting book to peruse before designing a rug.

TOOLS AND TOYS OF STITCHERY, by Gertrude Whiting, New York, Columbia University Press, 1928.

Presents uses and development of the many implements used in making laces and needlework. Fine illustrations. Text presented imaginatively.

STENCILING

EARLY AMERICAN STENCILS on Walls and Furniture, by Janet Waring, New York, William P. Scott, 1937.

Interesting historically.

HANDS AT WORK, by Emmy Zweybrück, Springfield, Mass., The Holden Publishing Company, 1942. (Distributed by The American Crayon Company, Sandusky, Ohio.)

A number of crafts are discussed, but stenciling is stressed. The illustrations are stimulating and informal in character.

THE SECOND STENCIL BOOK, by Frau Emmy Zweybrück, Sandusky, Ohio, The American Crayon Company, 1940.

This book shows examples of work done with chalk and crayons, as well as with paint.

THIS AND THAT

DECORATIVE IDEAS, by Ivy Penelope Roseaman, Leicester, The Dryad Press, 1937.

HOME DECORATION WITH FABRIC AND THREAD, by Ruth W. Spears, New York, M. Barrows and Company, 1940.

101 HOME FURNISHINGS AND HOW TO MAKE THEM, by Lucina Wakefield, New York and London, Harper and Bros., 1942.

LET'S DECORATE OUR HOME, edited by Anne Means, New York, Robert M. McBride and Company, 1941.

There are many usable ideas in the four books mentioned above which might furnish ideas for articles that would lend themselves well to decorative design applied in any of the craft media.

DESIGN TECHNICS, by Felix Payant, Syracuse, Keramic Studio Publishing Company, 1934.

A presentation of the methods employed when handling various media used for the execution of designs.

THE ENCYCLOPAEDIA BRITANNICA

This is always a good reference to use. Techniques for many of the crafts are discussed here.

SOURCE MATERIAL

ANIMAL FORM

LES ANIMAUX, by Armand Dayot, Paris, Charles Moreau, n.d. There are five volumes in this series.

A collection of drawings, photographs, and reproductions of sculpture. All excellent examples—they range from sensitive, realistic representations to advanced stylizations.

AUDUBON PRINTS

DESIGN IN NATURE, drawings prepared by the School of the Art Institute, Chicago, Field Museum of Natural History.

MUSEUM, Natural History Department.

For individual research.

NATIONAL GEOGRAPHIC MAGAZINE

NATURE MAGAZINE

ZOÖLOGICAL BOOKS

A thorough understanding of the anatomy of animals is a prerequisite to good drawing. Visit the zoo and draw!

PLANT FORM

ART FORMS IN NATURE, by Professor Karl Blossfeldt, New York, E. Weyhe, 1929.

Examples from the plant world photographed direct from nature. Every page is a challenge. About all that the designer need do is to combine forms. The photographs are exceptional.

BOTANY BOOKS AND SEED CATALOGUES

BOUQUETS ET FRONDAISONS, by E. A. Seguy, Paris, Massin, n.d.

ÉTUDE DE LA PLANTE, by M. P. Verneuil, Paris, Librairie Centrale des Beaux-Arts, n.d.

Each plant form is analyzed carefully for structure and shape. The finished interpretations of these studies belong to a period of art now past, but the studies themselves will never be outmoded. The plans given for units, borders, and allover designs are very useful.

FLORÉAL, by E. A. Seguy, Paris, A. Calavas, n.d.

The designs appear to have been done with a very free brush technique. The style is splashy and far from being conservative. Unusual color combinations have been used. Designs of this kind would adapt themselves well to the technique of contemporary stenciling or screen printing.

FORMEN DES LEBENS, Botanische Lichtbildstudien, by Dr. Paul Wolff, Leipzig, Karl Robert Longewiesche, 1933.

One hundred and twenty photographs of plant forms, every one beautiful in composition. The depiction of texture and detail is outstanding.

LA PLANTE EXOTIQUE, by Methurin Méheut, Paris, C. Massin and Company, 1931.

The freedom of the brush strokes and the delightful color will certainly prove inspirational. This same artist has prepared other portfolios of drawings of animals.

NATURE'S AID TO DESIGN, by E. S. D. Owen and Louise W. Bunce, New York, John Lane Company, 1907.

More photographs of flower and leaf form.

UNABRIDGED (OR ANY GOOD) DICTIONARY

For leaf, root, and flower forms.

MOTIFS FOR ADAPTATION

DEKORATIVE VORBILDER, a yearbook of decorative design, edited by Armand Guérinet, Paris, 25 volumes, 1894-1928.

KUNSTGEWERBLICHE, Schmuckformen für die Fläche, n.d.

The designs in this collection are very abstract and somewhat bizarre.

ORNAMENTATION AND TEXTILE DESIGN, by Alfred F. Barker, London, Methuen and Company, Ltd., 1930.

A book well supplied with photographs and drawings dealing with inspirational material ranging from architecture to nature forms.

PAPIERS, PEINTS, ET TENTURES MODERNES, by H. Clouzet, Paris, C. Massin and Company, n.d.

Good material to study with reference to space filling when making allovers. There are examples of interesting combinations of units, texture effects, and color combinations.

CONTEMPORARY

APPLIED ART IN FINLAND, World's Fair, New York, 1939-40.

L'ARREDAMENTO MODERNO, by Roberto Aloi, Milan, U. Holpli, 1934.

DECORATIVE ART, annual issues of the Studio Year Book, New York, The Studio Publications, Inc.

Any book or magazine which records trends in design will help to keep one abreast of the times.

DEUTSCHES HANDSWERKSGUT, by Walter Dexel, Berlin, 1939.

NEW IDEAS FOR SURFACE DECORATION, Philadelphia, H. C. Perleberg, Publisher, n.d.

HISTORIC

ARCHEOLOGY, any well illustrated text in this field.

DECORATIVE PATTERNS OF THE ANCIENT WORLD, by Flinders Petrie, London, University College, 1930.

This is in the nature of a scrapbook in which has been collected hundreds of motifs.

THE EVOLUTION OF DECORATIVE ART, by Henry Balfour, New York, The Macmillan Company, 1893.

Interesting for historical background.

PRIMITIVE ART SERIES, by Doris Rosenthal, New York, Brown-Robertson Company, n.d.

These motifs have been freely drawn and are much larger than material usually found in collections of this nature.

ROMANCE OF DESIGN, by Garnet Warren, Garden City, Doubleday Page Company, 1926.

NATIVE

ART AND LIFE IN NEW GUINEA, by Raymond Firth, New York, The Studio Publications, Inc., 1936.

The illustrations demonstrate character in line and space division.

BRODERIES DES PAYSANNES DE SMOLENSK, by Princess Marie Ténichev, Paris, Librairie Centrale des Beaux-Arts, n.d.

Especially interesting color combinations.

DESIGN FROM PEASANT ART, by Kathleen Mann, London, A. and C. Black, 1939.

This book shows motifs selected from various sources; then they are combined in a modern way so that they are suitable for present-day craftwork.

JAPANESE WOODCUTS

These are fine for color and allover patterns.

JAVANESE BATIK DESIGNS FROM METAL STAMPS, by Albert Buell Lewis, Chicago, Field Museum of Natural History, 1924.

This author has other books on allied subjects, all of which are good references.

PARACAS EMBROIDERIES, A Study of Repeated Patterns, by Cora E. Stafford, New York, J. J. Augustin, Publisher, 1941.

These are especially valuable for study of the importance of color value in design.

PERSIAN TEXTILES, by N. A. Reath and E. B. Sachs, Penn. Museum of Art, by Yale University Press, 1937.

WOMAN'S DAY, a periodical distributed by A and P Food Stores, New York, Stores Publishing Company.

The needlework section of this magazine presents one of the most intelligent approaches to handicraft for the average woman now available.

RELATED FIELDS

ANCIENT EGYPTIAN, ASSYRIAN, AND PERSIAN COSTUMES AND DECORATIONS, by M. G. Houston and F. Hornblower, London, A. and C. Black, 1931.

ILLUSTRATED BALLET PROGRAMS

LEON BAKST, costume designs by Leon Bakst, Berlin, E. Wasmuth, n.d.

PEASANT COSTUME OF THE BLACK FOREST, by Dora W. Pettigrew, London, A. and C. Black, 1937.

PEASANT COSTUME IN EUROPE, Vols. 1 and 2, by Kathleen Mann, London, A. and C. Black, 1931.

THE RUSSIAN BALLET in Western Europe 1909-1920, by W. A. Propert, New York, John Lane Company, 1921.

Fine source material for the use of color. It is dramatic—with an abundance of vitality.

SCANDINAVIAN PEASANT COSTUME, by Kathleen Primmer, London, A. and C. Black, 1939.

Abundant source material for headgear, as well as decorative notes for the entire wardrobe.

Index